mango
PUBLISHING

INNOVATING INNOVATION

Also by David Morey

Creating Business Magic

The Leadership Campaign

The Underdog Advantage

For further information,
please go to www.playoffense.com.

INNOVATING INNOVATION

LEADERSHIP TOOLS TO MAKE REVOLUTIONARY CHANGE HAPPEN FOR YOU AND YOUR BUSINESS

DAVID MOREY

Mango Publishing

Coral Gables

Cover & Layout Design: Jermaine Lau

For permission requests, please contact the publisher at:
Mango Publishing Group
2850 S Douglas Road, 2nd Floor
Coral Gables, FL 33134 USA
info@mango.bz

For special orders, quantity sales, course adoptions and corporate sales, please email the publisher at sales@mango.bz. For trade and wholesale sales, please contact Ingram Publisher Services at customer.service@ingramcontent.com or +1.800.509.4887.

Innovating Innovation: Leadership Tools to Make Revolutionary Change Happen for You and Your Business

Library of Congress Cataloging
ISBN: (print) 978-1-63353-844-3 (e-book) 978-1-63353-845-0
Library of Congress Control Number: 2018944503
BISAC category code: BUS071000 — BUSINESS & ECONOMICS / Leadership

Printed in the United States of America

This book is dedicated to my magical wife,
Xie Zheng—a change leader always.

TABLE OF CONTENTS

TABLE OF CONTENTS 8

FOREWORD 12

INTRODUCTION

MARKETING AND INNOVATION 15

CHAPTER ONE

STOP BEING A PUNCHLINE 23

CHAPTER TWO

SUBDIVIDE LIGHT 51

CHAPTER THREE

BUILD WORKSHOPS, NOT LABORATORIES 75

CHAPTER FOUR

CREATE A CULTURE OF URGENCY
AND SOFT LANDINGS 103

CHAPTER FIVE

DEVELOP PERIPHERAL VISION 129

CHAPTER SIX

INNOVATE BENEFITS, OWN THE FUTURE 155

CHAPTER SEVEN

SAIL WEST TO FIND EAST 181

CHAPTER EIGHT

BE A CHANGE LEADER, NOT A BUSINESS LEADER 207

CHAPTER NINE

EMPOWER, DON'T MANAGE 229

CHAPTER TEN

RELEASE EARLY AND OFTEN 257

CHAPTER ELEVEN

PUNCTATE YOUR EQUILIBRIUM 283

ACKNOWLEDGEMENTS 301

ABOUT THE AUTHOR 302

ENDNOTES 303

...matter is neither created nor destroyed. But it sure as hell is transformed. Even nature does not invent. It innovates. And this is what business demands we do today—at a rate and a tempo unprecedented in the history of industries and markets.... Innovation is not new, but it needs to be innovated. Today's markets not only demand this; in fact, they will show you how—if you let them.

—From Chapter One

FOREWORD

Change rules today. A leader's ability to navigate, manage, and lead change has never been more important, more powerful, and more urgently needed. Today, the leader who can best absorb, embrace, and ride ahead of the forces of change can transform markets, countries, and the world.

David Morey has written a must-read book. It is the battlefield manual for change leadership. It is the new primer for how to win.

Innovating Innovation builds on the guiding principles of Edison, Drucker, Jobs, and other breakthrough innovators and draws on David's own work in guiding nineteen winning global presidential campaigns and advising some of the world's top companies and business leaders. It builds on his underdog-insurgent model, developed with longtime business partner Scott Miller, and it evolves from his most recent work, *Creating Business Magic*, which leveraged and enhanced the strategies of magic with the principles of insurgency.

In the context of today's remarkable change-fueled disruptive environment, innovation by legacy companies is almost invariably stalled, misfocused, or altogether absent. Typically, innovation is bureaucratized and given no more than lip service—though plenty of that. It is pursued via doomed approaches born of incumbency, anachronism, and defensive orientation. Too often, innovation doesn't even get this far. It is never found, let alone harnessed. That is why innovation urgently needs reinvention. The concept itself needs a different, wider, more creative, more consumer-focused, and more pragmatic approach.

David argues that innovation is almost universally presented in overly narrow, technical, and backward-looking terms. It needs a new mental model, a wider scope, a broader grasp of human, perceptual, performance, marketing, creativity, and leadership factors, all of which must be unremittingly future-directed.

Innovating Innovation focuses sharply on the power of what David calls the "disruptive periphery," which is pitted against the "bureaucratized center." With unerring aim, David modernizes and synergizes the best of past innovation theories and practices, while adding his insurgent strategic and campaign-based model and blending in the unique creative problem-solving lessons he has honed not just as a top business and political consultant but as one of the world's leading magicians. *Innovating Innovation* details a step-by-step pragmatic framework to apply every insight to what leaders and businesses do every day.

In this beautifully written book, David distills the potent discipline of disruptive insurgent marketing and creative problem solving into a hands-on primer of practical principles. They will enable you to succeed in the most opportunity-rich and threat-intensive business environment in history. It will help you win while having fun.

Yoram (Jerry) Wind
The Lauder Professor Emeritus
Professor of Marketing

The Wharton School
The University of Pennsylvania

Yoram (Jerry) Wind joined Wharton in 1967 with a doctorate from Stanford. He is the Lauder Professor Emeritus and Professor of marketing. Wind also founded the Wharton Think Tank: The SEI Center for Advanced Studies in management and ran it for three decades, co-founded The Interdisciplinary Center (IDC) Herzliya Israel and acts as chair of their higher academic committee. He has edited top marketing journals, published over three hundred articles, twenty-five books, and received the four major marketing awards: Buck Weaver, Parlin, Converse, and AMA/Irwin Distinguished Educator Award. Wind was one of the original Legends in Marketing, with an eight-volume anthology published by Sage in 2014. He has consulted with over one hundred companies, is a member of the executive committee of SEI, sits on the advisory boards of various companies and nonprofit organizations, and testifies in intellectual property cases. Wind is a trustee of the PMA and chairs their marketing advisory group. His current research explores marketing-driven business strategy, the Network Challenge; reinventing advertising; creativity and innovation; and challenging our mental models. He is a 2017 inductee into the Marketing Hall of Fame.

INTRODUCTION

MARKETING AND INNOVATION

This book is about making innovation happen. Today, we are surrounded by remarkable examples of innovation, and a handful of great companies are driving innovation by the exponential dimension of their business models. In this context, everyone says they want innovation. But the truth? Innovation is broken. Most business leaders and businesses struggle to find ways to crack through their own corporate politics and bureaucratic silos, to move from defense to offense, to nurture real breakthrough, to drive bold creativity in ways that add new value to everything they do.

Innovation itself needs innovation. These pages teach, coach, and guide readers across eleven concrete and pragmatic steps that unlock and drive day-to-day innovation in your business and help you take long-term competitive advantage in your marketplace.

Innovation is old. As old as creation. It is the Big Bang. Anyone who has ever made a living selling anything knows that, in marketing, only one word is more powerful than "free." It is "new." In today's change-fueled environment, innovation is more essential to survival—let alone success—than ever before. Still, never have so many businesses gotten so much innovation so wrong. Everyone talks innovation, demands innovation, but—almost everywhere—it is stalled, unfocused, or totally AWOL. Given lip service, it is bureaucratized, limped after, and crawled toward via the most rutted and washed-out roads in existence—the worn ways of incumbency, anachronism, and timid defensiveness.

We need something better. It may be conveyed in three simple sentences that, together, are the thesis of this book:

Innovation needs innovation.
Innovation can be taught.
Innovation can be accelerated.

Today, innovation cries out for a different, wider, more creative, and more pragmatic approach. Innovation needs wide-eyed dedication to product benefits, not squinting recitation of product features. The approach needs a dramatic reorientation away from a stiflingly narrow, overly technical, and backward-looking focus to a wider and deeper vision—one that is resolutely human, keenly perceptual, and always performance-directed. Innovation needs a new translation into a set of future-directed terms redefining marketing and leadership.

Innovating Innovation: Leadership Tools to Make Revolutionary Change Happen for You and Your Business introduces the power of what I call the "disruptive periphery" versus the "bureaucratized center." It offers a comprehensive and step-by-step set of tools forged by more than three decades of work with change leaders in politics and businesses worldwide. These are tools that enabled me to help pilot 19 winning global presidential campaigns, advise 10 billionaires, counsel 5 Nobel Peace Prize winners, and work with the CEOs of numerous *Fortune* 100 and 500 companies to help add hundreds of millions of dollars of value to these and other businesses.

Innovating Innovation synergizes what is best in classic innovation theories with an insurgent strategic model inspired by one of my first corporate clients, Apple founder Steve Jobs. This insurgent model is about change leadership, not just absorbing or embracing change but, rather, leading change by moving relentlessly to the strategic offense. Moreover, using the great inventor Thomas Edison as our model, the book shows how to lead innovation to create the products of genius without the necessity for actual genius. It provides practical guidance on building and leading the teams, organizational structures, and cultures of market-made and market-making innovation. And it provides a roadmap to the *disruptive periphery*—the organizational margins at which real innovation happens.

Innovating Innovation is a framework to counter failure. It directs you, the reader, to the consumer, who is finally the only person who will tell you how to innovate the benefits to create a future you can own. This book invites you to *think different,* to become a change leader, to go the "wrong way" to get to the right places. And, in chapter 10, it shows you how to apply the pragmatic lessons of collaborative, responsive, and super-efficient Agile software development—exploiting concepts such as adaptive experimentation and open innovation—to absolutely everything. All this, together, will accelerate your leadership career and your company's success by stepping up from mere evolution to Punctuated Equilibrium, evolution as breakthrough.

You and your business require innovation as never before and unlike anyone else's. This is lesson number one. And in the space of eleven chapters, I offer lesson number two: You do not need to be a genius to deliver the performances, products, and services of innovation at genius levels in this most opportunity-rich and threat-intensive business environment in history. And finally, because time is money, and because innovation accelerated is innovation exponentially powerful, this book offers ways for leaders to drive velocity and make change happen faster.

This, then, is a step-by-step handbook for teaching and at times even tricking your organization, your culture, and your company into real-world change. It is the new battlefield manual for innovation.

• • •

Management consulting legend Peter F. Drucker wrote, "Business has only two functions: marketing and innovation. These produce revenues. All other functions are costs." Two things are true about this dictum:

1. It was true when he wrote it in his 1954 classic *The Practice of Management.*

2. It is even more urgently true today.

No business long endures, let alone prospers, by embracing any strategy that must be executed "at all costs." Drucker knew this, of course. That is why he called for innovation *and* marketing. In fact, he put marketing *before* innovation. This is because one of his greatest management innovations was to put marketing in the driver's seat precisely when it came to innovation.

Today, Drucker's legacy is evident as our most successful companies leverage marketing to shape technological innovation to create revenue. If a business is led well, marketing drives innovation not *at all costs,* but at the *right* cost, and innovation will, in turn, leverage marketing not *at all costs,* but at the *right* cost.

We can't all be Henry Ford, Bill Gates, or Steve Jobs. From all appearances, Ford, Gates, and Jobs created something out of nothing. Well, *we* can't create something out of nothing.

That's right. And, appearances to the contrary notwithstanding, neither did Ford, Gates, or Jobs.

Which brings me to Thomas Alva Edison. This book will unpack the way of thinking Edison brought to the 1,093[1] US patents issued in his name—an American record until 2015.[2] I argue that Edison's true genius was not only his legendary perseverance, but also his way of thinking and his process of invention.

In fact, it is common knowledge that Edison himself denied the sovereign power of genius. The only Edison quotation anyone ever repeats is: "Genius is 1 percent inspiration and 99 percent perspiration." So, I argue that Edison found ways to punch above his weight when it came to genius—both in terms of work ethic and in the way he thought about innovation and breakthrough.

From 1978 to 1986, actor Chris Robinson portrayed Dr. Rick Webber on the soap opera *General Hospital.* In 1984, Webber also appeared in a commercial for Vicks Formula 44 cough syrup. His pitch for the product began, "I'm not a doctor, but I play one on TV." Suppose, then, that Edison was not a genius, but only *acted like one* on demand and consistently enough to secure 1,093 patents between 1868 and 1931, the year he died: an average of seventeen inventions each year for sixty-three years. Based on those numbers, I am abundantly justified in proclaiming almost no one more prolifically innovative than Thomas Edison. Moreover, the scope of his innovation goes far beyond the numbers. Edison innovated a technology that created new, previously unimagined markets and a new reality in the human environment.

Chapter 1 of this book asks you to "Stop Being a Punchline." It is about the business necessity of innovation, on the one hand, and, on the other, everything that is wrong with innovation today. Chapter 2 asks you to do what Edison did when he decided—yes, when *he decided*—to create his most iconic invention, the incandescent electric light. He decided to "subdivide light." That was his phrase, and I know it sounds impossible, but he did exactly that. What is more, not only can you do it too, you can also lead others in doing it. (Spoiler alert:

It's a combination of innovation and marketing, marketing and innovation.)

You can think of the rest of this book as a set of variations on the theory and practice of subdividing light, using marketing to drive innovation and innovation to create new markets.

Chapters 3, 4, and 5 are about creating and leading the teams, working conditions, organizational structures, market platforms, and a culture of market-made and market-making innovation. Most of all, they are about creating a disruptive periphery, the organizational margins in which real innovation takes place.

Chapter 6 is about using the consumer to help you innovate the benefits that create a future you can own.

Chapter 7 begins with the example of Christopher Columbus to point you in the right wrong direction, so that you can do what Steve Jobs asked all his employees and his customers to do: *Think different.*

Being a *business* leader today is like clinging to your 8-track player. Hey, we have changed centuries, and chapter 8 is about being a *change* leader, so that you and your organization can own the future by getting there first.

Warren Buffett has told the insanely wealthy how to become even more powerful by giving away all their money. Chapter 9 will tell you how to become more powerful by giving away all your authority (to the right people).

In chapter 10, again, we apply the lessons of Agile software development to absolutely everything, and in chapter 11 we move from the short term to the long by exploiting a revisionist Theory of Evolution called Punctuated Equilibrium.

These eleven chapters are a battlefield guide to thinking like a genius even if you are not a genius. They are a doable and actionable set of steps for innovating innovation.

In this journey, we draw on some of history's great innovators as well as on my work, interviews, and studies with such people as Bob Iger, Chairman and CEO, the Walt Disney Company; Fran Tarkenton, founder, GoSmallBiz; Mike Milken, founder, The Milken Institute; Eugene Burger, the World's Top Close-Up Magician; John McLaughlin, Former Acting Director, CIA; David Copperfield, Las Vegas magician and headliner; Jerry Wind, The Lauder Professor Emeritus, The Wharton School; Scott Miller, Chairman and CEO, Core Strategy Group; Elon Musk, Chairman, SpaceX and CEO, Tesla Motors; Tim Cook, CEO, Apple; Bruce Springsteen, Rock Legend; and Mark Cuban, owner, The Dallas Mavericks—along with my company's extensive consulting work with some of today's most successful leaders of innovation, including Steve Jobs, Corazon Aquino, Bill Gates, Kim Dae Jung, Alex Gorsky, Rupert Murdoch, Mike Milken, Don Keough, Barack Obama, Bill Clinton, Sergio Zyman, David Bonderman, Pete Peterson, Phil Knight, Mike Roberts, Roberto Goizueta, Ray Smith, and many more.

Innovation isn't new, but it needs to be innovated. Today's markets not only demand this; in fact, they will show you how—if you let them. In these pages, I guide you through my real-world "Innovating Innovation" framework, which has been tested and proved across the battlefields of business.

CHAPTER ONE

STOP BEING A PUNCHLINE

As our case is new, so we must think anew, and act anew.

—Loser of multiple US elections

Six feet, four inches tall, gangly, but hunched now over his desk as he pens eighty-six meticulously written pages in fulfillment of his duties spelled out in Article II, section 3, of the Constitution of the United States of America. Nine hundred twenty-seven days before, he wrested his own party's nomination from three better-known and more privileged rivals—William H. Seward, Salmon P. Chase, and Edward Bates—and began to change one of the great losing streaks in American politics. Depending on how you count, he had lost three or five or, some even argue, as many eight elections before rising to the highest office in the land.[3]

One friend later observes the author's "whole soul" seems consumed in the writing of the words contained in his eighty-six-page document. In this era, the author's message will be hand-delivered and read aloud not by him but by the Secretary of the Senate. Only in the next century will the US president's State of the Union Address become a spectacle in which the American world leader stands before his nation via radio and then television, hoping not merely to report but to inspire.

The message of December 1, 1862 follows a crushing defeat of the author's own party in the mid-term elections, new and escalating cabinet power struggles, political unrest, and the horrors of Antietam, the bloodiest battle up to that point in the American Civil War.

Thirty days later, the author will sign one of the most famous edicts in the history of any nation: The Emancipation Proclamation. But the context for that signature to come must now be established with his own thinking, his own message, and with his own words, which include a long and fact-laden report on the progress of the war and the nation's governance, words that contain some of history's most famous statements and, in 1942, will inspire composer Aaron Copland to borrow excerpts in his evocative Lincoln Portrait. *Here is a small part of what the author wrote: "The dogmas of the quiet past are inadequate to the stormy present. The occasion is piled high with difficulty, and we must rise with the occasion. As our case is new, so we must think anew and act anew."*

At America's darkest of dark hours, no less a leadership authority than the sixteenth President of the United States, Abraham Lincoln, calls on his countrymen to "think anew and act anew." And today, more than a century and a half later, in governance and business, so are we once more called.

Why don't we just call it "Edsel"?

—Ernest R. Breech, Board Chairman, the Ford Motor Company

In the history of modern business, there is one failure that burns above the rest in symbolizing utter defeat. The trouble begins with the name—the name Henry Ford gave to his son, who had served as Ford Motor Company president from 1919 until his death from metastatic stomach cancer in 1943. For a person, the name was unusual, but not as bad as, say, Egbert or Poindexter. But for a car, *Edsel* rhymed with *Lemon.*

Remarkably, Ford Motor management put a lot of thought into it—or, rather, paid Foote, Cone & Belding to put a lot of thought into it. The advertising giant put so much thought into it that they came up with a laundry list of 6,000 names, and, as if that were not enough, Ford marketing research manager David Wallace asked avant-garde American poet Marianne Moore to make suggestions. These included "Utopian Turtletop," "Pastelogram," "Turcotinga," "Resilient Bullet," "Andante con Moto," "The Intelligent Whale," "Varsity Stroke," and, my personal favorite, the "Mongoose Civique." In the end, Ford chairman Ernest Breech, who complained that he had hired Foote, Cone to come up with *a* name, not 6,000, ended the search by surrendering: "Why don't we just call it Edsel?" Even the Ford family objected. No matter. Edsel it became.

Even today, if you send your browser in search of "Edsel" and gaze upon a picture of the car, you will find that an uncomfortable chill runs down your spine. It just *looks wrong*. Feels wrong, awfully wrong, like a high school chem lab experiment gone dreadfully, stinkily awry.

So, cast your imagination back to the late 1940s for the rarely told story of one of industry's most earnest misfires and America's single most famous innovation and marketing failure—a seventy-year-old inability to *think anew*.

The abridged narrative goes like this: The Ford Motor Company set out to create a car affordable for middle-class Americans that offered "futuristic" technology and looks to match. Great notion, but the two-lane blacktop to hell is paved with good intentions. Timing, design, marketing, and the cold dead hand of corporate incumbency transformed laudable aspiration into an unexpected, catastrophic, but well-deserved flop. Intent on innovating, Ford failed to follow through and thereby turned an innovative intention into a malignantly half-assed automotive punchline. Produced for only three years, which turned out to be three years too many, the Edsel achieved immortality as a symbol of marketing and innovation misjudgment.

Let's turn back to 1948. Henry Ford II and his top executives order what will later be called the "Forward Product Planning Committee" to begin researching design and production of a new medium-priced car to capture as much market share as possible from industry front-runner General Motors. Ford management's theory is that GM's wide range of price offerings is contributing to its success. The Korean War, between 1950 and 1953, breaks Ford's momentum on the project, but, nevertheless, the company performs a marketing study in 1952 that confirms an opening in the automobile industry's middle market. It is a gap of opportunity between the bottom-priced Ford and the higher-priced Mercury.

Over the next two years, the company founded by the innovator of innovators, Henry Ford, seeks to design and manufacture this "medium-priced" vehicle for somewhere between $2,000 and $4,000—a target lying in the crease between discount and luxury buyers. The category Ford has in mind is one the company terms “young executives.” Bogged down during the uncertainty of the Korean conflict, work chugged back into motion in 1954, when leadership on the project is transferred from the company’s engineers to its stylists.

From the beginning, then, the project is more about styling than technical substance, more about sizzle than steak. The point is that as Americans enjoyed their postwar mobility, they also came to crave symbols of status and success—emblems of affluence. So, more than ever before, style is selling automobiles. Little wonder that 1955 is labeled “the Year of the Car.” In America, manufacturers sell a record 7,169,908 automobiles. And in this Year of the Car, Ford’s rival, General Motors, sees its stock roar. It is in this desperate context that Ford focuses on what it calls the “E-car,” short for “experimental car.” Figuring that it will take something “special” to beat GM, on April 18, 1955, management assigns the task of design, development, and launch to its “Special Products Division.”

Headed by executive Dick Krafve, eager to make a name for himself, the mission is to innovate a car to match or exceed the Ford Thunderbird, a model then enjoying excellent sales—something executives believe is at least in part being driven by the car’s name, itself a product of extensive scientific research.

Strike one. Behind *Thunderbird* there was thought. Behind *Edsel* there is Henry Ford’s prematurely dead son.

After two years of work and at least a quarter of a billion 1957 dollars (the equivalent of 2.187 billion 2018 dollars), the Edsel is born in September of 1957. It brings with it a daunting ROI. Ford needs to sell 200,000 cars during the first year to *begin* to recoup its investment. The number sales actually hit is far different. Over the next *two* years and two months, the company sells roughly 100,000 Edsels, losing some $350 million.[4] In fact, in a period of fewer than 800 days, Ford manages to lose $3,200 for every Edsel sold—basically the cost of the car itself.

So, the folks at Ford made just about every mistake possible. But even what they could not control moved against them. Conceived in a boom time for auto sales, the car was launched during an economic recession that hit Detroit especially hard. All automakers in 1957 saw sales dip to between 75 and 50 percent of 1956 sales. And Ford managed to make this economic affliction worse by undercutting sales of the mid-priced Edsel with the ill-timed introduction of *another* mid-priced car, the Ford Fairlane, released just one year before. The Fairlane made no pretense to innovation, but it was a reasonably handsome vehicle that sold for less than the Edsel and was manifestly the better value. Consumers perceived the Fairlane for what it was—essentially an honest car.

By contrast, the Edsel not only failed to be special, it failed to be good. Its few true innovations served only to make it worse. Pushbuttons replaced the shifter for the automatic transmission. The buttons were mounted on the steering wheel hub, where the horn button was expected. This ergonomic faux pas resulted in many drivers shifting gears when they wanted to honk the horn. Another shortsighted design decision was embodied in the taillights of the 1958 Edsel station wagons. They were shaped like boomerangs and positioned in such a way that they created a terrible problem when the turn signals were operated. From a distance, the left turn signal looked like an arrow pointing right, and the right looked like an arrow pointing left. *Oops*.

In 1959, Ford brought in Robert McNamara as the first company president whose name was not Ford. He was supposed to turn the company around, and he began to cut Edsel's losses by ditching the separate Edsel division and consolidating the line into a single Mercury, Edsel, Lincoln ("M-E-L") Division.

McNamara pushed for a redesign to make the car look more like other Ford models. By 1960, the final year of its production, the Edsel was nothing more than a Ford with Edsel trim. That was just as well, since 1959 saw Edsel sales stall below forty-five thousand and McNamara cut the extravagant Edsel ad budget to near zero for 1960. Only 2,846 Edsels were sold in the automobile's third and final year.

REQUIEM FOR A LEMON

With the wisdom of hindsight, what can we innovative innovators learn from the sad tale of the Edsel? Six lessons, to which we will return again and again.

LESSON ONE: REMEMBER PERCEPTIONS RULE

The power of using consumer perceptions as your starting point is fundamental to Peter Drucker's strategic focus on marketing and innovation. It is also at the heart of my argument about today's need to innovate innovation itself.

Business Adventures: Twelve Classic Tales from the World of Wall Street, by John Brooks, is among the favorite business books of one of my former clients, Microsoft founder Bill Gates, and of Berkshire Hathaway founder Warren Buffett. Brooks offers a convincing and detailed argument to debunk the legend that the Edsel's marketing and innovation were based on scientific research. There was research, but nobody paid much attention to it. Then, when it came to manufacturing the car, what little of the research that went into design was mostly discarded so the car could be built on an existing chassis using existing machine tools and assembly lines. At a very basic level, therefore, the Edsel was a failure of both marketing and innovation. While marketing and innovation are together critical, trying to market a product shorn of any consumer-inspired innovation is a forlorn hope.

The blindness of Ford leadership did not prove temporary. Even after Edsel's failure, J. C. Doyle, an Edsel marketing manager, steadfastly refused to learn anything about the power of consumer perceptions. Years after the demise of the Edsel, Utah congressman Mo Udall remarked the day after he lost a particularly close election: "The people have spoken, the bastards!" Like Udall, Doyle concluded the people had spoken (the bastards!) and, to his dying day, he blamed the dopey American public for the Edsel's failed launch. As he told Brooks: "People weren't in the mood for the Edsel. Which is a mystery to me. What they'd been buying for several years encouraged the industry to build exactly this kind of car. We gave it to them, and they wouldn't take it. Well, they shouldn't have acted like that… And now the public wants these little beetles. I don't get it!"[5]

If we look at Ford's large market study of 1952 and the work of its "Forward Product Planning Committee" in 1954, it becomes apparent that, in designing the Edsel, Ford was focusing not so much on what consumers wanted, but on the gap between the company's offerings and those of its competitors. Ford executives should have been obsessed with potential customers. Instead, they were obsessed with their competitors. In single-mindedly concentrating on producing a mid-priced vehicle, they built a car for their competitors, not their customers. As former Procter & Gamble Chairman A. G. Lafley observed, there is a fundamental difference between *competitor*-focused companies and *customer-focused* companies. For example, in phone manufacturing, a *competitor-focused* company says they are in the business of "making smartphones." By contrast, a *customer*-focused company believes they are in the business of "connecting people and enabling communications any place, anytime…."

In fact, Brooks points out the market research was simply ignored, discarded, and replaced by whim, intuition, personal agenda, bureaucratic politics, plain-old guesswork, and, later, some old-fashioned snake-oil-selling methodologies.

THE LESSON: Successful innovation and business growth begin and end with consumer perceptions.

LESSON TWO: BE DIFFERENT OR BE DAMNED

As my former client, The Coca-Cola Company chairman Roberto Goizueta, once advised, "Be different or be damned." Notwithstanding its jarring looks, the Edsel actually represented a whole heap of same-old, same-old—particularly under the hood and from the inside-out. The January 1958 issue of *Consumer Reports* gave the Edsel its most damaging review. The editors hit it hard for sameness. Worse, they educated some 800,000 subscribers—and potential Edsel buyers—on what made the car tick. It "has no important advantages over other brands," they wrote. "The car is almost *entirely conventional* in construction.... The amount of shake present in this Corsair [the next-to-highest Edsel trim level] body on rough roads—which wasn't long in making itself heard as squeaks and rattles—went well beyond any acceptable limit... The Corsair's handling qualities—sluggish, over-slow steering, sway and lean on turns, and a general detached-from-the-road feel—are, to put it mildly, without distinction." *Ugh.*

And just when you think it cannot get worse, the Edsel came onto the market with another mortal wound, entirely self-inflicted. The vehicle was offered in eighteen different trim levels—Ranger, Pacer, Corsair, Citation, twenty-four door-hardtop, sedan, wagon, convertibles, six or nine passengers, and so on—smothering consumers in a confusing array of choice, far beyond what any sane buyer could want. Largely consisting of distinctions without differences, the lack of focus left consumers paralyzed, which is not what you want when the object is to get a showroom visitor to reach for his checkbook. When variety becomes a blur, indifference cancels out differentiation.

The thing is, Ford executives were less interested in designing and refining a distinctive product, image, and character and more intent on making the Edsel everything at once. Think of this as lazy innovation and lazy marketing, a dreary combination if there ever was one, shining a light on everything and everyone rather than focusing the spot on what is core to the success of your mission. The "everything approach" is easier, but doomed. In the words of Prussian monarch and strategic genius Frederick the Great: "He who defends everything defends nothing." If Der Alte Fritz could have seen an Edsel, he might have noted, doubtless in disgust, that it indeed defends nothing and offends just about everyone.

THE LESSON: A lack of focused differentiation will throttle any effort at innovative breakthrough.

LESSON THREE: INNOVATE FORWARD

As bad an idea as it represented, the Edsel's pushbutton transmission was at least capable of forward and reverse. Nevertheless, the car was resolutely aimed backwards. Whereas innovation is driven by forward momentum, the Edsel and its marketing were all about rolling to the rear. The car represented tried and tired conventional engineering wrapped in subjectively unattractive design billed as futuristic. Fueled by engineering sameness, it was promoted with depressingly conventional marketing strategies. As if to echo General of the Army Omar Bradley's famous 1951 rebuke concerning Douglas MacArthur's desire to extend the Korean War into China—"It is the wrong war, at the wrong place, at the wrong time, and with the wrong enemy." *Time* magazine in 1958 called the Edsel, "The wrong car for the wrong market at the wrong time."

Time was not just blowing rhetorical smoke. For instance, when the Edsel was on the drawing board, consumers seemed intensely focused on buying "big" and "bigger." By 1958, when the car finally limped off the assembly line, these same consumers were starting to look for smaller economy cars. The public's interest in gigantic, big-fin, chrome-encrusted, gas-guzzling cars was going stale. New, smaller, future-focused cars included the VW Beetle, the Nash Rambler, and the Studebaker Lark.

Congenitally conservative and shackled to the glacial pace of bureaucratic decision-making concerning matters of design and technology, Ford was innovating backward, not forward. It was not just that Ford suffered from an epidemic of wry neck, in which every head was turned backward and incapable of looking forward, the company's processes—planning, design, production—moved at the pace of a mastodon. Massive time lags between every step meant research findings were about as fresh as moldy bread by the time it came to apply them. During the two interminable years between conception and delivery, consumer trends toward smaller economy cars roared in like a rip tide, pulling the Edsel deeper out into the briny depths of oblivion.

The Edsel emerges for us as an argument for the kind of research approach I have used for such clients as The Coca-Cola Company, McDonald's, Microsoft, American Express, Verizon, KPMG, Nike, and many others. Importantly, this was not *research,* but *pre-search*—hypothesis and scenario testing rolled out into the future, pulling consumers as far forward as possible in their perception and thinking, driving market research to anticipate rather than react to consumer trends. Asking consumers, in effect, what *will* you want instead of what *did* you want helps us understand perceptions, attitudes, and behaviors and, most importantly, what might move consumers going forward.

THE LESSON: Aim your research and thinking forward, not backward, and put to work the same level of agility in dealing with change that today's consumers bring to their everyday lives.

LESSON FOUR: TRANSFORM YOUR BUSINESS

I argue in this book for a wide-angle view of innovation, far wider than your company's products, services, and technologies. Successful innovation today must take in a company's business model as well as the platform on which that model is implemented. Today, it is the platform that will drive breakthroughs and success.

Consider an example detailed in Ron Adner's excellent book, *The Wide Lens: A New Strategy for Innovation*. In the 1990s, Michelin innovated the self-inflating run-flat tire.[6] Sounds like a breakthrough if there ever was one. But Adner shows how Michelin's innovation process failed to contemplate, much less understand, how innovation must be adopted by the *larger* ecosystem into which it is delivered. Michelin's 1990s innovation was a *technological* breakthrough, but the innovation fell short of *commercial* breakthrough because repair shops, auto dealers, and auto manufacturers were not prepared to accommodate run-flat tires. Failure to innovate beyond the confines of your business model—failure to innovate the required platform out in the ecosystem—will doom success.

Return to the Edsel. The "car of the future" brought with it widespread confusion in terms of workers, parts, and processes. Moreover, self-sabotaging mistakes—the misguided attempt to build the "new" Edsel on assembly lines also assigned to turn out "old" standbys—landed right inside the Edsel engines and drive trains, which became proverbial for their unreliable mechanics, missing parts, and other failures of engineering and quality control. It got so bad that Ford began selling Edsels with a kit of extra parts packed in the trunk, along with instructions to dealer service departments on how to use them.

And, oh yes, the dealers. Ford wanted to brand the Edsel as special. Instead of making it special, however, Ford snatched away ownership of the Edsel from its own dealership system and added a new category of dealer to sell the Edsel exclusively. This uniquely self-inflicted orgy of cannibalism ate away at Ford's own long-established selling system. One thinks of the ancient Roman emperor who, when the people turned against him, settled into a warm bath, sliced open the veins in his wrist, and bled himself peacefully to death. Just so, Ford sapped away the force of synergy by not merely failing to leverage its existing dealer network, but by making such leverage impossible. This setup heaped inertia where momentum should have been at the very moment of the Edsel's launch.

And for those cars that did manage to drive off the showroom floor and into some suburban garage, their owners were quickly confronted by two things: electrical and mechanical problems *plus* dealer mechanics unequipped to handle them. The much-ballyhooed and universally hated "Tele-Touch Transmissions" presented customers with problems and dealers without solutions.

Amid the unfolding scenario of disappointment, Ford pressed dealerships to pre-order large quantities of Edsels in anticipation of a crush of demand. When the demand failed to materialize, retreating, and finally turning into outright rout, dealers rebelled, and the entire system, along with Ford's business model, seized up like an Edsel leaking dry of oil.

THE LESSON: In today's hyper-change environment, wide-angle, continual strategic transformation of your business model is not optional, but mandatory to marketing and innovation success.

LESSON FIVE: REMEMBER—CONTEXT IS EVERYTHING

As with so many failures of marketing and innovation, the Edsel was launched without proper regard for context. Two adages apply:

1. Timing is everything.
2. You can do the right thing at the wrong time, and it will be the wrong thing.

In a failure to understand the context into which they were selling, Ford made the mistake of moving heaven and earth to maintain consumer secrecy in conducting its market research. This was the same error The Coca-Cola Company made in designing and executing research for "New Coke" in the mid-1980s. Both Ford and Coke focused on what was for them "today," but it was, more accurately, "yesterday." In both cases, Ford and Coke failed to imagine, anticipate, and market test the consumer world of "tomorrow," the context into which they *will be* selling. They failed to undertake *pre-search.*

And it was even worse. The companies not only failed to look ahead to anticipate where their markets were heading, but both Ford and Coke failed in all their market research to test, analyze, and understand fully the larger context of how their product was to be positioned in its marketplace. Their obsession with secrecy meant they did not want to risk revealing and testing with consumers in market research the fundamental and *complete* offering that was Edsel, or the idea that New Coke will *completely* replace Coke Classic. In quest of secrecy, executives denied their company the real-world consumer insights that are the very reason for market testing. Secrecy superseded context.

Coca-Cola focused its research mainly on the "Pepsi vs. Coke" dimension of blind taste tests. And executives discovered the sweeter New Coke began faring better against its Coke archrival Pepsi than did Coke Classic. But, by omitting the key fact that New Coke will *take away* Coke Classic from its loyal drinkers, the company robbed itself of any meaningful measurement of consumer preference within this larger, crucial context.

Some thirty years earlier, Ford made the same mistake with its Edsel research. Like Coke, Ford was obsessed with secrecy, and so the company's endless market research never presented the entire Edsel package to respondents. The look, feel, brand, name, technical features, mechanics, drive dynamics—none of this was laid out. The equation was presented in fragments.

The absence of context left one thing both companies had in abundance: self-centered arrogance—a belief that top executives knew better than anyone else or any kind of market analysis. In the end, it was upon this commodity that most of the key internal decisions were made. Ford, for instance, failed to factor in a market and economy clearly changing during the months leading up to Edsel's release. Rather than adjust to the market, Ford released the car exactly as planned in the context of a different time, a different economy, and a different marketplace. More than three decades later, The Coca-Cola Company Chairman Roberto Goizueta faced a hostile press conference at which he announced the arrival of New Coke. Here, for the first time, the company's leader learned that media and consumers were uniting in their outrage at having something iconic taken from them without so much as an if-you-please.

In both cases, corporate arrogance was as hard to shed as a poker tell. It polluted any sense of the marketplace and descended on corporate vision like an old-school London fog. Arrogance, not the consumer, permeated all aspects of developing and marketing the Edsel and New Coke.

In addition, part of understanding and defining context involves the strategic principle that everything communicates. Even the smallest detail of marketing or innovation communicates loudly and profoundly. A single contradiction between promise and reality, once noticed by consumers, can undo hundreds of millions of dollars of marketing. In the case of Edsel, glaring assembly line errors, consumer confusion between the horn button and gear shift, misdirected turn signals, early and chronic oil leaks, sticking hoods, trunks that failed to open, buttons that needed a hammer to push them, and a pre-production average repair cost of $10,000 per car communicated more loudly and profoundly than any Edsel advertisement.

THE LESSON: At minimum, test, recognize, and understand the larger context into which your product, service, brand, or company competes. Better yet, develop and drive a strategy to control the dialogue and help define this larger context—and remember that everything communicates.

LESSON SIX: ALWAYS THINK ANEW

Edsel was a failure of imagination, a failure to think anew, to "think different." If Ford's intention had been to build another run-of-the-mill car, well, they certainly knew how to do that, and it might have cost the company a lot less money and grief. Instead, they faked innovation, and their Edsel ended up an eternal punchline.

Edsel's demise was all about the way Ford framed marketing and innovation. The roots of the car's failure grew from how people initially thought about the Edsel, how they imagined it, went about inventing it, refining it, marketing it, and ultimately failing with it. From the beginning, company executives and Edsel designers failed to understand that the 1950s was a decade in which everyone made their case based on newness. Therefore, these executives and designers were obliged to think anew and act anew. But they did no such thing.

Nevertheless, the Ford organization did learn from the Edsel episode. The failure of the Edsel helped produce Ford's legendary Mustang. Open your browser and click on some pictures of Mustangs through the fifty-four years of the car's production history. Compare the look of the Mustang to the Edsel, which limped across the earthly sphere for a mere three years. In both the Mustang and the Edsel, everything communicates. It is just that they speak entirely different languages.

One very important lesson Ford learned from the Edsel Apocalypse is that it was not all bad. Many new automobile features were introduced on the Edsel, and Ford did not throw all of them out with the car. By 1962, such features as self-adjusting brakes and the self-lubricating chassis became technical synergies throughout the Ford line. Add to this the hard-learned lessons born of Edsel's catastrophic quality control problems. These led the company not to tinker and tweak, but rather to reorganize all manufacturing under a single organization, thereby shifting the corporate culture to a focus on solving technical problems and human mistakes before they happen.

Of course, today, a cadre of collectors covets the car. Go shop for one of the fewer than 100 top-condition Edsels on the road at this writing. As of 2018, this icon of the failure of marketing and innovation, this Mt. Everest of lemons, which cost far too much at $2,500–$3,800 in 1958, can today be secured for your own garage from a trade collector for something over $100,000.

THE LESSON: Successful marketing and innovation demands three prerequisites: challenging assumptions, disrupting the status quo, and thinking anew.

INNOVATION IS BROKEN

Like the Edsel, innovation is broken today. It is in crisis. Innovation needs wide-angle, wholesale innovation. The problem is common these days. Attempts at innovation look backward. They react in an age when intelligent, proactive anticipation has never been a more critical advantage. To be sure, there is no shortage of books and articles and blogs on innovation. But you can safely ignore all that fail to focus *ahead* of where we are today. Innovation must foreshadow tomorrow.

So, we argue here for an anti-Edsel approach, relentlessly forward-focused and substantive. Not that looking ahead requires ignorance of the present or the past. What was once the future is now the present. That we live in this former future suggests that we live largely among products of successful innovation. Much as the Renaissance rejected aspects of its recent past (the Middle Ages), it recovered the innovation of its more distant past, that of Classical Europe.

Today, we can discover some proven ways to innovate and invent. These methods are inherently disruptive—that is, forward-focused. They are approaches that instinctively move out of the center of an organization, a society, a mindset, and go about innovation at what I call the "disruptive periphery."

That is where we will be spending most of our time in the pages that follow. We will:

- Adopt a wide and global approach to innovation
- Deploy the power of an insurgent strategic overlay

- Leverage customer- and marketing-centric views of innovation
- Borrow the pragmatic lessons from the still-emerging world of Agile software development

We will not reject the value of experience—when that experience has succeeded in outlining a future—but we will not reflexively defend any experience for its own sake. Some three decades of battle-tested global consulting and training go into the stew of the real-world strategic principles you are about to savor. I have plated it in a simple bowl of "how-to." Ingredients include:

- Proven change-leadership strategies counterpointed with insurgent organizational approaches
- Proactive marketing and communications strategies emphasizing customer-sourced perceptions
- Practical ways to "think different," including ongoing and new inputs, voices, questions, perspectives, passions, and experiments
- Executional steps to bring innovation and change to the pragmatic and personal level where they will take root and grow, bearing new advantages for your business

INNOVATION IS FIXABLE

Matter is neither created nor destroyed. That a thing is broken implies that it can be fixed—can be fixed, taught, and accelerated. This requires innovating innovation with new thinking, approaches, and strategies, all of which can be taught, so that innovation can be produced on demand.

We do need to face the fact that the challenge of fixing, teaching, and accelerating innovation has never been more urgent. Today, 50 percent of startups will fail in their first year, 80 percent by their fifth, and 96 percent by their tenth anniversary.

Then, it gets worse.

With only 4 in 100 new businesses still standing, only 5 percent of *those* will achieve $1 million in revenue, four tenths of 1 percent will rise above $5 million, and an even smaller fraction, 6 out of 100,000, will exceed $10 million in annual revenue.[7]

Given the odds, the need for more and better innovation is clear as day and bright as the sun. The management titan Peter Drucker has already told us what that better innovation will be: the "specific instrument of entrepreneurship" and "the act that endows resources with a new capacity to create wealth." Innovation is always an instrument *and* an act. As innovation pioneer 3M defines it, innovation is a simple equation: "New ideas + action or implementation = which result in an improvement, a gain, or a profit." I would change just one thing—the first instance of *or* to *and.* Innovation requires *both* action *and* implementation. In the first of these, innovation is an *act.* In the second, it is an *instrument.* There is an *act* and its *strategic application,* verb and noun, motion and tool.

The action and implementation of innovation is delivered in three ways:

> *By Leadership*: Defining your own innovation vision, values, and priorities by managing creative disruption (or disruptive creation) and by personally exemplifying the power of "thinking different."
>
> *By Company*: Creating and executing on a platform, driving a unique and effective business model, fueling

a change culture and organization, forming a uniquely powerful alliance, or inventing a new set of processes.

By Offering: Inventing new, relevant, and differentiated products, services, or technologies.

So, we have choices. But we must start fixing innovation right away. A recent Boston Consulting Group study finds 70 percent of CEOs interviewed put innovation among their top three leadership priorities. Great! Seven out of ten are already on board—except that the same survey reveals that a mere 16 percent believe their own company outperforms their peers in terms of innovation.

As World Economic Forum founder Klaus Schwab tells us, "We stand on the brink of a technological revolution that will fundamentally alter the way we live, work, and relate to one another. In its scale, scope, and complexity, the transformation will be unlike anything humankind has experienced before."

Faced with change at an exponential pace, we must all—CEOs and non-CEOs, inventors and non-inventors—take charge of innovation. Consider, for instance:

- **Airbnb**: Founded in 2008, born on the idea of renting air mattresses on the floor of its founders' San Francisco loft, it is today one of the world's largest hotel and real estate companies...yet it owns no buildings.
- **Uber**: Founded in 2009, an idea birthed on its founder's smartphone amidst his own frustration over not finding a taxi in the rain, it is today one of the world's largest transportation companies...yet it owns no vehicles.

- **Facebook**: Founded in 2004, inside a now infamous Harvard dorm room, it is today the world's largest media company, with nearly 25 percent of all internet users signing in to look for news, photos, music, or videos…yet it produces no content.
- **Bitcoin**: Founded in 2009, based on an academic paper by Satoshi Nakamito,[8] it is the world's first decentralized digital currency, with somewhere between 3 to 6 million unique customers…and, of course, it uses no central bank.
- **Alibaba**: Founded in 1999, it is today the world's largest retailer, featuring a billion different products on just one of its many portals, and managing as much as 80 percent of China's e-commerce market…but it has no inventory.
- **Salesforce**: Founded in 1999, it is at this writing among the world's largest marketing and sales companies, with over $10 billion in annual revenues…yet it neither employs nor offers any salespeople.

One glance at this remarkable list, and it is impossible to doubt the existence of exponential change all around us. The average age of these examples as of 2018 is thirteen years and, together, these relatively new companies represent over 1.3 trillion dollars of value.

For super achievers like Airbnb and the rest, innovation is happening earlier and faster than ever before. Our age of exponential change is an era of exponential opportunity. For example, companies such as Apple, Google, Amazon, Facebook, and Microsoft[9] are, at their best, driving innovation at an exponential pace. And Airbnb and the other digital enterprises that control much but own little or nothing are known as "platform businesses," digital (or digitized) business models that create connected ecosystems of producers and consumers, or, as the authors of *Platform Revolution* explain, the sheer innovative force of a platform is empirically impossible to ignore today. When it comes to disruptive innovation, platform beats pipeline, just as exponential thinking beats linear thinking. The elimination of gatekeepers atop platforms, just like the rejection of status quo thinking inside the world's most innovative companies, almost magically unlocks new sources of value creation. The proof is in the numbers, which are staggering. Today, more than half of US startups are platform businesses.[10]

Take, for example, just four US companies—Apple, Amazon, Facebook, and Google. Together, as of 2018, these companies have created $2.3 trillion—that's *trillion*—in wealth (in terms of stock ownership) and have entwined themselves in the daily lives of billions of people.[11] More specifically:

- **Amazon** in some ways has eliminated the consumer pain of shopping for things that are not fun. (Think toothpaste vs. Porsches) It is heading for a market capitalization perhaps twice that of its incumbent archrival, Walmart.

- **Apple** represents something of a religious offering to its loyalists and displays nearly unprecedented profit margins by offering low-cost products at premium pricing. At this writing, it is history's most profitable company.

- **Facebook** is, by the numbers, perhaps the world's most influential company—notwithstanding current privacy and security challenges. At present, one-sixth of the global population—about 1.2 billion people—sign in daily and spend an average of 50 minutes a day on the company's platform.

- **Google** has become the modern world's transcendent navigator—earning the trust of over 2 billion people, more than any other institution in terms of search and guidance. It is the Benjamin Button of companies, aging in reverse to become more relevant and valuable the more it is used, since it is through use that its associative database grows.

To put into context the ongoing platform-driven and disruptive innovation revolution, consider that the average employee at General Motors today creates $231,000 in economic value. Impressive—until you compare it to the $20.5 million in economic value created by Facebook employees today.[12]

Separately and together, this new "Big Four" of mega-companies is driving the most exciting and disruptive technological wave ever seen. Moreover, imagine the coming rounds of future breakthroughs in, for example, machine learning, artificial intelligence, mixed reality, quantum computing, green energy and, even more fundamentally, the future of our human minds.[13] Or just consider the extent of change already wrought by the power of platform. Founded in 1768, *Encyclopedia Britannica* defined the future of accumulated knowledge until 2012, when it ceased print publication and even shriveled into relative irrelevance as a paywall website thereafter. Back in 1999, Microsoft was sufficiently innovative to spend $450 million to develop an online encyclopedia. But even that was eclipsed just two years later when Jimmy Wales and Larry Sanger started Wikipedia, offering their web-based encyclopedia for free and today managing the fifth most-visited internet site in the world—one that is still maintained exclusively by volunteers.

Wikipedia and its ilk have prompted Wharton professor Jeremy Rifkin to forecast a paradigm shift from market capitalization to what he calls the "Collaborative Commons." Rifkin writes, "the Collaborative Commons is ascendant and, by

2050, it will likely settle in as the primary arbiter of economic life in most of the world."[14]

Those who hate today's modern monopolies can find a crumb of comfort in the fact that all this exponential change will not necessarily save even the biggest mega platform businesses from destruction. Consider that 88 percent of *Fortune* 500 companies from the 1950s are not just missing from today's list, they are gone, bankrupt, or out of business.[15] In the 1970s, IBM defined the business marketplace and was unstoppable. In the 1990s, Microsoft could do no wrong inside the electronics industry. And, in the 2000s, Enron looked to be the best or even only company ready to successfully ride the e-commerce wave of the future. Each of these companies either failed, went backward, or went bankrupt.

Today, the great majority of companies will fail to innovate and break through or they will move across a life cycle that takes them into thinking more like a status quo incumbent than a forward-looking insurgent.

And, in the meantime, outside, along some marketplace periphery, a wild-card company will be imagining a fresh-eyed innovation breakthrough that will someday turn the business world upside down. This is what the transistor did to the world of 1947, the integrated circuit to the world of 1958, the personal computer to the world of the 1990s, and the smartphone to the world of the 2000s. Perhaps here, out along this marketplace periphery, at a Starbucks table or garage or dorm room, will begin the gestation of the world's next trillion-dollar company.

HOW DO I CASH IN?

Creating or reinventing the next breakthrough mega-company almost certainly means putting to work some form of the insurgent innovation framework.

Driving innovation breakthrough means continually asking a version of the five fundamental questions that, in 1997, the newly appointed Apple CEO, Steve Jobs, asked his top executives when he began a well-nigh Shakespearian return to the company he himself created, the same company that, in 1985, had fired him. These questions formed the nucleus of the greatest corporate turnaround in the history of business:

1. What do you (really) do?
2. Why did you begin doing this originally—and now?
3. Who are you—and who do you need to be to win?
4. Where are you? (and where are your chokeholds?)
5. What's next? (What keeps you up at night?)

Fundamental to answering these five strategically loaded questions is a commitment to thinking and acting anew. This entails not a single magical moment or dramatic epiphany, but rather a step-by-step journey. And it means taking a first step and walking toward a commitment—a decision—to begin the battle to innovate. This is our next subject.

CHAPTER TWO

SUBDIVIDE LIGHT

And yet it moves.

—Attributed to Galileo Galilei

Over the course of some four centuries, the telescope, in its various technological iterations, has transformed the way we see both the universe and ourselves. The transformation became most dramatic since 1990 when the Hubble Space Telescope was launched and has since probed the very frontier of the universe, showing us reality as it existed some 13.82 billion years ago. This transformation has only multiplied as NASA launched its other "Great Observatories"—the Compton Gamma Ray Observatory in 1991, the Chandra X-ray Observatory in 1999, and the Spitzer Space Telescope in 2003.

Before these events, the most powerful perceptual and intellectual transformation wrought by the telescope came at the very beginning of its first years of use. In 1608, Galileo Galilei heard news of a Dutch spectacle-maker, Hans Lippershey, and the patent he filed for a device that could see beyond the sky. Within a day, Galileo got busy making his own version of this new, magical instrument. As with many inventions, the inventor and the innovator are not necessarily one and the same person. Lippershey deserves credit for inventing the telescope, but it was Galileo who made it an instrument of profound innovation.

Through this transformational lens—which in its first year allowed humankind to understand more of the universe than had been known over the preceding two thousand years—Galileo could see the mountains and craters of the moon and the daylit side of Venus. This revealed to him two earth-shaking facts. First, our universe was far bigger—and our place in it therefore far smaller—than previously understood. Second, those jagged mountains and pock-like craters were hardly evidence of the "perfect" and "eternal" work of a perfect and eternal God.

This convinced Galileo that the Polish astronomer Nicolaus Copernicus had been correct some hundred years earlier, when he said the sun and not the earth was the center of what came to be called the solar system.

The shift to the view of the sun as the center of the solar system took many years and, as innovation so often does, questioned, eroded, and even destroyed old beliefs. Chipping away at cherished faiths requires fresh faith in the new belief. And there is often a price to pay. In 1633, many refused to believe they on earth were not the center of everything. They took steps to suppress the heretical idea that it was not the sun moving, but rather the earth itself. Galileo was summoned to the Inquisition and ultimately compelled to retract his Copernican view. In a formal allocution, he was forced to say aloud that, in God's creation, the earth was stationary.

Aging and ill, Galileo did as he was told, denying that the earth orbited the sun. But legend has it that, after pronouncing the required allocution, he whispered more to himself than to those present, "E pur si muove"—"And yet it moves."

If we all did the things we are capable of doing, we would literally astound ourselves.

—Thomas Edison

The Copernican Revolution, validated by Galileo's *"E pur si muove,"* is a central example of what the controversial philosopher of science Thomas S. Kuhn calls a "paradigm shift" in his 1962 classic, *The Structure of Scientific Revolutions.*[16] Here he details the history and process of innovation, challenging conventional thinking about the progress of what he calls "normal science," arguing that scientific progress is more episodic than accumulative, with breakthroughs occurring during periods of "revolutionary science." Kuhn holds that, in revolutionary times, anomalies lead to new "paradigms," which make it possible to ask new questions of old data, thereby superseding the mere "puzzle-solving" of earlier paradigms.

Each new paradigm changes the rules. The paradigm shift is therefore the product less of linear thinking than an exponential or revolutionary displacement in thinking. When he proved Copernicus correct, Galileo set into motion revolutionary thinking that transformed the prevailing Ptolemaic paradigm—the geocentric universe. Viewed in retrospect, we may conclude that Copernicus led to Galileo, who led to Kepler's cosmology, and then ushered in Newtonian physics—progress begetting progress in serial fashion. Kuhn, however, argues that this linear interpretation is an ex post facto fiction. He sees this process of change as the product of revolutionary or breakthrough thinking. For purposes of analysis, he divides the process into phases:

- Phase 1 is the "pre-paradigm phase," wherein no consensus exists on any particular theory.

- Phase 2 begins the operation of "normal science," which puzzle-solves within the context of the dominant paradigm.
- Phase 3 witnesses the erosion of the dominant paradigm, which is shown to be increasingly unable to account for mounting anomalies. At this phase, the scientific community enters a crisis period.
- Phase 4 is the paradigm shift. In this period of scientific revolution, underlying assumptions are re-examined, and the new paradigm or way of thinking takes hold.
- Phase 5 is the "post-revolution" period, during which scientists return to normal science and solve puzzles within this new and now-dominant paradigm.

Fifty-six years after its publication, Kuhn's groundbreaking framework continues to prove durable. It applies to today's struggle over innovation. In some ways, the way we now think about innovation is entering Kuhn's Phase 3. That is, we are unable to account for mounting anomalies, which makes us feel we are entering a crisis period that demands a new approach, a new paradigm.

As Kuhn envisioned the process in the 1960s, true paradigm shifts are rare events. They may not even occur at the modest rate of one per century. This leaves you and your business plenty of room for puzzle-solving, incremental progress, and the accumulation of innovation that may someday reach the critical mass for a new, fresh Kuhnian paradigm shift. Kuhn further argues that the dominant paradigm so controls the agenda of thinking that it is sometimes impossible to break away from it, to "think different," to even imagine that it is the earth that revolves around the sun. In other words, the incumbent status quo is easy, addictive, and comfortable.

In this, Kuhn echoes our approach to driving change leadership and innovation. First, if we are to innovate in our businesses, we must not restrict ourselves to approaches to innovation that are ruled by the status quo. Second, we must look for constant, though linear, progress rather than waiting for that lightning strike of revolutionary progress—which may not come for another hundred years. Third, innovation today requires "chunking"—breaking into manageable, doable steps that allow us to keep driving innovation ahead rather than waiting for revolution to happen. If we can keep moving along a linear pathway of progress, we can create value at regular intervals and enjoy incremental success.

Assuming we are in Phase 3, experiencing the erosion of the dominant paradigm, we have no way of knowing how close we are to Phase 4, the paradigm shift. The digital transformation, in itself a paradigm shift, is driving the pace of change so rapidly and the scope of change so broadly that we may have good reason to believe that Kuhn's 1960s-based estimate of the relative rarity of paradigm shifts—once a century—is no longer accurate. While it is important to keep innovating rather than passively awaiting the revolution, we need to recognize that linear thinking will not suffice amidst a paradigm shift. As you push ahead, be prepared to spring at a moment's notice.

LINEAR INNOVATION: FIRST—COMMIT TO A WAY OF THINKING

Scientists Heather Barry Kappes of New York University and Gabriele Oettingen of the University of Hamburg argue that we humans need both to imagine *and* fantasize about the big things we are going to do *and* about how we are going to do them. It is not enough to simply imagine a desired future state. We must also fantasize about the steps to get there. In fact, Kappes and Oettingen conclude that both imagining and fantasizing about these steps help muster the energy required to succeed.

Sometimes, our challenge is that we don't believe we belong on a bigger stage or that we can innovate any kind of breakthrough, big or small. For example, Tina Seelig, a Stanford professor specializing in creativity and innovation, quotes studies indicating that "Up to 70 percent of people experience impostor syndrome at some time in their lives." They believe the stage on which they stand is too big and that they have no business being on it. Behavioral expert Olivia Fox Cabane goes further: "In the impostor syndrome, people feel that they don't really know what they're doing, and it's just a matter of time before they're found out and exposed as a fraud." She argues that this syndrome takes hold even at the highest levels of business and education, concluding: "I've heard that every time the incoming class of Stanford Business School is asked, 'How many of you feel you are the one mistake the admissions committee made?' two-thirds of the students immediately raise their hands."[17]

In business, the flipside of the impostor syndrome is an existentially total belief in yourself as a bold leader and successful innovator. Again, this is the role Chris Robinson played on the soap opera *General Hospital* and later in a Vicks Formula 44 cough syrup commercial pitch: "I'm not a doctor, but I play one on TV." Actor Robinson was no doctor, but he believed, as any good actor must, that he was no impostor but a bona fide MD. Thomas Edison, the inventor who declared genius to be 1 percent inspiration and 99 percent perspiration, even if he often publicly denied it almost certainly believed he did possess that critical 1 percent.

Belief in your existential legitimacy must be steadily fueled by your imagination, the lifeblood of innovation. Consider Martin Luther King Jr.'s "I Have a Dream" speech, delivered on August 28, 1963, before the Lincoln Memorial. King thoroughly imagined he had the legitimate right to dream that dream—and that was enough to persuade much of the world, opening a path to civil rights in the United States. Or think about Albert Einstein crediting his 1921 Nobel Prize and his development of the special theory of relativity to his own boyhood dreams about riding a light beam. He was confident that he had the right to dream such a thing—and he had the equation to prove it!

Or consider the iconic skier Jean-Claude Killy, who, in 1968, won all three Olympic alpine gold medals. He once told an interviewer about how, when he was recovering from a terrible downhill accident and was unable to ski, he continued to practice mentally. Was that a distant second best to being on the slopes? Common sense says *yes*. Yet Killy went from mental practice to delivering one of the best performances of his career.[18]

Killy's experience reminds me of Daley Thompson, who, like me, was a Decathlete. Unlike me, he won the Olympic Decathlon—twice. In 1984, he faced a high-drama athletic contest with his archrival, West Germany's Juergen Hingsen, for the unofficial title of "world's greatest athlete." Each man had more than once traded world records, even if the UK's Thompson had beaten Hingsen head-to-head on six consecutive occasions before entering the 1984 Olympics. When the competition for the gold, the 1984 Los Angeles Games, moved to the Decathlon's seventh event, the discus, Thompson was keenly aware that this was his worst event and Hingsen's best. Indeed, Thompson's first two throws were well below even his normally weak measurement.

But on this day of all days, when it counted, Thompson drew on his imagination to visualize a winning throw. He imagined he had the right to be a great discus thrower, and he hurled the metal-and-wood plate to a personal best on his third and final throw, crushing the West German's spirt and chance for gold.

"For that one moment," Thompson explains, "I wasn't interested in winning. Some people shy away from the high-pressure moments. It was what I had been looking for, a culmination of all I had trained for. Just to be faced with the situation in an Olympics—the feeling was incredible. And I'd faced it and overcome the thing I'm least competent in, the discus. I really hit the shit out of that discus."[19]

Jean-Claude Killy and Daley Thompson both practiced believing, visualizing each step toward success. When it counted most, their physical selves followed an internal belief and deep commitment they built from within. The truth is, it really does all begin with you. As a business leader, your own internal mindset and self-belief are your most powerful tools. Believing you are a bold and successful change leader and innovator is the first and fundamental step toward becoming…a bold and successful change leader and innovator.

Preparing internally to drive innovation breakthrough means taking yourself as seriously as you want others to take you. From working with top corporate CEOs and political leaders of many countries, I have discovered that each of them believes they are a top CEO or political leader. Their own affirmative self-image is a powerful driver, filter, and vision they aim at, move toward, and access. They take their leadership and their success earnestly, and this becomes a self-fulfilling element in leadership and success.

As business author and entrepreneur Tony Robbins reminds us, "Most people doubt their beliefs and believe their doubts."[20] Like the great and resilient athletes they were, Jean-Claude Killy and Daley Thompson used the power of visualization, the fuel of imagination, to give them the enduring self-confidence to face rejection after rejection. Innovators need thick skin to overcome the impostor syndrome by visualizing and believing in their own success. Knocked down, they *see* themselves getting up off the floor—and then they do just that.

Consider, for example, the number of times the founders of the following companies pitched investors before finally securing funding for their innovations:

- Skype 40
- Cisco 76
- Pandora 300
- Google 350[21]

Or consider the 302 rejections Roy Disney received from the banks he approached to fund his "new" amusement park, Disneyland. Or the Social Security check sixty-five-year-old Colonel Sanders cashed, which led him to pledge prophetically to himself: "I'm going to build something new with my life, I'm going to create something called 'Kentucky Fried Chicken.' "

Research shows that successful innovators deeply *believe* three things:

- First, innovation is *there*—it exists or will exist.
- Second, innovation *must* and *will* be found.
- Third, innovation will be *worth it* once it is found.[22]

Invariably, all three of these core beliefs are a part of innovation success—an inner belief that innovation can happen, will happen, and will be worth the journey. In fact, this inner belief—and the leader's ability to cascade and leverage it within the organization—has never been more important in creating and sustaining a culture of innovation and a successful business. Put another way, the ability to leverage belief is the minimal requirement to advancing leadership, company, and product breakthroughs and doing what it takes to grow a business: increasing the number of customers, the average transaction value, and the frequency of repurchase. It is essential to what pioneering marketer Sergio Zyman described as the job of marketing and innovation: "Sell more stuff, to more people, more often, for more money, more efficiently."[23]

Leveraging belief strips away the impostor syndrome and commits to an insurgent way of thinking about playing offense and driving innovation forward. Or else. At key times, this means channeling the do-or-die analogy constructed by Napoleon Hill in his 1937 classic, *Think and Grow Rich*. Hill applied the lessons of Conquistador Hernán Cortés. Back in 1519, as he landed on the shores of Mexico's Yucatan, he knew the odds were against him. He had to convince his crew of 600 sailors and soldiers that he truly believed and that they must as well. So, he scuttled his ships. With no means of turning back, there was no choice but to believe in victory. As Hill puts it:

> A long while ago, a great warrior faced a situation which made it necessary for him to make a decision which insured his success on the battlefield.... Addressing his men before the first battle, he said, "You see the boats going up in smoke. That means that we cannot leave these shores alive unless we win! We now have no choice—we win, or we perish!" They won. Every person who wins in any undertaking must be willing to burn his ships and cut all sources of retreat. Only by so doing can one be sure of maintaining that state of mind known as a burning desire to win, essential to success.[24]

LINEAR INNOVATION: SECOND—THINK INNOVATION NOT INVENTION

Sergio Zyman constructed a wonderfully fresh approach to innovation in his 2004 book, *Renovate Before You Innovate: Why Doing the New Thing Might Not Be the Right Thing*.[25] Too often, Zyman argues, the conventional quest for innovation amounts to a search for a shiny new object. Or, as Geoffrey Moore, author of *Crossing the Chasm*, puts it on the inside cover of Zyman's book: "Management thinkers, business writers, and global executives have too long been infatuated with the Next Big Thing. But the next thing is not always big and the big thing is not always next."

Extending Zyman and Moore's argument into today's business environment, we see that many companies habitually close their eyes and reflexively swing for the fences. They try to invent their way out of the ballpark with the Next Big Thing. In 2004, Zyman and Moore argued that such thinking is a mistake. Today, I argue it is more of a mistake than ever.

Instead of blindly swinging to invent the Next Big Thing, business leaders do better to focus on disrupting, renovating, and *innovating* their thinking, destination, battlefield map, attitudinal segmentation, brand positioning, customer experience, core strategy, and executional campaign. They are better off *innovating* rather than trying to *invent* their way to success.

As Kuhn might put it: Focus on "normal science," step-by-step progress, and "puzzle-solving," rather than "revolutionary science" and history's oh-so-rare paradigm shifts. Instead of inventing the Next Big Thing, focus on *innovating* every single day.

This is what America's most iconic "inventor," Thomas Edison, did. His ethos of *innovation*—in contrast to invention—underpins our argument. Take the light bulb. The most prolific inventor of our age, Edison set out, he said, to "subdivide light." In this quest, he was fueled by the deep-seated belief that he could really do this. But it did not take genius. Edison replaced *genius*—inventing something from nothing—with *analogy*, innovating something by spring-boarding off something else. He worked step-by-step to create the incandescent electric light. He played the part of extraordinary innovator, repeatedly. He was not sure he was an inventor, but he knew how to play the role of innovator—on demand. As we will see in the next chapter, he delivered a nearly endless series of innovations into the world. The process followed a set of doable steps. Some hit their mark, many others did not. No matter. He kept stepping, establishing with each step a vital connection between innovation and marketing.

Thomas Edison was very different from Albert Einstein, one of history's most revolutionary thinkers. Where Edison enlarged existing paradigms, innovating upon whatever came to hand, Einstein challenged paradigms—as when he approached gravitation not as Newton's attractive property of mass, but as a field of energy. Einstein and Edison are at opposite ends of the innovation spectrum. Einstein was a bona fide genius, a very rare force in history. Edison, by contrast, succeeded by *emulating* genius. He rationalized innovation, figuring out ways to furnish it on demand. For him, "Genius is 1 percent inspiration and 99 percent perspiration" was a business model.

We live in singularly interesting times. While the spacing between paradigm shifts is likely to become compressed, the pace of business cannot await even the first signs of the next revolution. Success in business depends on moving along the spectrum of innovation closer to Edison's evolutionary end and farther from Einstein's revolutionary edge. The sweet spot is squarely within the space of progressive innovation rather than going all in on the next revolution. Progress is more achievable than paradigm.

Nobody, by the way, has a corner on paradigmatic thinking. Isaac Newton's notion of gravitation as a property of matter with mass truly opened to contemplation a new universe. The idea that seemingly inert matter possessed a *force* of gravity was a profound paradigm shift. But could Newton have even imagined Einstein's new paradigm, of gravity not as a force, but a field that shaped the very universe?

Paradigm shifts, like revolutions, end. Even Einstein's undoubted genius for invention had bounds. The paradigm he shifted he could shift only so far. He imagined much that defies imagining—the equivalence of mass and energy, the gravitational field, and the space-time continuum—but paradigm became wall when it confronted the emerging science of quantum mechanics, especially "entanglement," the quantum theory that entangled subatomic particles remain connected so that actions performed on one particle affect another, even when separated by vast distances. Until late in life, Einstein scoffed at this as "spooky action at a distance" and famously countered entanglement by declaring: "God does not play dice with the universe." So, there are limits to the paradigm-shifting prowess of even history's heroes of invention.

In a more pragmatic realm, consider the Wright brothers, whom we explore in greater detail in chapter 4. While their invention of manned, powered flight was surely paradigm shifting, the Wright brothers followed their breakthrough with an obsessive rush to prevent further change. Masters of innovation, they succumbed to the plague of incumbency. Their breakthrough success narrowed the field of their insurgent imagination, and they became an upstart startup turned establishment incumbent, using the courts to retard the further development of aviation. Innovators they were, but the Wrights made innovation no part of their business model, which included a barrage of suits meant to tort rival innovators into submission. Their efforts set American aviation technology back twenty or thirty years.

LINEAR INNOVATION: THIRD—USE AGILITY TO THINK, ACT, AND PLAN THE FUTURE

Along with the inner conviction that you can innovate, and along with channeling Edison-style systematic innovation, today's unprecedented business environment demands new levels of agile thinking. Progressive innovation may not aim directly at paradigm shifting, but even less does it cling to the cushy comforts of incumbency. The great University of Alabama football coach Paul "Bear" Bryant symbolized the requisite agile thinking when he described how he recruits great football players: "I want players who are agile, hostile, and mobile."[26] Agility and mobility proved vital in the building of Bryant's 323 wins—still a record for college football.

Agile thinking, disruption, and innovation rarely emanate from the status quo. Incumbents are not structured, staffed, or motivated to "think different" precisely because they *are* the leaders in their categories or marketplaces. Today, change is not fundamentally critical to the incumbent's current state of survival. They still have their yachts, to which they can retreat to count their treasure.

By contrast, as we argue in chapter 8, today's insurgent or outsider has never had greater advantage. Because they have no legacy system or model to protect, insurgents are naturally given to agile thinking and are positioned to exploit low-overhead opportunities and the democratization of information, technologies, and platforms. They can afford to attack any market and redress any point of consumer pain. They can afford to drive change by the relative absence of other choices. They have little to lose.

Even in the apparently peaceful valley that lies between outright paradigm shifts, today's business environment is volatile. The air of tranquility is superficial, hiding the certainty that the incumbent will be disrupted by the insurgent. Lolling on his yacht, the incumbent does not understand that he is cursed. The insurgent, meantime, burning the midnight oil in a studio apartment, relishes his great advantage. As Steve Forbes argues, "You have to disrupt yourself or others will do it for you."[27]

My position is that you can afford neither to embrace the status quo nor to await a paradigm shift. You must engage in a program of progressive innovation and disruption. To do this requires continually refreshing your perspectives, always putting agile thinking to work. Today's successful leaders must be vigilant to identify new voices, questions, perspectives, passions, experiments, experts, inputs, and books.

Take, for example, the eminently agile thinking of the sometimes controversial Elon Musk, already one of history's greatest innovators. He was once asked how he created such groundbreaking companies as SpaceX, Tesla, Inc., OpenAI, Neuralink, The Boring Company, SolarCity, Zip2, and PayPal.

"I just started reading books," he answered.

Innovation is not "out there" any more than the next paradigm shift is "out there." Innovation begins with innovating your own mind.

In addition to agile thinking driven by curiosity and fed by the acquisition of knowledge, innovation demands cross-disciplines, combining subject-matter expertise and approaches across and among multiple fields. Walter Isaacson, who has written bestselling biographies on innovators, credits cross-field knowledge as the commonality among the likes of Ben Franklin, Steve Jobs, and Leonardo da Vinci. Innovation demands mixing your own creative stew, thereby breaking your own status quo patterns and limiting beliefs. You cannot innovate your enterprise without innovating yourself.

But it does not come from nothing. God began (apparently in Latin) with the words *Fiat lux*—"Let there be light." God is God. Edison, who was Edison, began not by creating light, but by subdividing it. Over thirty years, in focusing on ways to "think different" in terms of marketing and innovation, my own client work has always begun with one core question: "*Where's the pain?*"

Whatever else you have or lack, you can own as your starting point the pain of the consumer. Identify their pain—what bothers them, what hurts them, what they miss, what they long for—address their pain, and the solution can deliver the next billion-dollar IPO to any marketplace.

In the late 1990s and early 2000s, my work with some of the American firms that became the great American internet companies centered on the founders' answers to a specific source of consumer pain. In a few cases, such as LinkedIn and Google, the answer delivered not just pain relief but a new inflection point within the business world. These were the paradigmatic movements within the rolling paradigm shift that is the digital transformation. My job was to facilitate innovation within the breakthroughs by helping CEOs and their companies reposition perspectives and change assumptions—in short, to "think different."

Innovating your mind requires disrupting your own thinking so that you can creatively disrupt your customer's thinking, your business model, your industry, and the competition. For example:

- Create an "A" and "B" competitive teams to test and rethink your core strategy.
- Devise a "Red Team" exercise to attack and disrupt your own best-laid plans.
- Formulate a variety of "Outsider" sourcing strategies for innovation, creativity, and imagination.
- Above all, focus on the most important consumer-focused question in business: *"Where's the pain?"*

But let me pause here, because I am in danger of misleading you. You need to innovate your mind. But essential to this innovation is discovering your customer's pain. So, this brings the number of people involved in the innovation to two: you and your customer. Still, this is not enough. One of the myths of innovation is that it is the product of some lone genius. The truth is that innovation is never solitary. At minimum, it is an action of two people: you and those whom the innovation will impact. But, as in most endeavors, the minimum is rarely sufficient. One of the fundamental realities of innovation is that innovation takes a team—and not a single-minded team. As General George S. Patton Jr. liked to say, "If everybody is thinking the same way, nobody is thinking." Innovation requires a widely diverse *team* to succeed.

My first corporate client, Steve Jobs, was brilliant, no doubt, but he didn't *invent* the Macintosh. He didn't even originate the Macintosh project. Human-computer interface guru Jef Raskin started it. Jobs and Raskin, in turn, were just two members of a team of extraordinary technicians, engineers, and software developers. Jobs was a brilliant visionary, who knew what he wanted and where he needed to point his team to get there. But it was the Macintosh *team* that turned a disruptive vision into a technological and marketable reality.

Innovate your mind to innovate your company. We need a middle term in this formulation. *Innovate your mind to innovate your team to innovate your company.*

Jobs pointed his team in the direction where he wanted it to go. Do *you* know what direction this is? Wipe the beads of sweat off your brow. The answer is self-evident. It is the direction in which success lives. So, reboot your view of what success looks like, and then point your team in the direction of that vision.

Successful innovation demands a clear vision—a sharp definition—of success. We've all seen those blooper reels where the heroic wide receiver takes the ball over the goal line—only to discover that he has run in the wrong direction. You must define the correct goal line for your team. You must tell them what it looks like. You must point them toward it.

Do not edit the work of the team. Just keep them pointed the right way. Every effort they make must be made with the same "end" in mind—success—and performance must be judged by metrics that count how much closer the organization is to the *correct* goal line.

Call it "destination planning." If an innovation campaign delivers a win, how will everyone know? What are the metrics of this final success and the successes along the way? By what date must success and each intermediate success be delivered? How will key constituents of this innovation relate to each success?

To succeed, each definition must describe how each stakeholder group will think, feel, and behave differently because of each success. "Success" is a sweet and smooth term. Make it sweet and granular by defining success in the most specific and meaningful terms possible—for the organization, for your customers, and for individuals. The context is simple: "If we achieve all our goals over the next twenty-four to thirty-six months, what will our success look and feel like...for us and all our key constituents?"

Write your own answers to these fundamentally important strategic questions:

- What business are we in now—and what business, or businesses, will we be in because of successfully innovating and transforming our company?
- What will be the metrics of our innovation success? For various aspects of the business? For key individuals?
- How will our constituents—employees, management, stakeholders, customers, business media, competitors—think, feel, and behave differently because of our innovation success?
- What will a "battlefield map" look like for us? What, in terms of innovation, are key competitive threats? What are transformational opportunities? What quick gains can be found to generate business momentum?
- When are the key milestones over the next twenty-four to thirty-six months? What is the "By When?" of this innovation campaign?

STAND ON THE SHOULDERS OF INNOVATION GIANTS

So, I said it. Innovation is not a solo endeavor. Below is a hand-selected sampling of strategic questions and answers from other thinkers about innovation. I am not saying that these are essential to everyone all the time, but they are some of my favorites. Steal what works for you.

In *Innovation and Entrepreneurship* (1985), Peter Drucker argues that consumer values and customer values are at the heart of innovative entrepreneurship. He advises entrepreneurial innovators to combine customer/consumer values with these key "sources for innovation opportunity":

- Unexpected events.
- Incongruities between the expected and the actual.
- New process requirements.
- Unanticipated changes in industry or market structure.
- Demographic changes.
- Changes in perception, mood, or meaning, and new knowledge.

No entrepreneurial innovator can afford not to read every word written by Clayton Christensen, beginning with those in *The Innovator's Dilemma: Why New Technologies Cause Great Firms to Fail* (1997). This Harvard professor argues that even companies that do everything right can fail in their efforts to control and succeed in their markets. Nevertheless, key to success is what he terms "disruptive innovation"—innovation that does not merely add something new to a market, but does something completely unexpected. When you accomplish this, your product does not merely accompany those of your competitors, it displaces and replaces them. In *Seeing What's Next* (2004), Christensen offers a pragmatic three-part innovation model:

- First, predict changes in the industry.
- Second, understand the competition and the difficulties they may face.
- Third, determine a company's longevity.

In his 2016 *Competing Against Luck*, Christensen disrupts Drucker by arguing that disruptive innovation is not so much about predicting what the customer wants now and will want next, but rather understanding what jobs customers hold now and will hold in the future. The predictive "Jobs to Be Done" structure, Christensen claims, underpins the success of such companies as Amazon, Uber, Airbnb, Chobani, and many others.

In *The Myths of Innovation* (2007), Scott Berkun outlines ten innovation myths that demand to be disruptively rethought. They are of such linear and exponential value I will devote the final words of this chapter to him:

- *The myth of epiphany*—because all ideas come from other ideas, and not all ideas make for success.
- *The myth that we know history*—given that history is often shaped to fit how we want to see the present.
- *The myth of a method*—arguing not everything is within our control, and failure happens even if everything is done right.
- *The myth we love new ideas*—because conservatism often prevails.
- *The myth of the lone inventor*—given that innovation does not happen in isolation, but rather with the collaboration of teachers, friends, teammates.
- *The myth that good ideas are rare*—because we are in many ways built for creativity that must be nurtured.
- *The myth that your boss knows more than you do*—arguing bad bosses focus on conformity, while good ones empower innovation.

- *The myth that the best idea wins*—given that marketing, politics and other factors help determine what idea succeeds.
- *The myth that problems are less interesting than solutions*—because a creator must focus on the problem to find solution.
- *The myth that innovation is always good*—pointing out that all inventions and innovations have caused good for some and bad for others.

CHAPTER THREE

BUILD WORKSHOPS, NOT LABORATORIES

Mozart pisses me off…

—Billy Joel

One of the late twentieth century's greatest musical performers, composers, and songwriters admits openly that his own creativity came earlier in life and flowed forth in fits and starts, with titanic phases of prolific originality and, since his 1993 release of his last album, River of Dreams, far less frequent bursts of new songs.

Born on May 9, 1949, and raised in blue-collar Hicksville, Long Island, Billy Joel began taking piano lessons at the age of four. Soon, he became less interested in reading other people's musical notes or even in learning how to read music at all. He would become a six-time Grammy Award winner, a member of the Rock and Roll Hall of Fame, and a 2013 Kennedy Center Honoree. He would sell more than 150 million records worldwide. And he began by improvising minor changes in works by the likes of Schubert and Brahms, workshopping his own versions of such masters.

"I found reading to be intrusive to the musical process," Joel recalls.[28]

This outside-the-music-box creative process still holds, as Joel prepares for his record fiftieth sold-out monthly concert at New York's Madison Square Garden: "I write backward—I write the music first and then I write the words. Most people write the words first and then they write the music."[29]

"Everybody is different," he continues. "Some writers can write reams of great books and then J. D. Salinger wrote just a few. Beethoven wrote nine symphonies. They were all phenomenal. Mozart wrote some forty symphonies, and they were all phenomenal. That doesn't mean Beethoven was a lesser writer, it's just some guys are capable of more productivity, some guys take more time. Mozart pisses me off because he's like a naturally gifted athlete, you listen to Mozart and you go: 'Of course. It all came easy to him.' Beethoven, you hear the struggle in it. Look at his manuscripts, and there's reams of scratched-out music that he hated. He stops and he starts. I love that about Beethoven, his humanity shows in his music. Mozart was almost inhuman, unhuman."[30]

Joel has not released any new music since 1993—but today, he is playing before bigger sold-out crowds every year (including monthly runs at Madison Square Garden in New York City) since returning to the road in 2013 to continue a fifty-year performing career.

Make no mistake. This does not mean the creativity and workshopping stops: "I'm still composing music, which is my first love anyway," Joel confesses in a June 17, 2017 Rolling Stones *interview. "I never stopped writing music. I just stopped writing songs…."*

Dance like no one is watching.

—Mark Twain

The Wizard of Menlo Park, holder of more than a thousand patents, Thomas Alva Edison, left us an important clue to his extraordinary creativity: Build a workshop, not a laboratory. We will dig into this in a moment. It is a big part of what makes Edison such an extraordinary model of innovating innovation. Laboratories are for geniuses. Workshops are for mere mortals who like to build things. The symphony was to Mozart what the laboratory is to a scientific genius—a place where creativity just happens naturally. No wonder Mozart pisses off a working-class musical innovator like Billy Joel. Mozart is not human, so how can a mere mortal emulate him? Beethoven, on the other hand, struggled for every one of the "mere" nine symphonies he wrote, pounding them out in the chaos of his distinctly untidy combination living quarters and workshop. Billy Joel, then, found him human, a fellow creative convict sentenced to hard labor.

As for Edison? Like Billy Joel, he continually riffed on the work of others. God created light. Edison just figured out a way of subdividing it to make it more useful. Sir Humphrey Davy invented the first electric light, an arc lamp. Commercially, it was all but useless. Edison riffed on it until it became not only useful, but the "killer app" around which he created the first electric power utility, including generators, power grid, and a metering system to allow for equitable billing. Subdivided, light became a fungible commodity. This was no work of poetic inspiration but, rather, the product of a workingman's sweat.

Behold Billy Joel. You can see him as an artist deserted by creative inspiration back in 1993. Or, you can see him as a performer who managed to subdivide inspiration, commoditize it, and deploy it over fifty years and counting. He may have never made his peace with Mozart, the supernatural natural, but he saw in the example of Beethoven a reason to struggle and sweat.

For us ordinary innovators, working men and women who get our daily bread by creating on demand, it is to Billy Joel and Beethoven and Edison that we look. Let the likes of Albert Einstein admire Mozart. Einstein pisses *me* off. Try to reverse engineer Einstein's process of deductive reasoning that produced his famous "thought experiments," and you will find them almost useless as objects of emulation. The imperative "Think like Einstein" makes as little sense as asking a man to give birth to a child. He is just not built that way. Like Mozart, Einstein is too gifted, rare, and natural to help those of us in urgent need of an idea.

But then there is Beethoven. Work the problem. Wrestle the music out of the idea. Or Edison. Find the 1 percent inspiration that drives the 99 percent perspiration needed to innovate something. Edison, like Beethoven, walked as we walk. The exhaustive historical record around his process of invention paints a clear picture of how the Wizard of Menlo Park operated.

Edison first opened shop in Newark, New Jersey, but his genuine innovation in the business of innovation came in 1876, when he built what some historians call his industrial research laboratory in what was then the semi-rural village of Menlo Park, New Jersey. In fact, "laboratory" is a misnomer. It is well worth a visit to Dearborn, Michigan, where Henry Ford established Greenfield Village, an outdoor museum of American history and culture. He dismantled Edison's Menlo Park facility, inside and out, transported the pieces to Greenfield Village, and meticulously reconstructed it there. Today, visitors walk through the building. While there are bottles of chemicals, beakers, and flasks—the furnishings of a nineteenth-century lab—the overall look of the place is that of a workshop. When you examine period photos of the place in action, you see men in shop aprons, not lab coats. The credentials they hold are not PhDs, but experience as master machinists, telegraphers, metalworkers, and industrial tinkerers. They are technologists, and Edison gathered them in his workshop to execute a mission: streamline, systematize, and regularize the processes of invention and innovation. Plant, nurture, and harvest ideas. Do not let a single one die of neglect. Just purge the enterprise of the vagaries of hit-or-miss inspiration and luck.

Edison called what he built an "Invention Factory," and there was nothing else like it—and would not be, probably, until Bell Labs (today called Nokia Bell Labs) was established in 1925 in New York City, and later distributed across several New Jersey locations. Until Bell Labs, Edison's Invention Factory was the only dedicated private R&D facility in the world. Yet, as radical as the idea was, its true brilliance lies in the fact that it is a far less radical departure from Edison's own era than it might seem. As always, Edison built on existing models. He innovated rather than invented. He never conjured up something from nothing. He was Beethoven, not Mozart—Edison, not Einstein.

Active during the height of the Industrial Revolution and the early years of modern mass production, Edison borrowed from an approach that was certainly on the retreat, the pre-industrial tradition of individual craftsmanship. His Invention Factory was staffed by uniquely skilled craftsmen and apprentices, workers who could diligently execute Edison's orders and conduct trial-and-error experiments in innovation while, at the same time, contributing their own wisdom and instincts. Edison wanted craftspeople and problem solvers, not cogs. An indispensable feature of the Invention Factory were notebooks and pencils laid out on the work benches at the start of every day and collected at the close of business. Edison asked his workers to write down any observations and ideas that occurred to them as they worked. He was anxious to capture every thought, every insight. Not a minute of the imaginative brainpower for which he was paying should be lost.

Not that he wanted daydreamers. Edison expected his workforce to achieve new levels of scale, speed, and reliability. He was determined to produce "a minor invention every ten days and a big thing every six months or so."[31] Wishful thinking? If so, it was borne out by results. Over his sixty-one years in active business, Edison averaged one patent every twenty days—remarkably close to the objective he set, especially if you consider that not every "minor" invention was separately patented or patentable.

What was Edison's greatest invention? There are so many that it's difficult to pinpoint one above the rest. Most people would choose his most iconic achievement, the incandescent electric light. And, if you consider that this simple invention gave rise to the electrification of the world—a paradigm shift if there ever was one—they would be right.

Contrary to popular thought, however, I suggest that Edison's most important invention was the one he never even thought to patent. It was the innovation of innovation achieved with the Invention Workshop. It was a place and a system and an ethos that disrupted traditional concepts of creativity. Gone was the mystification of genius and inspiration and luck. The replacement was a set of procedures and mandates that both required and enabled imaginative creation on demand. This leap forward began with a step backward, into the pre-industrial culture of individual craftsmanship. But it was the reinvention of invention, rendering it more reliable, regular, and consistent, and laying the predicate for the R&D empires that distinguish today's most profitable and admired enterprises.

CONFORM TO NON-CONFORMITY

In his book *The Originals: How Non-Conformists Move the World*, Adam Grant makes a compelling case that each of us can channel our own inner non-conformist. Grant's work is a masterful roadmap for creativity, focusing on how ideas are created, traditions disrupted, and barriers of resistance broken down. He argues that all of us possess the DNA for creative thinking and innovation. In Grant's world, we are all originals.

I nominate Thomas Edison as historic proof of this argument. His workshop methodologies made creativity happen. He summoned forth innovation when and how he wanted it. Most impressively, he left behind the schematics of how he did it. His wide range of inventions—including the electric light, the electric power industry, the phonograph, a telephone transmitter and receiver that vastly improved on Alexander Graham Bell, the movies, and a range of basic materials from wax paper to a better Portland cement—were the result of a creative process far from unique and quite capable of our emulation.

Take the time and effort to dig into Edison's most "miraculous" inventions, the paradigm shifters, and you will find the existing technologies or analogies to existing technologies that underlay each of them. Late in his life, for instance, in 1927, Edison focused obsessively on innovating rubber, which, with the mass-production of the automobile (innovated by his good friend Henry Ford), had become among the most important materials of the twentieth century. Natural rubber was costly, and it had to be harvested from some of the most remote and inhospitable places in the world, jungle environments that were unhealthy, far from transport, and, often, politically unstable. Many inventors were desperately looking for artificial alternatives to natural rubber.

Edison took a different tack. Instead of trying to invent "manmade" rubber, he looked for natural alternatives to natural rubber. Finding these, he realized, did not require genius, inspiration, or an equation. The answer was *out there* in the world. Finding out where required a lot of work, and so he launched a global research study that came to include some 17,000 plant specimens. Eventually, he targeted goldenrod, a latex-bearing plant both abundant in and native to the United States. While Edison was never able to commercialize the goldenrod idea, it stands as an example of his systematic approach to innovating without inventing. Like many others, he sought to innovate in the rubber industry. In this, he conformed—yet he conducted his search in a most non-conforming manner, one that assumed the answer already existed in the world and was therefore discoverable.[32]

The search for a natural alternative to natural rubber is typical of what we might call Edison's open-source operating system, a pre-digital version that drives today's information revolution, which Amazon Web Services CEO Andrew Jassy calls "the largest technology transformation in our lifetimes." If the answers were *in* the world, Edison resolved to add even more answers *to* that world. While he patented everything he made, he also worked very much in the open, writing diaries, memos, instructions, details, and marching orders, almost all of which he circulated among a small band of workshop assistants. They, in turn, were encouraged to record everything they did and thought.

As schoolchildren, we are all taught early the "difference" between an explorer and an inventor. The explorer *discovers* what is already there but never known before. The inventor *creates* something new in the world. As an *innovator* misnamed an inventor, Edison erased much of the difference between explorer and inventor. He sought answers in the open-source database and operating system that is the world, and he used these as platforms on which he built innovations. The incandescent electric light was just an idea until Edison found precisely the right material to use as a filament. He searched out and tried more than 10,000 different substances. Talk about "99 percent perspiration"!

Edison's open-source seek-and-ye-shall-find approach to creativity on demand can be expressed in seven key lessons to apply to innovation today:

"FRUIT STAND" YOUR IDEAS

Forget Mickey Rooney's and Spencer Tracy's memorable movie portrayals of Edison as a naturally gifted, maverick boy-genius who could see every invention before it happened. The truth was that Edison never felt he understood a thing if he knew it only from a theoretical perspective. This meant that he only deployed theory founded on firsthand observation and physical experimentation. Edison would have approved of what is today the practice of "fruit standing." Instead of laboring to invent a theory behind a new product, build a prototype. Then *"fruit stand"* it, producing it on a small scale and trying it out on a limited group of consumers. Watch how it takes hold and attracts buyers—or fails to.

Edison often turned to modeling, experimenting on a small scale before embarking on a full-size endeavor. The smaller-scale, proof-of-concept step was riskier than performing thought experiments, but it provided much more information. For Edison, innovation required understanding the real world, seeing and feeling it, and then determining what might solve a problem or advance an innovation. To innovate, Edison had to get his hands dirty. But keeping the scale small reduced cost and risk.

PROTOTYPE FROM THE BOTTOM UP

Edison almost never innovated from the top down but workshopped his ideas from the bottom up. Pencil in hand, he imagined an idea. He sketched an approach to translate it into three-dimensional practicality, and then he handed the work to one of his craftsmen, with instructions to build a prototype. Once a working model was made, the adjustments and modifications could be added in a real-world context. Either the prototype was made to work, or it was set aside, and a new approach tried. And "set aside" is the correct term, because Edison rarely abandoned an idea or a prototype, and he never outright discarded any of them.

Today, we should note, most conventional R&D processes work top down. The example of Edison is an argument either to try the bottom up approach or to craft a hybrid that combines top down and bottom up. For example, start with theory, but set a goal of moving from theory to prototype as rapidly as possible. Take whatever observations are made based on the prototype and plug these back into the theory for analysis, revision, and refinement, which must be quickly embodied in a revised prototype.

LEARN BY DOING

People who worked with Edison always said that there was something of the boy about him. Maybe it was his dirty fingernails. Like the rest of us, he learned best by doing. At the age of twelve, he strung a half-mile-long telegraph line between his parents' house and that of a friend. The boy devoured a popular book of his era, Richard Parker's *Natural Philosophy*, which advocated a pragmatic approach to such subjects as electricity and magnetism. Toward this end, the book was heavily illustrated, and we can easily imagine young Tom putting a real-world plan to work in stringing his telegraph line. Learning by doing is a powerful element of Edison's approach.

TRY EVERYTHING

Edison the explorer preferred to whittle-away, uncovering innovation instead of building out to create it. He called his method "cut and try." The long search for the ideal filament is a prime example. It was brute force discovery. He set out to obtain samples of every conceivable substance—including hair from an employee's magnificent beard—tried each, recorded the results, and celebrated whatever worked: "Whatever worked…worked," he used to say. And in his own day, scientists sometimes scoffed at this labor- and time-intensive effort. They had a point—but a point somewhat dulled by the fact that this method succeeded.

Edison did not try to pull out innovation from his head. Instead, he thought broadly and peripherally, front-loading innovation as if pouring a miscellany of materials into a funnel, beginning wide and progressively narrowing down to solution. The chief costs of this approach are labor and time, but the value of a wide-mouthed innovation funnel can be a breakthrough of maximum magnitude because it results from the widest set of possible options. As Billy Joel once explained immodestly of his own creative process: "It's like Michelangelo sculpting marble. Inside that marble is the sculpture, he's just got to find it."[33]

The costs notwithstanding, there is a bonus in the try everything approach. It is the confidence of certainty. If what you create is the product of theory, you cannot be certain that you have found the optimum solution. If, however, you have "tried everything," you can be confident that you have reached the best possible outcome, based on the technology and knowledge at the time.

CAPTURE ALL IDEAS

Edison *collected*. Even if an idea was not immediately a solution to a problem, his larger approach was to record everything and discard nothing. Sooner or later, an old idea might find a new application.

Like most inveterate collectors, Edison started young. As a boy, he carried a pocket notebook, in which he jotted down or drew up ideas as they occurred to him. Edison believed that an inventor needed a strong, amply stocked memory. Recall was, for him, key to invention. Nevertheless, he never trusted anything to memory. He wrote it down. As mentioned, he distributed notebooks and pencils throughout his workshops so that everyone could record the activity of their minds and imaginations. The lesson: Capture every idea. Get them all down. Discard nothing.

For an innovator who produced one civilization-changing product after another, Thomas Edison never became fabulously wealthy—a Jobs, a Gates, a Bezos. He lacked the gene of acquisitive wealth. Nevertheless, he collected everything else, hoarding ideas, patents, breakthroughs, failures, craftsmen, scientists, workers, assistants, and equipment. Creativity was most creative, he believed, when it was loaded down with everything you could throw at it or bring into it. His ambition was to stock his workshop with every material or chemical known to humankind. Whatever might be needed had to be on hand. In an era well before the global internet could even be imagined, Edison sought instant access to everything his world contained, taking open-source as far as it could be taken on a pre-digital planet.

ACCEPT PROBLEMS AS GIFTS

Edison welcomed failure. In practice, Edison could rarely determine whether a design might work or fail until it was moved to prototype. Picture him walking across his workshop floor, asking each worker what was going wrong, and then creating a plan to fix it.

Edison extended his problem-solving approach to existing products. He carefully analyzed customer complaints and used them as the basis for creating solutions to address consumer pain points. Often, this produced incremental improvements that were themselves patentable.

Edison understood that innovation begins with *dissatisfaction.* Satisfied people want nothing. Such is the definition of satisfaction. But one man's itch is a pharmacist's ointment. Edison used consumer pain to fuel innovation. He understood that most marketplace needs could be met by incremental innovation rather than full-blown invention. That was just fine, because it was cheaper and faster. Two of his most commercially successful innovations were incremental improvements to the telephone, which had already been invented by Alexander Graham Bell. Edison drove steadily toward step-by-step innovation, even if it fell short of a revolutionary breakthrough.

EXPLOIT DISASTER

They called it "Edison's Folly"—the inventor's ten-year quest to create an industrial plant capable of separating iron from the lowest-grade ore. Had it worked, Edison's 1,094th patent might have changed another aspect of our world by delivering unheard of quantities of cheap iron or steel.

But it didn't.

Unfazed by large-scale fiasco, Edison focused on putting failure to work by recycling the costly physical plant he had built. Iron and steel were high-need building products. What other materials did builders want? There was wood, but Edison saw no way of innovating that. And there was cement, specifically Portland cement, the basic ingredient of all concrete, mortar, and stucco. Edison believed he could introduce an important innovation in this familiar product. He embarked on a radical new design for a rotary roasting kiln to manufacture the cement, a kiln much bigger than any in existence and employing an innovative "coal gun" technology to fuel it. The cement was familiar, but the new kiln was radically new. Without a technological precedent from which to start, Edison employed trial and error to arrive at the best practices for operating the kiln. His goal was to produce 1,000 barrels of Portland cement daily, compared to the 150 to 200 barrels existing kilns produced. It took three years of trial-and-error to attain this goal, which produced not only more cement, but *better* cement. Edison recouped much of what he had lost in the failed iron-extraction venture.

THE EDISON ATTITUDE

Fruit-standing and then scaling-up your ideas, innovating from the bottom up with prototypes, learning by doing, trying everything, capturing all ideas, using problems as gifts, and exploiting disaster are all valuable lessons. But equally important is the attitude Edison brought to them. Building your own Invention Factory begins with attitude—*how you think.*

THINKING LIKE EDISON

The example of Edison teaches us that workshopping is a state of mind, an attitude, a way of thinking. Where Einstein was an inventor, Edison was an innovator. If Einstein was a revolutionary, Edison was a change agent. Both challenged and changed the status quo by historically remarkable measures, but they did so with different ways of thinking.

We might see the story of Einstein and Edison as a tale of two mental methods, illustrating the creative tension between deductive and inductive reasoning, or what might be called *deductive invention* and *inductive innovation.*

Deductive invention begins with the general and then moves down to the specific—as, for example, in the case of Einstein's 1905 breakthrough work in creating four scientific papers that transformed all scientific thinking. It begins with a general statement, or a hypothesis, and moves through Kuhn's process of scientific discovery and experimentation, testing and re-testing an existing paradigm, or way of thinking, and examining the possibility of reaching a specific and logical conclusion. In the case of Einstein, deductive invention begins with theory and moves to the specific, to observations that confirm the theory. The burden of deductive invention is to get the premise or premises right from the very beginning. Short of this, there is no invention, no breakthrough, no innovation, no change.

By contrast, inductive innovation is what went on not in Einstein's brain, but inside Edison's Invention Factory—the methodical workshop approach to driving innovation. It begins with specific observations and works up to the general principle, the opposite of deductive invention. It begins with data, data often created and tested inside a workshop. From specific data, it moves to generalization. We make observations, discern a pattern, generalize our findings, and infer a theory. The burden of *inductive innovation* is tied to our concrete world, to what we can see, sometimes short of what we can imagine.

All of science and all of innovation are bound to the continual interplay and tension between deductive reasoning and inductive reasoning, between deductive invention and inductive innovation, between theory and observation, and between Einstein and Edison. All dance together, even as they come alive in separate parts of our quest for advancement and change.

Einstein freely admitted his preference. All four of his 1905 paradigm-busting papers—written and published during his so-called Annus Mirabilis ("miracle year")—begin by making plain his intention to use deductive reasoning. Each paper begins with the jostled state of the relevant theoretical thinking of his day. None alludes to experimental or inductive data. And each paper moves quickly to state grand principles and minimize the role of data. In fact, in a 1919 essay, "Induction and Deduction in Physics," Einstein admits very openly where he stands on our innovation continuum:

> The simplest picture one can form about the creation of an empirical science is along the lines of an inductive method. Individual facts are selected and grouped together so that the laws that connect them become apparent... However, the big advances in scientific knowledge originated in this way only to a small degree... The truly great advances in our understanding of nature originated in a way almost diametrically opposed to induction. The intuitive grasp of the essentials of a large complex of facts leads the scientist to the postulation of a hypothetical basic law or laws. From these laws, he derives the conclusions.[34]

Later in life, Einstein went even further toward deductive reasoning and the power of theory: "The deeper we penetrate and the more extensive our theories become, the less empirical knowledge is needed to determine those theories."[35]

Unarguably, our world benefits more from Einstein's way of thinking than most of us can understand. But my argument is that innovation today cannot depend exclusively on Einstein's attitude, on the primacy of deductive reasoning and on deductive invention. We mere mortals must workshop our way to *inductive innovation*, change, and breakthrough.

CREATE A WORKSHOP ENVIRONMENT

In the dance between deductive invention and inductive innovation, between theory and observation, between Einstein and Edison, our music must be the notes of radical open-mindedness. One of history's greatest investors, Ray Dalio, has been called the Steve Jobs of the investment world. In his 2017 book, simply titled *Principles*, he lays down his outline for successful business. He argues persuasively that success in business comes down to recognizing and breaking down every vestige of status quo thinking and other barriers to change, including our own egos, blind spots, and limitations. He goes on to argue that we must synergize our deductive and inductive instincts to build an environment friendly to innovation. He calls this practicing "radical open-mindedness." His pragmatic approach is summarized in the seven following principles:[36]

- Don't be afraid of not knowing.
- Take in relevant information. Then decide.
- Forget looking good. Focus on achieving your goal.
- Realize you can't produce without first learning.
- Empathize with other views to gain perspective.
- Remember the best answer—not your own best answer—is the goal.

- Balance arguing and understanding and use each wisely.

These seven battle-tested principles overlap with and reinforce our own operating system for change leadership and business success. Workshop environments such as Verizon's "Video Services," Google's "X," Amazon's "Lab126," Raytheon's "Bike Shop," Nike's "Innovation Kitchen," Staples' "Velocity Lab," Xerox's "PARC," and Apple's "Mac Group" remind us of Edison's inductive innovation lessons. To be sure, there is something different in the air in these places, some of which I've worked in or visited. All are informal workshops, not bureaucratized laboratories. They are out-of-the-box factories for innovation.

THINK INNOVATION

Our ability to workshop important change walks around with us inside our heads every day. It is a way of thinking, and when you think in the workshop way, what thoughts may come!

In 1970, for example, a vice president of a luggage company named Bernard D. Sadow, returning from a family vacation to Aruba, lugs two big, clumsy suitcases through an airport—soon to become his own real-world workshop—when something catches his eye. A slight, short man effortlessly rolls a heavy machine on a wheeled skid.

Something clicks. Sadow workshops an innovation—in his head, in the airport. He turns to his wife, indicates the man with the skid, and tells her, "That's what we need for luggage." When he gets back to the office, he builds an Edison-like prototype. Taking the casters off a wardrobe trunk, he weds them to a large travel suitcase, puts a strap on the front—and it worked.

He rushes to secure a patent (no. 3,653,474, "Rolling Luggage," applied for in 1970 and secured in 1972), but it doesn't fly off the shelves. Sadow does manage to get a big order from Macy's, which takes out ads touting "the Luggage That Glides." *Luggage* and *Glides* are two words not normally put together. And that was it: the consumer breakthrough the rolling luggage needed.

Now this is where I am supposed to write "The rest is history," and, of course, it is. But history is not stone, and innovation is relentless. Sadow's "gliding" luggage was a big improvement on "lugging" luggage but pulling a suitcase on a leash could cause a swerve and a crash, especially if you were running to catch a plane. That was where Robert Plath, an innovation-minded pilot who flew 747s for Northwest Airlines, entered the picture. In the 1980s, he worked in his own home workshop to custom-build his own iteration of the rolling suitcase. This one ditched the leash and instead put the wheels on the edge of the luggage, added a long, adjustable, fully telescoping rigid handle. You could tip the bag up to just the angle that worked for you, and you could control the bag, even at a run, as you rolled it across the airport floor and into a flight toward product innovation. In 1987, it hit the market as the Rollaboard, and it left Sadow's gliding pull-along in the dust.

Why? The advantage Sadow's innovation offered over conventional luggage is obvious—but so is its disadvantage. Seen one way, luggage that "glides" is a minor miracle. Seen another way, it's luggage out of control. Plath added control to the miracle.

But how did he get there?

Both Sadow and Plath used workshopping. The difference is that Plath workshopped more extensively and effectively. Sadow, a tourist, relied on deductive invention, beginning with a completely new solution. Plath, a pilot, forced to live with his own luggage problems every day, used inductive innovation that allowed him to workshop a better way. Where Sadow was a tourist with imagination and a luggage business, Plath was a pilot with a home workshop—located in his garage—one not unlike those in which such legendary companies such as HP, Nike, and Apple were born.

By the 1990s, the changing context of air travel made Plath's innovation look smarter and smarter. Airlines were deregulated, which made pricing more competitive. A free market generally drives down prices and, as they fell, more people regularly flew. As more people flew, more chaos ensued, more middle seats, more testy flight attendants, and more crowded airports. Anything that relieved customer pain looked better and better to frequent flyers. Plath's Rollaboard became increasingly appealing, especially as airlines, having driven ticket prices down, sought to recoup losses by charging for absolutely everything else—including checked luggage. The Rollaboard concept was especially adaptable to luggage you carried on board. Now, fast-forward today, to our new status quo, and watch four-year-olds bravely dragging their own miniature rolling suitcases alongside their parents. You can see it as a form of symbolic tribute to Plath's workshopped, garage-born breakthrough—and as an indication that the Rollaboard concept owns the future—at least until someone, somewhere (in some other garage, perhaps) innovates an even better solution.

Luggage is low-tech. While technology has spurred and speeded much innovation, Sadow and Plath show that high-tech is not necessary to it. But it helps.

Jack Dorsey was a young man of the 1980s. Growing up, he tinkered with CB and police-band radios, the high technology of the era, and a field that appealed to professionals and hobbyists alike. Dorsey, the young enthusiast, took special note of the lingo emergency workers used to communicate quickly and clearly. They used "blasts," monosyllables, shorthand codes to tell people where they were located and what they were doing. Somewhat more than a decade later, Dorsey transformed his early enthusiasm into a career. He became a software developer in San Francisco and Oakland who specialized in programs to help police and other emergency dispatchers to direct cars around the Bay Area. As he worked, deductive invention called out to him. If he could report on the whereabouts of a cop car or an ambulance, why couldn't he do the same about himself? As Amazon's Jeff Bezos did years later, Dorsey asked himself: "Why not?"

Workshopping his own answer, Dorsey cobbled together software and plugged it into the cutting-edge phone of 1999, a RIM 850, an early Blackberry device capable of sending and receiving emails. He quickly developed a way to send outbound, text-based messages. The only problem? Nobody was listening.

While relaxing in beautiful Golden Gate Park one day in 1999, Dorsey sent out a message about what he was doing, seeing, and exactly where he was. The response, naturally, was silence. No one was on the other end of the "line." Six years after this silence—six years and a new century—as Pagan Kennedy recounts in *Inventology: How We Dream Up Things That Change the World*,[37] time and context were finally as kind to Dorsey as they had been to Plath and his controllable rollable. Six years after hearing only silence, Dorsey was now collaboratively workshopping his innovation at a company called Odeo, and the external forces of change were beginning to move in his favor. Millions and millions of cellular phones were now using SMS or Short Message Protocol. Finally, people were transmitting—*and* listening.

It took two weeks of workshopping for Dorsey and his colleagues to assemble a social network to seize the long-delayed moment. After many years, what began as something like Bernard D. Sadow's pull-toy suitcase was about to become something else altogether—something called Twitter. Eventually, Dorsey and his workshopping colleagues would add an "@" symbol, typing shortcuts, hashtags, and retweets. And, in 2016, that workshopping would have a consequence as unanticipated as it now seems close to inevitable. Inveterate tweeter Donald Trump was elected the forty-fifth president of the United States.

SHARPEN YOUR TOOLS

How do you put together your own workshop? How do you staff it? And how do you empower these people with think-outside-the-box energy and permission? Chapter 5 details my own "Skunk Works" approach to peripheral innovation: a development model and team that operate outside the center of their own bureaucracy. For now, however, my seven workshop principles to help drive your own innovation forward are given below.

FIRST, CHANNEL EDISON

Balance the creative tension between deductive invention and inductive innovation, between Einstein and Edison, and put to work the seven lessons of Edison that frame our approach to consistent, real-world, and on-time innovation: fruit-stand and scale your ideas; prototype from the bottom up; learn by doing; try everything; capture all ideas; use problems as gifts; and exploit disaster.

SECOND, BUILD A WAR ROOM

Yes, the phrase "War Room" has graduated from buzz word to cliché, but that does not mean the concept doesn't work. It does. In my consulting work, I build War Rooms within companies to develop strategy, drive change, focus communications, and discipline execution. You should organize one of your own, a War Room for innovation. It is a system for strategic, creative, and innovative thinking, for brainstorming, testing, refining, and launching innovation.

The War Room's mission? To challenge conventional thinking and status quo behavior. So, put some of your best, most insurgent, most talented, and boldest people inside your War Room. Fill it with change agents.

THIRD, GO BOLD

Don't let the tyranny of the "How" get in the way or stall you. Focus instead on the liberating energy of "What" and "Why"—or the even more boldly empowering "Why Not?"

This means playing offense. Important research shows that strategically and developmentally playing only 15 percent more offense can make the difference between good and great innovation, which does make the difference between good and great companies. Prioritize and attack innovation.

FOURTH, MODEL SUCCESS

Most great innovators, most great entrepreneurs, model relentlessly. Success leaves many clues. We need only find them. For example, in the early 1970s, Howard Shultz, founder of Starbucks, refined and extended his company's approach by modeling. He took salient features of high-end Italian cafés and used this model to displace the outworn model of the conventional coffee shop. Earlier, in the mid-1960s, Subway founder Fred DeLuca modeled his sandwich shop franchise chain on the most successful delicatessens to create an experience different from incumbent fast-food giants like McDonalds,

Burger King, and Wendy's—while, of course, remaining in the fast-food category.

If you want to succeed, model someone or something that has already succeeded—and make it work in the new context you desire.

FIFTH, LEARN, MEASURE, AND ACCOUNT

Borrow the lessons of *The Lean Startup*[38] and build into your workshop the discipline and focus of "validating learning." This consists of running frequent experiments—like Edison, of course—and allowing people to test and retest each element of their vision.

In business, as in life, we focus on what we measure. Measurement helps us set milestones, prioritize work, drive breakthrough, and prove success.

SIXTH, BRAINSTORM.

Design your workshop to stream a continuous, well-planned flow of new voices, questions, perspectives, passions, and experiments. Relentlessly brainstorm consumer problems and innovation solutions. Workshop your chief competitor's status quo and brainstorm a differentiated and better way.

Done right, brainstorming is all about asking bigger and better questions, thinking more exponentially, and then beginning to categorize the resulting ideas into clusters. For example, a hundred ideas can be bundled into three "mega-shifts," three big-idea changes to your status quo. These three are then workshopped and tested for their potential to create your own powerful innovation advantage.

SEVENTH, TRAIN YOUR CREATIVITY

Innovation is almost never accidental. (But never ignore a good accident! Write it down.) Almost always, innovation must be planned and prepared for. Rely on spontaneity, and you will find yourself the victim of spontaneous combustion.

For companies like InVentiv Health and clients such as Johnson & Johnson, Merck, and Eli Lilly and Company, I measure innovation attributes, put people into workshops and training, and then re-measure how innovation is becoming more effective and efficient. Such evaluation includes two key steps:

STEP ONE: Measure, drive, and then re-measure what I call "moving toward" attitudes:

- Hunger, curiosity, and drive
- Competitive focus and energy
- Comfort with change
- Willingness to challenge status quo habits
- Optimistic focus on the future
- Obsession with customer satisfaction
- Motivated to address customer pain
- Aggressiveness and boldness
- Strategic and planned risk taking
- Pride in communications abilities
- Extroverted and highly motivated
- Willingness to go "out of the box"
- Agile and fast-moving
- Bold and open

- Motivated to be proactive
- Action focused

STEP TWO: Drive innovation by doing these:

- *Use destination planning.* Per chapter 2, this will enable you to define the win and articulate what successful innovation looks and feels like.
- *Ask why?* Why must this succeed? What must we believe to innovate? Studies show that 80 percent of successful innovation and entrepreneurship is psychology, while only 20 percent involves tools, tactics, and techniques. So, get the answer to your *Why?* down cold. Why *must* innovation happen?
- *Check alignment.* Are your own and your workshop team's emotions and beliefs lined up and all aimed at a single definition of the win? Is there any old baggage to jettison? Ensure that you and your innovation team are aimed along the same trajectory for success.
- *Model breakthrough.* Write down two or three innovations you admire, that inspire you and your workshop colleagues. Successful innovators often model and emulate other successful innovators. These are the formulas for success they borrow.
- *Take massive actions.* Walk out of your workshop after a very focused planning session with a list of 5 to 10 massive actions you will take to drive innovation *immediately*. The key to action and momentum is to begin the moment planning is done, as in that very night! Waiting is death. So, don't wait. Take an action immediately, even a

small action, to put momentum on your side and drive innovation forward. Momentum is magical. It is what sustains urgency, and urgency drives all innovation.

CHAPTER FOUR

CREATE A CULTURE OF URGENCY AND SOFT LANDINGS

Create panic early.

—Richard Branson

One school headmaster predicted he'd either end up in prison or become a millionaire. He was right and wrong. In 1971, a young Richard Branson was convicted and briefly jailed for tax evasion, but he soon shot right past millionaire to become a billionaire many times over.

Today, the founder of Virgin Records, Virgin Mobile, Virgin Cola, Virgin Cars, Virgin Media, Virgin Blue, Virgin Trains, Virgin Express, Virgin Nigeria, Virgin America, Virgin Holidays, Virgin Vacations, Virgin Hotels, Virgin Voyages, Virgin Limited Edition, Virgin Megastores, Virgin Money, Virgin Atlantic, Virgin Galactic, Virgin Fuels, Virgin Comics, Virgin Health Bank, Virgin Radio Italia, Virgin Healthcare, Virgin Racing, Virgin Sports, Virgin Orbit, Virgin Startup, Virgin Care, and the Virgin Earth Challenge, Sir Richard Branson, personifies the power of using urgency to drive innovation.

"Create a sense of urgency," Branson offers, "not complacency."[39]

Branson's history of business innovation is unprecedented. The founder of 135 companies that have gone bankrupt, he quickly reminds us that "40 are doing well." His philosophy—and the focus of this chapter—is summed up in a simple imperative sentence followed by a compound question: "Let's give it a go. What's the downside and how can we protect it?"[40]

Branson is restless by nature and design, sometimes channeling this restlessness outside the business world. He has, for example, moved from challenge to challenge, physical to engineering, speed to endurance. He boated to a world record for crossing the Atlantic, and then he tried to cross it in a balloon—training in preparation for three years: skydiving, water survival, and, yes, ballooning.

In July 1987, Branson began pushing even harder—building the largest balloon ever made—as tall as a 21-story building—and using it to ride a jet stream at a never-before-attempted wind speed of 200 miles per hour. Later, he'd try to be the first to cross the Pacific in a hot-air balloon. Four times he tried to bring Jules Verne to reality, by attempting to circumnavigate the globe in a balloon. Once he set a world record for the fastest crossing of the English Channel in an amphibious vehicle.[41]

But let's go back to that July morning of 1987. Branson is in real trouble. He's brought along a co-pilot, Per Lindstrand, an experienced balloonist—probably to make up for the simple fact that he himself has barely flown a hot-air balloon before.

The adventure started out flawlessly. Sailing through the air nearly 3,000 miles over a day and a half, Branson and Lindstrand are now well on their way. Then, suddenly, the winds of luck shift. As they begin to attempt to land, trouble hits in multiples. First, the ejection capsule that is supposed to get them safely to earth fails, forcing them to fly out and over the Irish Sea. Several times, their balloon dips into the icy chop of the Irish water, bouncing up to sixty feet above the waves. The experienced Lindstrand's advice is unsubtle: Jump!

He does. But no sooner does he jump than the balloon, bearing Branson, rockets upward to a spine-chilling 12,000 feet. The multi-billionaire can do no more than stare at the ever-retreating sea.

I am dead, *he thinks.*

Briefly he debates skydiving out of the capsule—but, based on a prior near-death training incident, he decides to play it safe.

"I climbed back into the capsule and just desperately tried to make sure that I was making the right decision," Branson remembers in a TED interview.[42]

All he can do now, 12,000 feet above the Irish Sea, is to recall, recover, and channel the ways he has before surfed hundreds of business crises. Calming and steading himself, he realizes that above him is a balloon that in some ways is like a large parachute, and so, wishful thinking or not, he convinces himself the best bet is to steer it down anyway he can through the clouds—willing it, slowly and uncertainly, guiding it back down to the water. As it hovers 50 feet above the Irish Sea, he jumps.

Rescued from the chilling waters, Branson swears off ballooning—for a full two hours, before beginning to plan something even more daring.

Protect the downside, and the upside will take care of itself.

—Warren Buffett

Opfer müssen gebracht werden! "Sacrifices must be made!" Those were his last words.

It is August 9, 1896, and Otto Lilienthal had been piloting a new glider, jumping off from the Rhinow Hills near Berlin, on a crystal-clear day punctuated by a partial solar eclipse, maneuvering this new thing—that was almost an airplane—by the only means his design made possible: aggressively shifting his own weight as he lay prone over the wing.

Suddenly, the wind gusts hard, tilting his craft up into the air, even as he tries to lurch his body in the opposite direction, trying to wrestle the awkward flying machine back to earth.

It is a losing battle.

Like Branson, he is fifty feet above the earth. Unlike Branson, he has no Irish Sea beneath him to cushion the crash. At first, he does not seem all that badly injured. But his faithful mechanic, Paul Beylich, lifts him gently and lays him down in a carriage. They drive to Stölln, where a physician diagnoses a fracture of the third cervical vertebra. No sooner is this determination made than Lilienthal loses consciousness and is loaded aboard a train for downtown Berlin. The next morning, he is carried to the clinic of the eminent surgeon Dr. Ernst von Bergmann. But it is too late for surgery. Some thirty-six hours after the crash, Otto Lilienthal drifts in and out of consciousness.

"*Opfer müssen gebracht werden!*" he says to his brother Gustav, who is by his side.[43]

The small universe peopled by aviation enthusiasts in 1896 quickly heard or read the news of Lilienthal's fatal accident. It made an especially powerful impression on the proprietors of the Wright Cycle Shop, of Dayton, Ohio. Wilbur later recounted the conversation he had with his brother, Orville. He told his brother that the German had been doomed from the beginning because he counted on nothing more than the shifting weight of his own body to achieve what Wilbur Wright called "equilibrium" in flight.

Both Wrights intensely watched the flight of birds, but Wilbur was the more acute observer. He concluded that "birds use more positive and energetic methods of regaining equilibrium than [merely] shifting the center of gravity." What he observed was that they achieved control and maintained equilibrium largely by turning the leading edge of one wingtip up and the other down.

We can imagine the Wrights' conversation turning to a conclusion something like this: *It is not crazy to try to fly, but it is crazy to try to fly something you cannot steer.* In fact, the death of Otto Lilienthal leads them to the eminently sane conclusion that the key to manned flight is, first and last, *control*. Solve *that* problem, and you will fly—as well as live to talk about it.

To a resident of the twenty-first century, there is something quaint about two "bicycle mechanics" attempting to fly. But, in fact, at the end of the nineteenth century and beginning of the twentieth, the bicycle was high technology, and the Wrights pursued their craft of bicycle sales and service with great sophistication. The leap from bicycle high technology to aeronautical high technology was not nearly as great as it now may seem. They drew on their intimate knowledge of the bicycle—crossing disciplines, as so many great innovators do—to arrive at a solution for control. The brothers themselves explain it in their book, *The Early History of the Airplane*:

> The balancing of a flyer [that is, an airplane] may seem, at first thought, to be a very simple matter, yet almost every experimenter had found in this one point which he could not satisfactorily master. Some experimenters placed the center of gravity far below the wings. Like the pendulum, it tended to seek the lowest point; but also, like the pendulum, it tended to oscillate in a manner destructive of all stability. A more satisfactory system was that of arranging the wings in the shape of a broad V, but in practice it had two serious defects: first, it tended to keep the machine oscillating; and second, its usefulness was restricted to calm air. Notwithstanding the known limitations of this principle, it had been embodied in almost every prominent flying machine that had been built. We reached the conclusion that a flyer founded upon it might be of interest from a scientific point of view, but could be of no value in a practical way.[44]

In his excellent book *How to Fly a Horse: The Secret History of Creation, Invention, and Discovery*, Kevin Ashton cites Wilber Wright's telling observation in *The Early History of the Airplane*: "When this one feature"—control—"has been worked out the age of flying machines will have arrived…."

It arrived, Ashton observes, when the Wright brothers successfully imagined an airplane as "a bicycle with wings." They synergized what they knew about cycling with what they did not know about inventing a horse that can fly. They continued to study bird flight, persuaded that the flight of a bird provided clues about the flight of a man. Again, as Wilbur noted, they watched especially how birds balance in flight by raising a wingtip, lowering another, as a flying horse might someday raise a wing, lower another, and thereby stay safely in the air, soaring higher than either Wilber or Orville Wright could ever imagine.

As Ashton recounts, the Wright brothers created early panic, forcing urgency into their process of innovation. At the same time, they bore in mind the broken back of Otto Lilienthal, and they worked hard to protect themselves from that fatal downside. We can outline their mental steps something like this:

Problem: Balance an aircraft to allow it to soar.

Solution: Borrow lessons from birds to bicycles.

Flight was not a novelty to the Wright brothers. As young boys, they loved nothing more than to fly kites. Nobody in Dayton thought it odd when, decades later, Wilbur Wright rode through the streets with a five-foot kite on his handlebars. He had built it to show Orville what a "warped-wing approach" to flying might look like.

The popular image of the Wright brothers as tinkerers is partly accurate, but only partly. They both devour every book they can get on the theory of flight—even if, unsurprisingly, there are not many such books available. No matter, the Wrights use and apply theory rather than dwell on what they do not have. Instead of relying on what we call in chapter 3 "deductive invention," the Wrights turn out an urgent but incremental flow of inductive innovations. They move step-by-step, from one incremental breakthrough to another. Like Edison, they prototype each inside the workshop of the Wright Cycle Company.

Even driven by urgency—for the Wrights are convinced that the world is on the verge of powered, manned heavier-than-air flight, and they want to be the first in the air—it takes two years to scale up Wilbur's kite to accommodate a pilot. They experiment and prototype. They advance and they retreat. No matter, with each advance and each retreat comes new and powerful knowledge. It is the knowledge gained, and not the "failure" or "success" achieved, that drives the ultimate breakthrough.

By 1901, after a series of experiments, driven as fast as they could drive them forward, the Wrights have worked out most of the mathematics of aerodynamics, framing the paradigm of flight that is still applicable today. The numbers come to them inductively. Acting on a flash of insight, they create an incremental invention second in importance for the evolution of flight only to the airplane itself. They build the world's first wind tunnel and use it to make exhaustive tests of innumerable wing shapes. The fan that generates the wind is powered by a modified stationary bicycle. Using it, they calculate and discover that a flying horse's wings must be much bigger than anyone else has before understood. They also come to understand that its cross-section must be cupped, so that the wind passes over the top of the wing much faster than under it. In this way, a region of low pressure is created above the wing and high-pressure under it. This lifts the wing—and anything attached to it. In effect, the wing rises to fill the semi-vacuum created by the air flowing swiftly over it.

Now, how to get and keep the wind flowing?

The brothers urgently and safely transfer the calculus of the wind to the design of a propeller. Their intention is to power flight. As Ashton explains: "Just as the brothers thought of an airplane as a bicycle that flew, they thought of a propeller as a wing that rotated."[45] This allows them, from almost their first attempt, to design a propeller that not only works but, to this day, remains the basis of how planes with prop engines fly.

Through their urgently driven pipeline of innovation comes the kite of 1899, the glider of 1900, the glider of 1901, the glider of 1902 and, finally, the Wright Flyer, the airplane of 1903. Each step they take is a step, not a leap, toward the takeoff from Kill Devil Hills up into the Kitty Hawk sky.

The culmination: At about 10:35 a.m. on the morning of December 17, 1903, on the dunes of North Carolina's Outer Banks, Orville Wright takes off in Flyer I and makes two powered flights, the longer of which lasts only 59 seconds. It is incredibly modest by today's standards, but at the time it is revolutionary. A human being has made a sustained powered flight—and has lived to tell about it.

The Wright brothers continue to improve their designs, and in 1905 they fly the world's first truly practical airplane, in a flight of a spectacular 39 minutes and 23 seconds.

The magnitude of this innovation is almost impossible to quantify. Before the Wright brothers, the human-navigable domains of our world were land and water. After the Wright brothers, we travel within a third domain: the sky. This paradigm shift was achieved by two persistent mechanics possessed of an urgent drive to innovate, an abundance of daring, and a willingness to discover and work within the life-or-death bounds of aerodynamics.

THE BOYD LOOP

Robert Perkins is a top researcher, strategist, political consultant, and a former US Air Force flight instructor. He teaches us the power of something called the Boyd Loop, or OODA loop, which is central to how the US trains fighter pilots to do battle.[46]

Developed for the USAF Flight Weapons School (FWS) by a legendary maverick military strategist, Air Force Colonel John Boyd (1927-1997), the Boyd or OODA loop is still applied to combat operations at both the strategic and tactical levels. By extension, it is also regularly used in business, litigation, and sports.

But the key is that OODA was intended first and foremost to train combat jet fighter pilots, and that means it is a model of operation fueled by urgency. OODA stands for—

Observation: collect data

Orientation: analyze and synthesize data

Decision: based on perspective

Action: execute the decision

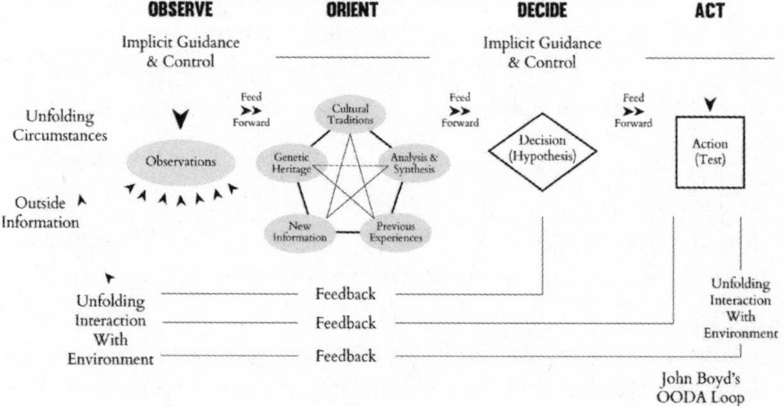

Figure 4-1

This is a decision-to-action loop, and, put simply, the fighter pilot who completes the OODA loop fastest wins. He kills the other pilot. Over the years, the military began studying how to build a fighting force capable of completing the OODA loop faster than the adversary in any situation, not just in aerial combat. Later still, the OODA loop was extended into the realm of high-stakes civilian endeavor.

The OODA loop is about agility more than raw power. It rewards accuracy and, even more, speed. Researchers who have studied Boyd's innovation have discovered that three elements are key in executing the OODA loop:

- First, you must approach strategy development with "radical uncertainty." You must be ready for and open to anything and everything. This helps you increase both the speed and accuracy of assessment, decision, and execution.
- Second, you must increase the urgency and speed of driving strategy into decisions and actions.
- Third, it is essential that you trust the steps of the OODA loop, and that this trust empowers you to "drive power to the edge," enabling battlefield decisions that you know will be as good and fast as they can be.

Successful innovation today—as in the days of Wilbur and Orville Wright—depends on the kind of urgency and speed found in the OODA loop. This urgency and speed are especially critical to successful innovation in the context of today's volatile change environment. As the molecules of innovation change and change again, the more agile and faster navigators will be those best positioned to succeed and win. In my consulting practice, I work with clients to drive the strategic planning and innovation loop as rapidly as possible. In homage to the OODA loop, I call it the DMVDA loop:

Define the Win: Do the kind of "destination planning" described in chapter 2.

Map the Battlefield: Analyze and synthesize perceptions, data, and dynamics.

Validate Hypotheses: Test strategies and messages.

Define the Strategy: Formulate comprehensive strategy.

Activate/Review/Refine: Drive War Room execution.

For businesses, the faster, the more urgently, you drive strategic innovation across the DMVDA loop, the better.

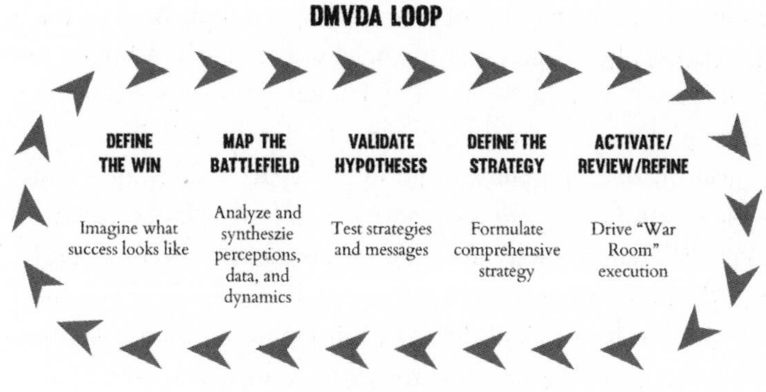

Figure 4-2

DO WHAT BOEING DID

Let's take to the air again. Consider Boeing's historic bet some sixty years ago to shift the company's focus from military to civilian aircraft. At the time, it seemed crazy. In 1952, Harvard Law graduate and Boeing CEO William McPherson Allen convinced his board of directors that focus and urgency will pay off, and, and with an intial $16 million investment, the company created the Boeing 707, the first US transatlantic commercial jetliner. It changed the course of aviation history, presaging Steve Jobs's willingness to bet ahead of where consumers were and urgently focus on producing something totally new. For Apple, it was the iPod, the iPhone, and the iPad. In the case of Boeing, Allen literally bet the company. Without a single order in hand, he authorized total investment of $185 million in the yet-to-be-created 707—some $36 million more than Boeing's net worth at the time.

"I think it's the biggest business decision of the twentieth Century," recounts Boeing's corporate historian, Michael

Lobardi.[47] At the time, Boeing's chief competitor, Douglas Aircraft Company, had been building civilian aircraft since 1934. Douglas was clearly better positioned to take advantage of the economic opportunities linked to civilian aircraft. Boeing, for its part, had endured a series of financial setbacks—the Clipper, the Stratocruiser, and the Stratoliner. The safer choice for Boeing was to stick to military manufacturing. But Allen refused. His bet was on Boeing's culture and its ability to build some of the world's best, fastest, and most accurate military planes. Allen believed Boeing's focus and urgency could be redirected onto design and prototyping in the form of the Dash-80 (as the future 707 was designated) and then workshopping, building, refining, and flying a single consumer-focused product, the 707.

But even Allen did not neglect to provide some downside protection at a key moment. He knew the new USAF heavy jet bombers, the B-47 Stratojet and the B-52 Stratofortress, needed the availability of a tanker aircraft for midair refueling. The Dash-80 airframe fit the bill, and so the risk in development of the civilian 707 was cushioned somewhat by development of the KC-134 Stratotanker. The resulting military orders bought Boeing time and helped protect against some of the worst possible outcomes.

The rest, as they say, is history. On October 28, 1958, five years after its inception, the maiden commercial flight of the Boeing 707 took off, with a first-class seat selling for $505 and a back-of-the-plane economy ticket for $272. Every US President from Dwight D. Eisenhower to George H. W Bush flew on a modified version of the 707 designated Air Force One. Indeed, the 707-320 was like nothing the aviation world had ever seen: 153 feet long with a 146-foot wingspan and the capability to fly 3,735 nautical miles in one go.[48] It was launched in a benefits-focused print and advertising campaign: "Only seven hours to brush up on your French!" And it foreshadowed the focus of

B2B companies such as Intel on consumer benefits. The tagline went "If it ain't Boeing, I ain't going."

PLAY OFFENSE

How do you channel Richard Branson's restlessness, the Wrights' stubborn focus, and the boldness of Boeing's decision to bet the company on the 707? The answer: create a culture of urgency.

Today, with change swirling around all businesses and business leaders, our only choice is to adopt an insurgent model of strategy and innovation as part of an offensively oriented playbook. In a time when change comes faster and faster, consider the cost of ignoring change, resisting it, or trying to defend against it. Calculated in terms of loss of control, loss of morale, loss of conviction, loss of share, loss of momentum, and loss of your future, the cost of failing to be urgent is incalculable. Falling back on your current and temporary advantage of market leadership is a dangerous complacency. Lack of urgency is the number-one challenge facing business innovation today. Urgency is the difference between successful innovation and outright failure.

Learning to think, plan, and act like an insurgent is the only way to survive and thrive today. In terms of innovation, if you are playing defense, you are playing by somebody else's rules and on somebody else's home field. You are playing not to win but to keep from losing. It is no longer sufficient to make one bold move in the marketplace or to drive a single innovation initiative against your competition. Building an urgent cultural bias in favor of playing offense on innovation requires uninterrupted movement forward—a relentless series of attacks on the status quo—whether of the market or yourself. Put simply, you must instill an insurgent spirit inside of your company's culture. How? Let me draw on many of my battle-tested principles reiterated throughout this book.[49] Here are five:

- First, define success and define the enemy.
- Second, set an example of bold initiative.
- Third, take what they give you.
- Fourth, take control of the dialogue and never let go.
- Fifth, never act like an incumbent.

FIRST, DEFINE SUCCESS AND DEFINE THE ENEMY

Your employees and constituents cannot play to win if they do not understand the stakes of the competition. What does winning mean? I suggest you define it in three ways:

- First, what will a "win" mean for your customers? And how will it make their lives better?
- Second, what will a "win" mean for the company and all its stakeholders?
- Third, what will a "win" mean for the individual employee?

In chapter 2, I presented "destination planning" to develop achievable goals on the road to innovation and business success. Destination Planning requires defining the goal, as well as the steps that will get you there, five yards at a time. In planning, try not to allow any one objective to be too daunting. Arrange your actions in order of the difficulty of the challenge. Then take on the least difficult first and establish momentum by getting a few easy wins. Define success in terms of a victory of action over inaction, innovation over paralysis, decisiveness over timidity, and urgency over complacency.

If you want to build a culture of urgency in your company, your employees and constituents will need an opponent on whom or on which to focus. The enemy does not have to be a person or an entity. It can be a problem that consumers face in the marketplace. It can be a problem that innovation will solve, or that consumer education will solve. It can be a problem created by the domination of the market by one or two big incumbents. In this view, the enemy is paucity or stagnation of choice. Microsoft's 1980s mission statement—"A computer on every desk and in every home"—was about how digital technology was going to increase choice through an information revolution. Choice will make all people's lives better.

SECOND, SET AN EXAMPLE OF BOLD INITIATIVE

Creating a culture of urgency depends upon change leadership at the top of a company. When you are the boss, your people will often *listen* to what you say, but they will almost always *do* what *you* do. The insurgent approach mandates leading by example. Think Richard Branson, think the Wright brothers, think Boeing's William McPherson Allen. Then set an example of bold action. *Do* something!

Incumbent executives feel an incentive to play defense. Their mindset is protective. They are focused on holding on to what they have. For this reason, their strategy is not aimed toward victory, but toward avoiding defeat. In contrast to leadership aimed at avoiding mistakes, taking bold action both requires and creates leadership differentiation. Research consistently reveals that the leadership of the CEO makes up 49 percent of a company's brand and reputation. In other words, 49 percent of a company's brand boils down to what and how its leader communicates. Ask yourself: *Does your customer want a brand known for bold innovation or the brand known for trying to avoid a stumble*? (Note: That is a trick question. Only the brand associated with bold innovation is the known brand. The other is known only as Brand X—the generic, the commodity.)

In taking bold action, in driving thought leadership forward, impress upon your organization that you all face a simple but demanding choice: Change or be changed, innovate or die. Play by the other guy's rules or set the rules yourself.

Based on some thirty years advising political campaigns, I cannot think of a single major campaign won by a candidate who played defense. Winning campaigns fight forward. They play offense, offering the candidate as a change leader. When it comes to playing offense, follow the advice of Southwest Airlines founder and CEO Herb Kelleher: "Don't play *not* to lose—play to *win*!"

THIRD, TAKE WHAT THEY GIVE YOU

As an insurgent innovator, you must make something happen. You must disrupt the marketplace. Obviously, you should not try to do this by sheer force or random effort. It makes no sense to define challenges that cannot be overcome. In combat terms, it is no good running your people up a hill they cannot take. In the Civil War's Battle of Kennesaw Mountain, on June 27, 1864, the Union's General Sherman foolishly attacked uphill and lost about 3,000 men compared to 1,000 for Confederate commander Joe Johnston. When Sherman asked his subordinate commander, George H. Thomas, to renew the uphill effort, the hard-fighting "Rock of Chickamauga" replied, "One or two more such assaults would use up this army."[50]

A great football coach once preached to his team over and over: "Take what they give you!"[51] His point? Look for the other side's weakness and play to it. In reshuffling their defense to take away an opening, they will open-up another opening—and another—and another. The untrained and ungentlemanly

Confederate General Nathan Bedford Forrest was famous for this probably apocryphal formula for victory: "Be there the firstest with the mostest." Forrest was considered a wild man, heedlessly brash. In fact, his unbridled aggression was strategically calculated. A cavalryman, he understood that the greatest asset of cavalry was mobility. It could ride out front of the main force and serve as "the eyes of the army." That was well recognized by all competent commanders. The thing that made Forrest different was his willingness to use his cavalry aggressively, to skirmish hard—not in a doomed effort to break through superior numbers, but to probe for the enemy's weak point, so that the main body of the army that followed the cavalry could put its mostest *there*—and do so firstest.

And by mostest, Forrest meant going all in. Civil War-era commanders typically committed no more than a quarter to a third of their force to an attack, leaving the rest in reserve to defend against a counterattack or in case of unexpected resistance. Not Forrest. He threw virtually all that he had against the enemy line's weak point. It was against the rules. No less an adversary than Sherman—perhaps the Union's fiercest warrior—called him a "devil," who "must be hunted down and killed if it costs ten thousand lives and bankrupts the federal treasury." He also deemed him "the most remarkable man our Civil War produced on either side."[52]

Forrest took whatever weakness his enemy offered. So, too, did Southwest Airlines. Famously, this industry insurgent avoided competing in the hubs of the major airlines. When founder Herb Kelleher was drawing the concept of Southwest Airlines on the back of a cocktail napkin in a bar, the strategy might have been most accurately described as "take *whatever* you can get."[53] Necessity really is the mother of invention—just as desperation is its daddy. Yet today, the insurgent brands in the market's bottom tier create most of the innovative thinking in every category. Some of these insurgents can and do ride breakthrough innovation right to the top.

At the market's top tier, the big, incumbent brands have the scale and resources to fight big set-piece infantry battles for the patronage of the masses. But attrition in these wars is very costly. Top-tier incumbents find they are gaining less ground with every charge "over the top." ("One or two more such assaults would use up this army.") Yes, top-tier competition is getting to look a lot like trench warfare—slaughter without measurable progress. Except that while the two top-tier brands devour each other, trading one or two points of share, the smaller guerrilla brands maneuver around them, decimating their flanks. No wonder that, more and more, the big incumbents are trying to match the strategies, tactics, and innovations of the little insurgents. They are trying to achieve the efficiency and effectiveness of innovation, marketing, and distribution that the insurgents have. And they are quickly trying to develop the motivation to seek opportunity the way the little insurgents do. Why? Stark marketplace terror.

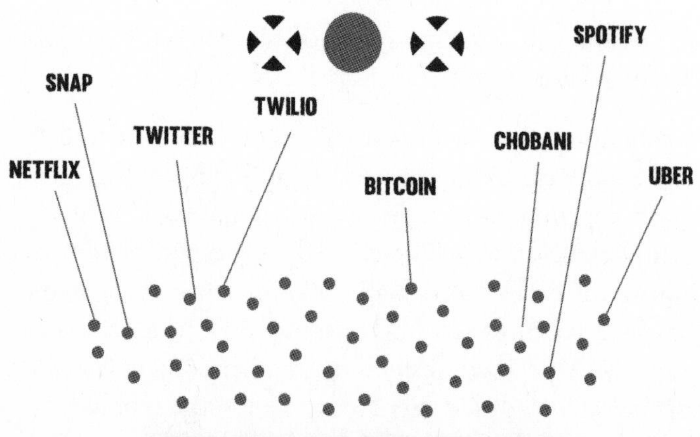

Figure 4-3: 3 top-tier incumbents leave only one—as insurgents brands rise.

FOURTH, TAKE CONTROL OF THE DIALOGUE AND NEVER LET GO

In politics, the candidate who controls the dialogue wins the election. In business, control the market dialogue and you win the market.

In today's reset environment, control is gained by innovation and change, and the good news for the insurgent is that *the incumbent doesn't want to innovate and change, and they will resist innovating and changing at almost all costs.* This gives you one hell of an advantage—akin to knowing that the Heavyweight boxing champ will throw only the left. Keep circling to the right and hooking your right, and you will tear him up.

If the incumbent hates change and innovation, then you, as the insurgent, must love change and innovation. Just beware the incumbent who comes to love change and innovation—as, for example, at this writing, Google or Amazon or Apple or Alibaba. Getting control away from this type of incumbent market leader is very difficult.

As the insurgent innovator, another assumption you can make is that the incumbent has fallen behind changes in consumer attitudes. Today, in virtually every marketplace, consumers' desire for refreshment and change is greater than the incumbent's willingness or ability to satisfy it. Why? Because the incumbent's desire is the status quo, which means that he is generally averse to innovation and change.

Incumbents aren't stupid. In fact, for many decades, the biggest companies, the market leaders, did not need to innovate—not with their marketplace domination. When change was forced upon them by the innovations of a market insurgent, they just followed the change, using their muscle to eventually overtake and trample the smaller competitor. Today, however, market change moves faster and faster, carried on the viral wings of digital interconnectivity.

Today, the early adopter segment in every marketplace is instantly informed about new choices and is very quick to move to them. The magnetic pull of big brands on these early adopters is weaker than ever. Moreover, the current innovation cycle of newness is compressed. Each round of changes in the market value proposition comes faster as more new ideas and innovations are introduced. Contrast this to the situation of only a decade ago, when a newly introduced product advantage might enjoy a year without matching competition. Recently, you could count on six months, then thirteen weeks, a month, and, today, in many cases, a few days or even a few hours. Often, the enormous consumer demand at the high early adopter margins is devoured by the small insurgents before the lumbering giants can even move toward it. The successful insurgent takes this market foothold and continues to grow—and grow.

Fundamentally, the only way to create urgent innovation and control the dialogue is to drive change *ahead* of what consumers are thinking. No wonder hockey great Wayne Gretzky's "I skate to where the puck is *going to be*, not to where it has been" is already a cliché. The desire and willingness of insurgents to understand the consumer's wants and needs must exceed that of the incumbents. A deft and agile insurgent should be able to find a way to fit into the gap between what consumers really want and need and what the incumbent is willing or able to deliver.

FIFTH, NEVER ACT LIKE THE INCUMBENT

History and fiction are filled with stories of the humble, hardworking challenger who becomes the champ and "forgets where he came from." In fiction, at least, the wayward insurgent comes to his or her senses just before the final credits roll. Actual history, however, is not so kind to insurgents who take on the character of the incumbents they replace. Here's how to avoid that terrible fate for yourself and your company:

- *Never, ever declare victory.* Celebrate the small victories, but never declare the war won. Picture President George W. Bush declaring victory in Iraq on the deck of USS *Abraham Lincoln* beneath a banner emblazoned with "Mission Accomplished." That was on May 1, 2003—when, as it turned out, the Iraq War had another eight years and seven months before it ended not in victory, but US withdrawal. It's better to keep the spirit of battle going.

- *Do not stop setting doable goals.* After several doable goals have been achieved, managers often slack off, but nobody tires of achievement. Keep innovating, setting up goals, and knocking them down.

- *Do not let anybody get between you and your customers.* Stay on them like holy on the Pope. Understand these customers' needs and wants so well that you anticipate them. How? Make sure you are in ongoing dialogue with them.

- *Do not stop hating "bigness."* Most companies hate big, bureaucratic companies until they become one. Keep the hatred alive. As you build and fuel your culture of urgency, keep the organization as flat as you can.

KEEP INNOVATING URGENTLY

Beautiful, bold, audacious, and witty American film star Tallulah Bankhead once proclaimed: “If I had to live my life again, I’d make the same mistakes, only sooner.” Building and putting to work a culture of urgency helps you make mistakes—just sooner, faster, and better. Emulate the urgency of the ever-restless Richard Branson, the determined Wilbur and Orville Wright, and Boeing’s bet-the-company William McPherson Allen to create a culture of playing offense on innovation. But heed the wisdom of history’s greatest investor, Warren Buffett, who advised protecting your downside while playing more and more offense. Sometimes this demands that leaders drive focused and urgent innovation, not so much on their own products and services, but on their company’s business models. Companies that follow this thinking, such as Amazon and Netflix, continue to perform especially well.

Look as well at what former client and Walt Disney Company Chairman and CEO Bob Iger has done since 2005. Iger gives cultural permission to fail as he transfers to employees his belief that the company’s true magic is inside *their* brains, works through *their* hands, and is made manifest in the fruits of *their* labor. Iger continues to maintain a culture of urgency as he extends his own retirement a fourth time, continuing to triple annual profits, and announcing one of the most audacious acquisitions in history: the proposed purchase of Rupert Murdoch’s 21st Century Fox.[54] As Disney gets bigger, Bob Iger intends for its culture to become no less urgent.

The attitude of Steve Jobs was much the same as that of his close friend Bob Iger. Despite the impression that he focused generally and broadly, in fact, when it counted most, Apple’s CEO zeroed-in narrowly and intently. On July 9, 1997, at the beginning of the greatest turnaround in the history of business, he began whittling down a troubled Apple from over 100 strategic priorities to just three "things that mattered most."

A NEVER-ENDING BATTLE (IF YOU ARE LUCKY)

Urgency of focus is always a battle. The war to remain an insurgent has no end—if you are lucky. Our great role models, the Wright Brothers, also stand as a cautionary tale of the consequences of ending a battle that must always be fought.

Wing warping was a breakthrough solution to controlling flight, but it was as imperfect as most first-generation inventions are. An alternative had begun to emerge in 1902, the year before the Wrights first flew. New Zealand inventor Richard Pearse designed ailerons. Hinged tabs on each wing, these had the potential for achieving control more efficiently, reliably, and easily than warping the entire wing. In 1904, a year after the Wrights' first Kitty Hawk flights, the French aviation pioneer Robert Esnault-Pelterie made a successful flight with an aileron-equipped aircraft. More aileron experiments followed, prompting the Wrights to patent wing warping in 1906 and then to argue that their patent protected the very concept of "lateral control," whether it was achieved by wing warping or ailerons. In 1908, when American aviator Glenn Curtiss flew a spectacular demonstration of aileron-controlled flight in his *June Bug*, the Wrights sent him a warning of patent infringement. This led to years of costly lawsuits and countersuits, which held back the development of American aviation. Only US entry into World War I in April 1917 broke the Wright stranglehold on innovation. Patriotic American aircraft manufacturers banded together to form a patent pool, so that all US aircraft makers could get down to the business of making planes for the war, fixing royalties at 1 percent for the use of patents. By this time, the United States entered World War I with aircraft so woefully obsolete that American combat pilots flew French and British aircraft exclusively.

Worst of all, however, the Wrights fell into the deadly mindset that had killed Otto Lilienthal. They obstinately refused to abandon their wing-warping system, even after it repeatedly proved fatal. Between 1908 and 1914, more than twenty aviators were killed in crashes almost certainly caused by a loss of control due to the inadequacy of wing warping. In 1914, the US Army officially banned the technology. As for the Wright Company, founded in November 1909 with a terrific innovator's advantage, it was out of business in 1916 and merged with the Glenn L. Martin Company as Wright-Martin, having spent its brief seven years of operation in patent litigation instead of innovation.

Never stop innovating urgently. While protecting the downside, double-down on efforts to think "out of the box," to "think different," and to think in the direction of our next chapter: *peripherally*.

CHAPTER FIVE

DEVELOP PERIPHERAL VISION

A computer on every desk and in every home.

—Bill Gates, circa 1980

His best friend prefers drinking Coca-Cola, sometimes for breakfast. But he prefers Diet Orange Crush. And Diet Orange Crush is the unhealthy carbonated fuel that reenergizes his twice-a-year ritual of getting away, out into the periphery, in this case, in 1995, to a modest, two-story clapboard cottage in the woods and on a lake where distractions of friends, family, and incoming emails are banned so that focused, proactive, and strategic innovation might flourish.

Bill Gates and Warren Buffett sometimes alternate between being the world's richest men, and each may prefer different types of unhealthy carbonated drinks, but both share a love of recharging their intellectual and creative batteries to think different, to drive change, and to seize opportunity. "Read 500 pages like this every day," Buffet advises one interviewer as he points to a stack of books. "That's how knowledge works. It builds up, like compound interest."[55]

Back in the heyday of Microsoft, the company he founded, my former client Gates Foundation creator Bill Gates needed to build up more compound interest by getting away to stay ahead of the pack. He began getting serious about developing peripheral vision in the 1980s, with a quiet visit to his grandmother's house near Seattle, Washington. By the time he reached his apex as Microsoft's change leader, he regularly developed his peripheral vision out in the woods, away from the daily distractions of media, work, and phone.

So, go back to 1995. Gates has helicoptered in and driven along a narrow, winding road through a Pacific Northwest cedar forest to begin another "Think Week." In retreat from the world of centralized bureaucracy and SOP, amply stocked with Diet Orange Crush, Gates gets away. He gets away to the periphery, where he can focus on the critical topics facing Microsoft. He will spend this day reading extensive briefing papers, thinking, daydreaming, receiving no incoming emails. He plays offense exclusively, hitting send to deliver outbound edicts to his Microsoft troops.

This day begins in bed absorbing papers by Microsoft engineers, product managers, and anyone who wants to get their leader's peripheral but creative attention. Gates scribbles notes atop the covers, skips breakfast, reads more papers, drinks more Diet Orange Crush, sits at his kitchen table, eating, reading, thinking, the view of the Olympic Mountains just outside the window.

Toward the end of this "Think Week," during eighteen-hour days, Gates has read almost a hundred papers, just short of his record of 112, one memorably entitled: "10 Crazy Ideas to Shake Up Microsoft." Now, it's early morning and a recharged Gates makes a decision born inside this cottage in the woods. Microsoft, Gates imagines, must pivot toward, not away, from the internet. He hits send and broadcasts a now-famous May 26, 1995, memo titled "Internet Tidal Wave."[56] *It will lead Microsoft to develop its own internet browser, Explorer, which will crush sector-owning rival Netscape. Among others.*

This is Gates's woodland retreat—"It's the world's coolest suggestion box," remembers Stephen Lawler, a Microsoft general manager.[57] *Here, through the years, Gates gave the go-ahead for the highly profitable Xbox Live, imagined his first book,* The Road Ahead, *and repeatedly refocused his company's strategic direction, creating its tablet PC, more secure software, and an online video game business. "I really wanted to be alone, just reading," Gates reminisced to David A. Kaplan in an interview in 2012.*[58]

Ten years after his last official "Think Week" and eighteen years after he stepped down as Microsoft CEO, Gates is busy disproving F. Scott Fitzgerald's adage: "There are no second acts in American life." In fact, Bill Gates and the Bill & Melinda Gates Foundation will this year spend $4 billion on initiatives battling malaria, HIV, and other global health challenges. They have already given away more than $40 billion. Along with the money the Coca-Cola drinking Warren Buffett has donated to the Gates Foundation, this charitable giving has pushed both Buffett and Gates down one notch on Forbes' "The World's Billionaires" list to #2 and #3, behind Amazon founder Jeff Bezos.

No matter. Gates is today one of the two or three most influential leaders in history, having made an impact on the information revolution and now revolutionizing the way we tackle the global challenges of hunger and health. Implicit in this work is a call to us all to move out along the creative periphery, to think different, to develop better peripheral vision.

Out in the periphery, it is as if the water tastes different there...

—Robert Shapiro, Chairman, Sandbox Industries

He should have been fired. It is 1933, and Clarence Leonard "Kelly" Johnson has just started working for a struggling company called Lockheed, a small airplane manufacturer with only five engineers. Johnson's first day does not go well.

He knows he shouldn't, but he can't help himself. Everyone, including his own professor and mentor at the University of Michigan, Edward Stalker, head of the university's department of aeronautical engineering, agrees Lockheed's new Model 10 Electra all-metal airplane, on which the reorganized Lockheed has literally bet its future, is right on track.

Johnson speaks. "It's unstable."

The room goes quiet—and stays quiet just long enough to become very uncomfortable. It is Johnson who breaks the silence, going on to make his case that the airplane is based on a bad design.[59]

Silence. Johnson's boss, Lockheed chief engineer Hall Hibbard, a graduate of MIT, arguably the world's most prestigious engineering school, now has a choice to make. His first impulse is horror. But before he acts, he reminds himself that his mission is to recruit "new young blood…people fresh out of school with newer ideas."[60] Instead of making this Johnson's last day, Hibbard makes it his first. Thinking out of the box, challenging the conventional status quo, Hibbard challenges Johnson to act on what he had just said. Hibbard stakes out the ground for a system for peripheral innovation. Instead of firing Johnson, he gives him an assignment.

Fix the plane, he tells him. Kelly Johnson responds by immediately going out to his creative periphery. He drives 2,400 miles to the University of Michigan with a model of the Electra in the backseat of his car. Like the Wright brothers thirty years before, Johnson needs a wind tunnel, and the best one is at Michigan. Johnson tests the model seventy-two times in search of a creative solution to a problem only he can see. In the end, he invents a never-before-seen twin tail to fix the plane's stability problems. He removes the single conventional vertical stabilizer and redesigns the horizontal stabilizer, making it longer. Then he puts vertical stabilizers near the tips of the horizontal stabilizer, giving the aircraft two fins. It is a radical design, which provides this beautiful and innovative aircraft, the first truly modern airliner, with the flight stability it needs.

Hibbard's written response to Johnson's new idea is an expression of joy, gratitude, grace, and a fine thank you to an out-of-the-box innovator who saved an airplane, a company, and untold lives:

> You will have to excuse the typing as I am writing here at the factory tonight and this typewriter certainly is not much good.
>
> You may be sure that there was a big celebration around these parts when we got your wires telling about the new find and how simple the solution really was. It is apparently a rather important discovery and I think it is a fine thing that you should be the one to find out the secret. Needless to say, the addition of these parts is a very easy matter; and I think that we shall wait until you get back perhaps before we do much along that line.
>
> Well, I guess I'll quit now. You will be quite surprised at the Electra when you get here, I think. It is coming along quit well.[61]

Skunk Works, two words, capital *S* and *W*, is a registered trademark of the company today known as Lockheed Martin, but the exploits of Kelly Johnson and his Skunk Works are so famous that, to this day, the phrase "skunk works" or the word "skunkworks" is used to describe any gathering of disruptive innovators outside the center of their own bureaucracy.

Johnson's record of innovation at Lockheed lasted nearly forty-five years and was driven by fourteen "rules and practices." Rules, yes, but created by innovator-practitioners, not bureaucrats:

- The Skunk Works manager must be delegated practically complete control of his program in all aspects. He should report to a division president or higher.
- Strong but small project offices must be provided both by the military and industry.
- The number of people having any connection with the project must be restricted in an almost vicious manner. Use a small number of good people (10 percent to 25 percent compared to the so-called normal systems).
- A very simple drawing and drawing release system with great flexibility for making changes must be provided.
- There must be a minimum number of reports required, but important work must be recorded thoroughly.
- There must be a monthly cost review covering not only what has been spent and committed but also projected costs to the conclusion of the program.
- The contractor must be delegated and must assume more than normal responsibility to get good vendor bids for subcontract on the project. Commercial bid procedures are very often better than military ones.
- The inspection system as currently used by the Skunk Works, which has been approved by both the Air Force and Navy, meets the intent of existing military requirements and should be used on new projects. Push more basic inspection responsibility back to

subcontractors and vendors. Don't duplicate so much inspection.

- The contractor must be delegated the authority to test his final product in flight. He can and must test it in the initial stages. If he doesn't, he rapidly loses his competency to design other vehicles.

- The specifications applying to the hardware must be agreed to well in advance of contracting. The Skunk Work's practice of having a specification section stating clearly which important military specification items will not knowingly be complied with and reasons therefore is highly recommended.

- Funding a program must be timely so that the contractor doesn't have to keep running to the bank to support government projects.

- There must be mutual trust between the military project organization and the contractor, the very close cooperation and liaison on a day-to-day basis. This cuts down misunderstanding and correspondence to an absolute minimum.

- Access by outsiders to the project and its personnel must be strictly controlled by appropriate security measures.

- Because only a few people will be used in engineering and most other areas, ways must be provided to reward good performance by pay not based on the number of personnel supervised.

The key to adapting the 14 rules and practices is to focus on their essence. Get your Skunk Works out of the larger bureaucracy, give it real and delegated authority, keep it small, create a simple drawing, a crystal-clear vision of what must be done, set a "By When?" cut bureaucratic red-tape, assume responsibility, build mutual trust, fund the project properly and accountably, and use only the "best athletes" available.

This is the boss we all wish we had. Instead of firing Johnson as a troublemaker who isn't a "team player," the intellectually mature, managerially savvy Hibbard promoted him to become Lockheed's sixth engineer. Now, flash ahead, to 1943, and the height of World War II. The US Army Air Forces face a life-and-death challenge. The British have decoded secret German messages indicating that Hitler's engineers have built a jet-powered fighter plane. The Messerschmitt Me 262 *Schwalbe* (Swallow) can reach 559 miles per hour, which is about 150 mph faster than most conventional propeller-driven Allied fighters. The Nazi plane has gone into mass production. It is agile, and it is armed with machine guns, rockets, and bombs. The substance of the intelligence is clear: if deployed in sufficient numbers, the Me 262 will be a war-winning aircraft.

Re-enter Kelly Johnson. He is now assigned the job of countering German innovation by building a jet-powered aircraft to outfight the Nazis. But he must do it fast. And he must do it secretly. Without the luxury of time to build an annex to the Lockheed plant, Johnson puts a bunch of old boxes inside a circus tent hidden next to a wind tunnel at the company's Burbank, California, factory. The boxes serve as desks, the tent provides shelter and secrecy. The whole thing is so ugly and makeshift that one engineer christens it the "Skunk Works"—or "Skonk Works," which is the way cartoonist Al Capp spelled the name of a ramshackle Dogpatch factory in his universally popular *Li'l Abner* comic strip.

Like *Li'l Abner's* Skonk Works, which ground shoes and skunks together to produce oil, Kelly Johnson's Skunk Works must do the impossible. And so they did. Just forty years after the Wright brothers' first flight and a mere 143 days since the group barely imagined a jet aircraft, test pilot Milo Burcham climbed into a piece of peripheral imagination. It was a P-80 Shooting Star named *Lulu Belle,* America's first combat jet. With stubby wings and nary a propeller to be seen, it reached 502 miles per hour on January 1944—not quite as fast as the German fighter jet, but sufficiently fast and maneuverable to be competitive in a dogfight.

Burcham flies low and can see his colleagues watching him from the ground, going slack-jawed as he streaks just above them. It is the fastest aircraft in the Allied inventory. Although the P-80 will not go into full production before the end of the war, the Skunk Works' P-38 Lightning, a twin-engine propeller-driven fighter with a radical twin-boom fuselage design, had been earning a reputation since the start of World War II as one of its greatest combat aircraft. And after the war, Johnson and his crew will go on to develop the likes of the Cold War's U-2 spy plane and the SR-71 Blackbird, still the fastest aircraft ever built.

Bill Gates's woodland getaways were a solo version of the Skunk Works, a journey to the periphery of innovation via an actual journey to the periphery. Steve Jobs's famed "Mac Group," set up in a Cupertino, California strip mall, physically separate from official Apple headquarters and topped by a Jolly Roger pirate flag, was another. Here, his engineers found the perfect place to imagine and build a computer that shifted the PC paradigm.

Considerably.

THE PERIPHERY ROCKS TODAY'S MARKETS

Today, the only way big incumbent companies can innovate is by learning to use insurgent strategy to drive a campaign that leverages innovation breakthrough. In short, they must innovate and market like an insurgent, not an incumbent. For most of the nineteenth and twentieth centuries, the assumption was that the natural tendency toward stability rules all markets. By the beginning of the twenty-first century, it became clear that change rules. As the information revolution has continued to ramify, instability became the norm.

To know is to change. To know infinitely more and know it instantly is to change profoundly. That is why change rules markets today. Unsurprisingly, the rules of change greatly favor the insurgent, who embraces and adores change. Insurgents are at home in the periphery, where change is most robust. The incumbent, by contrast, is comfortable only in the center of a marketplace and therefore hates change, which is a threat. To swim against change these days, however, is to flail against a riptide. *That* is the real danger to incumbents. The traditional structure of markets is crumbling under the weight of the information revolution.

Once, virtually all markets could be visualized as three concentric circles:

- *Inner:* This circle held two or three nationally known, mass-marketed leader brands. These brands established the "category brand," the understood attributes and benefits that define the category. These category brands became the table stakes for playing in the center of the marketplace.
- *Middle:* This circle held as many as several dozen "follower" national brands in the slipstream of the inner concentric circle brands. The brands here tended to share the same positioning—namely, "Me too!" In fact, this remains the world's most popular brand positioning. Any differentiation is achieved by price.
- *Peripheral:* This circle held the zillions of smaller, customized, personalized niche brands—often, local, regional, or startup companies.

DRAWING OF INNER, MIDDLE, PERIPHERAL CONCENTRIC CIRCLES

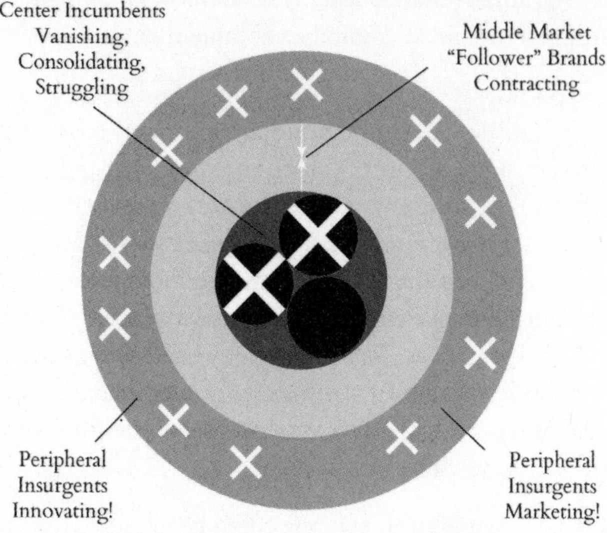

Figure 5-1: center incumbents leave only one–as peripheral insurgents rule.

The movement from one of these circles to another was formerly glacial. Once you reached the inner circle, you were almost frozen in place. Today, the information revolution has had the effect of a sudden global warming. Nothing will ever be the same. A torrent of information has given consumers infinitely more choices in every marketplace. This has changed the way consumers move in markets.

At present, they are moving in two directions: First, to the center of the market, to one sure-thing big brand guaranteed to be available, affordable, and acceptable. Today, one leader brand dominates its category more often than during the past half-century. In most categories, the number two and three and four brands suck wind, often falling into the middle circle. Second, the same consumers are now moving just as strongly to the peripheral circle, where they can fill out their personal-choice menus with brands customized and localized to their needs and wants. Each menu contains one big brand and maybe five or six small-brand options. No wonder that most of the vitality and innovation in today's markets bubbles up from this periphery.

What are we to make of this bidirectional movement to the center and to the periphery of markets?

- *The middle circle is being squeezed out.* At present, the middle market is going or gone in every single marketplace we know about. If you want to find stubborn, chronic unemployment in the US economy, look in the crushed middle.
- *Life flourishes only in the center and the periphery.* The brands in the center innovate and go to market very differently from the brands in the periphery, but the brands in the middle circle have held on to their own imitative, lower-rent versions of center-circle companies for too long.
- *To play at the center of the market, bring buckets of money.* Center-circle marketing is mass marketing. Expensive, it is the approach that has defined the most successful brands for about a century. This is changing.
- *At the periphery, desperation and high-stakes poker define innovation and marketing.* So-called experts derisively call the periphery the territory of "niche" marketing. But niche marketing has been increasingly successful with sophisticated and cynical consumers. Today, this is *all* consumers. Consider the early success of Airbnb, Alibaba, Facebook, Uber, Bitcoin, Shake Shack. At their early and super-fast growth stages, their innovation created new markets and niches and their marketing was

nontraditional and non-mass. Marketing experts decided to call it "un-marketing." Far more accurately, it is simply non-mass marketing, which is to say insurgent marketing—the strategy we will talk about in chapter 6.

- *The growing success of marketing for brands in the periphery depends directly on the diminishing success of marketing for brands in the center.* Insurgent marketing depends on today's growing consumer savvy and cynicism about mass marketing's tired tactics. Consumers of all ages are on to the game. It is like the big, incumbent brands in the center of the marketplace are playing three-card monte with just two cards.

The disruption of the traditional market structure and movement to the center and the periphery make marketing the biggest brands increasingly expensive, even as they dominate their markets more and more. According to generally accepted economic theory, it just ain't supposed to be this way. But it is.

There may be great comfort in tradition and a traditional view of the marketplace of business. But you can end up riding tradition right over the falls. Truth to tell, the safest thing to do today is the scariest. Emulate Richard Branson in his out-of-control balloon drifting over the Irish Sea. Jump.

PERIPHERAL INNOVATION PROGENY

The Skunk Works model has inspired many peripheral efforts, such as Verizon's "Video Services," Google's "X," Amazon's "Lab126," Raytheon's "Bike Shop," Nike's "Innovation Kitchen," Staples' "Velocity Lab," and Xerox's "PARC." None has yet been more successful than Steve Jobs's Mac Group of the 1980s. Jobs understood that IBM, creator of the PC, was not just the industry incumbent, it was the center of its own marketplace. Jobs understood: Apple David and IBM Goliath. He understood the moral of the original story. Strength and incumbency could be weaknesses. No question, IBM had the lead in computing. But, within computing, *personal* computing was the cutting edge.

The product of innovation, innovation was at the core of *personal* computing's value proposition. Although IBM had invented the personal computer (the PC), Big Blue was, Jobs saw, institutionally averse to the disorganized innovation required to deliver on the edginess of its own invention. IBM was to the PC what the Wright brothers were to the airplane—absolute innovators, who almost immediately became so incumbently protective of their innovation that they stopped innovating. Both the Wrights and Big Blue acted as "center-of-every-bureaucracy" incumbents. And both rapidly slipped from leading edge to trailing edge of the very categories they had innovated.

By all appearances, IBM made for an incredibly intimidating competitor. It was already the standard business desktop computer, and IBM anointed Microsoft DOS as *the* operating system software for *the* desktop computer. Moreover, the businesses buying IBM's PCs were looking less for innovation than affirmation. During the mainframe epoch, "Nobody ever got fired for buying IBM" was the aphorism universally mumbled, like a rosary, throughout corporate America. Big Blue made no bones about carrying it into the era of the desktop. IBM assumed that, mainframe or PC, IBM was to remain the standard.

But Jobs saw things differently. He recognized that IBM's marketplace supremacy came at a cost—not necessarily or immediately to IBM, but to the consumer. There was a difference between IBM "big iron" (mainframe computers) and IBM PCs, obviously. Yet, apart from size and cost, there were also great similarities. Both the IBM PCs and the IBM mainframes were text-based machines using text-based operating systems. This meant that computer users who bought IBM—the machine nobody ever got fired for buying—had to be willing to put in some hard labor to learn the language of the computer to communicate with it. As IBM saw it, the PC was a junior version of a mainframe.

Now, look at the little Mac at the time my company began working with that machine's leader and champion. This computer was not just an example of insurgent, peripheral innovation, it was a born revolutionary. It was conceived, if not born, in a garage, and, like Facebook, it might as well have been delivered in a dorm room. Steve Jobs had marched out of Apple in a fit of paranoia just a couple of years before we began working with him. He was scared. Computing, he realized, was moving away from fun and kids and elementary schools, the territory his company had staked out, and it was moving into businesses. That meant adults, which, ultimately, enabled a move on to *everything*. Advantage: IBM.

Jobs had a choice: to be better or not to be at all. He needed to reposition Apple to capture that *everything.* There was no time to get the organization to move behind him. Instead, he moved out of the building, marched across the street from Apple HQ, and opened a modest set of offices in a little business strip mall. Over its flat roof, he raised a black skull-and-crossbones. *This* was the Mac Group and, under its wind-snapped Jolly Roger, Jobs presided over the making of a Macintosh that was different from the IBM PC in every way possible. He let his paranoia drive innovation to disorganize the IBM corporate mindset. Text-based MS-DOS was native to machines, but it was a foreign tongue to human beings. Working in a strip mall physically on the periphery of Apple HQ, Jobs and his team created the anti-text operating system. They called it a graphical user interface (GUI—pronounced "Gooey"). Instead of requiring the user to learn a language friendly to a machine, the GUI "talked" to the user, in sign language. The screen served up icons and menus, and users clicked on their choice of action using a new version of something called a mouse.

Very soon, the Mac and its GUI were creating legions of insurgents, who loved—yes, loved—their Macs and proclaimed that the initials *IBM* stood for Incredibly Boring Machine. Advantage: the outsider. *Machine* serves *man.*

Steve Jobs was a visionary. That means he saw a lot. But he did not see everything. Not content with having blown up the text-based universe of DOS, he decided to make the personal computer not just personal, but intimate. Whereas the IBM PC was effectively a 1960s-computer terminal given an upgrade in autonomy, but still intended to connect to Big Iron, the Mac was made so it could not connect to anything bigger, even a network. (The internet did not yet exist, and even Steve Jobs did not imagine it.) As for measuring the user's output, Jobs did not allow anything as objective as quantifiable productivity. Instead, he emphasized more self-indulgence: creative expansiveness. It betokened the truth that innovators working on the periphery cherish an attitude of difference, have a desire to move faster, and welcome change as opportunity. They are the very embodiment of the recruiting profile of legendary Alabama football coach Bear Bryant. Again, he wanted players who were "agile, hostile, and mobile."

INNOVATION: AGILE, HOSTILE, AND MOBILE

Maybe "hostile" is a little strong, so let's say "aggressive." That was the Mac, and that was Steve Jobs: Nothing he did was passive or coincidental. He left nothing to chance. Everything he said, everything he did communicated the American, democratic, disorganized species of innovation that can be imagined along the periphery. From the defiant Jolly Roger to the 97-key Imperial Bösendorfer grand piano Jobs presented as a gift to the Mac team, to the Mac OS, to the triumph of the mouse over the keyboard, and to the spectacular public statement that launched it all, everything conveyed a unified message of innovation.

Fundamentally, the Apple Mac's outsider spirit fueled Jobs's innovation and change leadership. And in our work with Jobs and Apple, we developed the full pattern of the "insurgent vs. incumbent campaign model." It was all about a marketplace center focused on "Bigness Leadership" versus an innovative periphery focused on "Change Leadership."

The in-the-center Bigness Leaders share the following attributes:

- *They literally worship bigness*—size, scope, market share, and gross revenues.
- *They are used to being number one* and have developed a great deal of arrogance about this position.
- *They are centralized and bureaucratic*, believing in the hierarchy of the marketplace, even as they believe in the hierarchy of their own corporate cube farm.
- *They are excessively formal*—to the point of making every process into a ritual of superstitious behavior—"this is the way we do things because this is the way we do things." Their culture is a form of corporate religion.
- *They are oh so cautious.* They've got a lot to lose, so why take chances? Incremental gain? They'll take

it, no matter how slowly it creeps. After all, they've been the leader forever and intend to remain the leader forevermore.

- *They are driven by heritage*, owing their success mostly to the past and therefore driving into the future with their eyes firmly fixed on the rearview mirror. The reverence they feel is for "the good old days."

- *They hate change.* When you are the market leader, you do not want things to change at all. Indeed, if you are number one, change means becoming number two—and that's the *best* case. Therefore, most big companies cannot innovate themselves out of a paper bag—because, what is innovation if not disruption of the *status quo*?

The peripheral innovation of the Macintosh division of Apple Computer became the insurgent template for thousands of startups that followed in personal computing hardware and software, the building of the internet, and the emergence of mobile technology. The Mac model inspired the innovators Warren Buffett cited when he was asked why he believes in America's ability to succeed, invent, and imagine. Precisely the opposite of the "in-the-center" bureaucracy-worshipping incumbents, these change leaders:

- *Worship better and greater*, rather than bigger and bigger.

- *Take chances.* Accustomed to being number zero, they swing for the fences. They are bold. And why *not*? They don't have all that much to lose.

- *Are informal*, working out of flat organizations. Most of them have not had the chance to create a hierarchy, and few of them ever will. They work as a team toward the revolutionary goal of unseating the incumbent and disorganizing the norm. Their own cultural glue? It is all about being a part of something great.

- *Value speed and mobility over size.* They are okay with errors of commission, but they are horrified by the errors of omission that could put them out of the game.
- *Are vision-driven,* focusing on the future, because that is where change is going to take them. The future is where success lives. The past is where nobody lives.
- *Love change* because, to an outsider-insurgent, change means opportunity. When the market's molecules are in motion, everything is up for grabs.
- Think Different

"Think different" was the Apple motto under Steve Jobs. But, in fact, outsider insurgents do not just *think different*, they play by a different set of rules than in-the-center incumbents. Here briefly are the rules for thinking outside your own center and disorganizing innovation.

THINK "CHANGE LEADER"

Today, you must make a commitment to avoid acting like the in-the-center incumbent leader, no matter how overwhelmingly you may dominate your market. The only unstoppable leader is the one playing by outsider insurgent rules. Don't act like a leader. Act like you did on the way to leadership.

No law bars the leader of the center from creating and implementing peripheral insurgent strategies. On the contrary, our experience says you *must* do this. In business, the companies doing this—Amazon, Starbucks, Google, Uber, Alibaba, Airbnb, Twitter, and others—are now market leaders. Sometimes, they themselves invented those markets.

NOTHING FAILS LIKE SUCCESS

As Tony Robbins says: "We either party or ponder. When we're winning, we party; and when we're losing, we ponder.... and the key is to ponder at the same time we're winning." In fact, the human body craves sweets, but sweets, they say, are bad for us. They rot the teeth, bulge the belly and, after a short-lived high, let us down. The danger of sweet, sweet victory comes the moment when the newly winning crew is doing high-fives at their victory party. The truth is, "Nothing fails like success."

Up until just a few years ago, Microsoft was assailed by the insistent drumbeat of unhappy investors who had watched the company's stock petrify in the wake of ceaseless insurgent innovation from Apple, Google, Facebook, Twitter, and Amazon. Microsoft's troubles began when it started reflexively protecting what it had instead of repeatedly betting the company on innovation. In the days when he was Microsoft's hands-on chief, Gates delivered an annual speech to the employees, each year recommending a new target worth "betting the company" on. The company gambled accordingly, and it became an indefatigable pursuer of the bets it made—even when it had already managed to run the table.

The temptation to stop scrapping and start basking is hard to resist. As Clayton Christensen warns: Stop creating and you get disrupted. It's the unavoidable gravity that is peripheral insurgency. Consider Microsoft after Gates: When Ballmer took over at Microsoft, Google was just two years old, Facebook was four years from being founded, Twitter six years off, and the release of the iPhone was seven years in the future. Every one of these outsider insurgents snuck up on the in-the-center incumbent Microsoft.

In trying to extend the domain of Windows, Ballmer was essentially trying to protect Windows. The protection strategy just does not work anymore. Balmer next seemed to try to turn Microsoft into a hedge fund, developing follower brands in gaming, search, tablets, and mobile to hedge against his huge bet on the immortality of Windows. No dice.

Today, Microsoft has a more peripheral insurgent leader. CEO Satya Nadella has changed the game since taking the reins on February 24, 2014. He has the company potentially marketing and delivering new software and services to everyone, on any device, leveraging Office 360 Cloud, Windows 10, Surface Pro 4 Tablet, and Xbox 360. While nearly doubling the company's stock price and value reflects these accomplishments, this nevertheless follows the company's 50 percent loss in market value over the preceding thirteen years. Nadella still has a high mountain to climb in his innovative assault.

DISRUPT BEFORE YOU ARE DISRUPTED

As much as today's startups need to harvest their natural insurgent advantages, today's incumbents must also learn to adopt insurgent strategy. Both challengers and incumbents can benefit from disrupting their own SOP by disorganizing their own innovation.

Why do most businesses need to behave like out-in-the periphery insurgents? For most of the last century, the assumption was that a natural tendency toward stability rules all markets. Now, well into the twenty-first century, nobody is talking about stability anymore. All the talk is about change.

GET OUT OF THE "CENTER"

Change rules, and the rules of change greatly favor peripheral insurgents, who love change. The in-the-center incumbent sees change as a threat and therefore hates it. Too damn bad. The concept that once made them great exists in what Robert Shapiro, former client and CEO of Monsanto, and now change agent leader of Sandbox Industries, calls "The cool sacred center of the corporation." This is where the incumbent's truth lives. In the cool sacred center, disruption is not tolerated, and change is the enemy.

BUILD YOUR OWN SKUNK WORKS TEAM

The first rule of creativity and innovation is that no one person does it. Disruptive creativity requires a diverse team. Innovation happens not just *outside* bureaucracies but *inside* teams. It is not the province of solitary geniuses.

Perhaps the wildest peripheral innovation team consisted of Lee Felsenstein, an electrical engineer, community organizer, and antiwar activist, who got together with political agitator Fred Moore and engineer Gordon French to start the Homebrew Computer Club on March 5, 1975. At subsequent meetings of the club, two young computer hobbyists, Steve Wozniak and Steve Jobs, demonstrated their latest invention: The Apple I. "Without computer clubs," Wozniak later admitted, "there would probably be no Apple computers."

APPLY YOURSELF

The goal of my work and this book is to sow peripheral and insurgent innovation wherever possible. The magic of innovation does not exist inside the center of America's corporate hallways. Magic-making innovation must be disorganized—disrupted and conjured along the creative periphery. Here are seven major ways to mobilize peripheral disorganization:

1. *Get away*. Find your cottage in the woods and, twice yearly, imitate Bill Gates at the apogee of Microsoft. Bring the work on which you need to catch up, segmented by the prioritized, the most forward-thinking, and the most important. Leave behind the tyranny of the most urgent and the less strategically valuable. Focus on the more strategically important parts of your business, your career, your next rung up the ladder. Get away and get out along your own periphery to think, focus, strategize, create, and, above all, play offense.

2. *Do the doable to create momentum.* Consider beginning with a "Think Day" or a "Think Weekend." Just be sure you well isolate yourself, cut the cord of media and phone distraction, set up a theme or focus, prepare what you need to read and absorb, organize a routine, including how you will eat, so distractions are at a minimum.

3. *Skunk Works yourself.* Build your own Skunk Works. Become part of an outsider team or create your own. Make it small but include misfits and disrupters—the folks who create but also sometimes get bogged down. Put several of your best proven talents alongside your most promisingly creative people. Insist everyone convene in another place, another city, another country to escape your own organizational center. Charge them to "think different" and to invent something bolder than can be imagined.

4. *Continually disrupt your thinking.* This means, yet again, seeking out and absorbing new mentors, angles, inputs, and ideas. This is what Ray Dalio calls "Open-Mindedness" vs. "Closed-Mindedness." In *Principles*, Dalio makes the case for remaining curious, not being afraid to have your own ideas challenged, being open to the (slight) possibility that you might be wrong, listening and absorbing, really absorbing, what others around you are saying. Humility, listening, and absorbing what others say is integral to driving forward peripheral ideas and innovation. Put your imagination ahead of your day-to-day urgently unimportant distractions.

5. *Challenge your own status quo.* Emulate the US intelligence community by running some Red Team exercises. A Red Team is an independent group that challenges your organizational status quo to improve effectiveness. You might task your Red Team to explore cutting-edge strategies or breakthrough technologies. Red Teams are great for everything from testing cybersecurity systems to writing articles about alternative futures. Ask a Red Team to compose the newspaper headline that sums up what success will look like for your organization five years from today.

6. *Focus on the "new rules."* The ugly, glorious truth that big incumbent companies at the center of the market must face is that innovation takes place on the margins. Your challenge today is to create a "disruptive periphery" in your company, cultivating those margins without killing them. Bail your own Skunk Works out of the larger bureaucracy. Give it real, delegated authority. Keep it small. Cut

bureaucratic red tape, assume responsibility, build mutual trust, fund it properly, and accountably. Use your best available athletes.

7. *Google your future*. Google whatever your industry is…in 2025. Write your own additional links and chapters to this definition of the future. Imagine it. Think different, as if you were standing out in the same periphery in which your future archrival stands. Play offense with your peripheral imagination about the benefits that will matter most to your customers.... In 2025.

CHAPTER SIX

INNOVATE BENEFITS, OWN THE FUTURE

What incredible benefits can we give to the customer?

—Steve Jobs

It is 1997, his hair is long, and he wears a version of his signature black t-shirt, and faded and patched jeans that don't quite fit, let alone stand the test of time. He is on stage, facing questions.

"Mr. Jobs, you are a bright and influential man," a questioner begins.

There is an edge to his voice, and Steve Jobs instinctively picks up a stool and holds it up as if to defend himself. Is he being funny? Then he gulps some water from a bottle he'd rather throw at the questioner. He is not really being funny.

The man continues: "But it's sad and clear that you don't know what you're talking about."

Jobs pauses for an incredibly long ten seconds. You can see he is gathering himself, deliberately rejecting the pugilism of his younger self, who might have thrown first the bottle and then the stool at the inquisitor. Instead, Jobs moves into a more mature jiu-jitsu maneuver, beginning his response by agreeing with at least part of the statement just hurled at him. He really does not know what he's talking about. That's the point.

"One thing I've always found," Jobs begins, "is you've got to start with the customer experience and work backwards to the technology. You can't start with the technology and try to figure out where you're going to try to sell it. And I've made this mistake probably more than anybody else in this room. And I've got the scar tissue to prove it."

Jobs goes on to explain that, in trying to come up with a vision for Apple, he and his team asked: "What incredible benefits can we give to the customer? Where can we take the customer? Not starting with 'let's sit down with the engineers and figure out what awesome technology we have and then how are we gonna market that?' "[62]

I've learned that people will forget what you said, people will forget what you did, but people will never forget how you made them feel.

—Maya Angelou

Two men transformed the way we had been shopping for at least the hundred years before they arrived on the scene.

"There is only one boss," Sam Walton said around the time he founded Walmart in 1962. "The customer. And he can fire everybody in the company from the chairman on down, simply by spending his money somewhere else."[63]

"We see our customers as invited guests to a party, and we are the hosts," Jeff Bezos offered some time after he founded Amazon in 1994. "It's our job every day to make every important aspect of the customer experience a little bit better."[64]

Both of these innovators, starting several decades apart, not only went to the top of the *Forbes* list for the world's richest people, they got there in precisely the same way—by focusing on their customers, on their customers' perceptions, and on the way their customers feel pain and see benefit. It was not so much that neither man knew what he was talking about before listening to the customer. It was that neither had anything to say.

Walmart began in 1950 as "Walton's 5 & 10" in Bentonville, Arkansas, and Amazon began in 1994 in a garage—like HP, Apple, and Nike—a Bellevue, Washington garage, out in the periphery, where creativity and innovation so often flourish. By 2015, Amazon overtook Walmart in market capitalization, but both companies continue to flourish, with their eyes squarely on customers and their perception of benefit.

Brad Stone's book *The Everything Store: Jeff Bezos and the Age of Amazon* tells the inside story of the company's fixation on customers.[65] Publication of the book preceded the widely circulated August 15, 2015 *New York Times* article "Inside Amazon: Wrestling Big Ideas in a Bruising Workplace," which painted an unflattering picture of the company's internal culture, prompting Bezos himself to suggest that anyone who believes the story is true should contact him directly. Both the book and the article agree on Amazon's obsession with its customers—at times, perhaps, at the expense of employees, stakeholders, partners, and other constituents.

Stone's first meeting with Bezos began with the author handing him a fictional press release imagining how the book would be presented to readers. This borrowed Amazon's own practice of writing a press release on how a new product or service would someday be seen by customers. Imagining future benefits with a future press release borrows from the approach of Steve Jobs as well as Amazon: begin with the customer and work backwards from there.

Stone recalls that Bezos laughed so hard he spit, but in the book, Stone revealed a previously unpublished memo from Bezos to his senior staff. Titled "Amazon.love," it analyzed why some companies are loved, literally loved, by customers while others, even high-performing companies, are not. "Some big companies develop ardent fan bases, are widely loved by their customers, and are even perceived as cool." Bezos offers Apple, Nike, Disney, Google, Whole Foods, and UPS as examples, which he contrasts to "unloved" companies, such as Walmart, Microsoft, Goldman Sachs, and ExxonMobil. The memo details what makes the first bunch loved. Bezos argues they are polite, reliable, inventive, and above all customer-obsessed. They see the world through their customer's eyes. By contrast, the "unloved" companies are perceived as inventive, but more for their own benefit, rather than for that of their customers.[66]

THE PERCEPTION OF BENEFIT

Successfully innovating benefits demands focusing less on yourself and more on your customer. It requires focusing less on how things work and more on what they do to help customers, on obsessing less over product *features* and more on product *benefits*.

You might want to gauge your own focus on customer benefits by measuring it against a list compiled from my work in both politics and business: six consumer drivers that underpin every focus group and in-depth interview my longtime business partner, Scott Miller, and I have conducted over the last decade in more big cities and backwater hamlets than we can remember. These six consumer drivers are as true for voters as they are for customers. We call them the six Cs: Control, Choice, Change, Customization, Convenience, and Connection. Today's explosion of product information and offerings makes understanding how consumers see "benefits" increasingly difficult and more volatile. These six drivers aim toward the benefits that must inform all your innovation efforts: *control, choice, change, customization, convenience, connection.*

Control is at the center of consumer's sense of benefit. Today, consumers make decisions that afford them a greater sense of Control—over their personal safety, economic security, health and wellness—in short, Control over their future. They assert such Control often in opposition to powerful and incumbent institutions. Everything from a computer to a retail experience to an athletic shoe to a brokerage statement can give a consumer the feeling of Control. It is a matter of product innovation, development, and positioning.

Orbiting around *Control* are the five following satellite drivers:

- *Choice* provides more consumer control, even if it may add to consumer confusion. Interestingly, choice neither restrains nor forces the hand of today's increasingly knowledgeable consumer. Instead, it provides cost, quality, and value comparisons, particularly if the offered choices are bundled and navigated to give the consumer the feeling of even more control. Technology is an enabler here. The internet has trained us all to expect choice, and if consumers do not get it, they are going to go out and find it themselves and on their own terms.
- *Change* usually leads to more choices and newer choices. Change formerly produced anxiety in many consumers, but ever since Steve Jobs revolutionized personal electronics, and Jeff Bezos provided a friendlier guidance and navigation retail experience, consumers have anticipated change far more positively. It is no accident that, these days, the negative dynamics of political leadership have been making change especially attractive to voters—and thereby to consumers. "Anybody *but*" has become a viable, and often winning, candidate, in the US and globally.
- *Customization* is now more attainable than anyone could have predicted even a few years ago. During the bygone era of mass marketing, consumers accepted as immutable Dictum of the Tube Sock: "one size fits all." With the technology-driven and Google-led penetration of controllable web search,

that dictum has been crushed by the idea that "*I can find the* one *size that fits just* me."

- *Convenience* is a long-known consumer driver, but it is too often taken for granted in a world of increasing *choice*. Although early adopters, consumers at the forefront of market trends, will seek out a new idea, once they adopt it, they expect to find it distributed ubiquitously and conveniently. Moreover, in contrast to the prevailing experience of the early days of the personal computer, consumers now expect their initial usage experience to be easy and painless. They will not tolerate the burden of thick and impenetrable instruction manuals in seventeen different languages.
- *Connection* is not a new consumer driver, either, but it is now empowered by the information revolution and by the new tactics and new media that go along with it. The urge to associate with "people like me, people I like, and people I'd like to be like" still pulls consumers toward brands, as well as voters toward candidates. Connection, particularly atop digital platform companies, has become increasingly important in an age in which people spend nearly half their day staring into television and computer screens.[67]

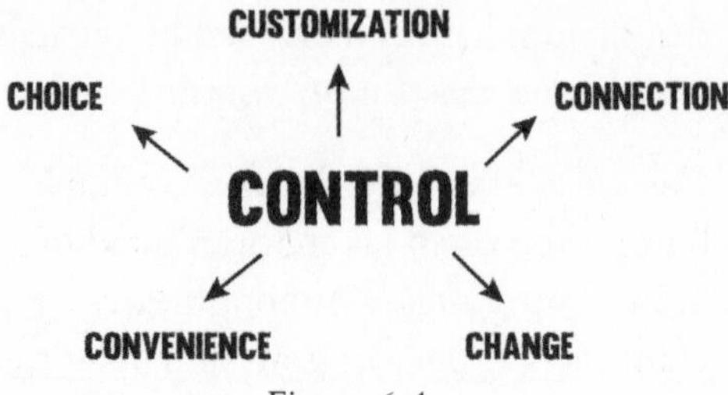

Figure 6-1

Do you want to achieve a high level of innovation and marketing success? Tape these six consumer drivers onto your bathroom mirror and War Room wall. They are your map to missing benefits and un-resolved consumer pain.

WALK A MILE IN THEIR SHOES

Fundamental to standout innovation and leadership today is this single discipline: Stop looking at yourself and start looking at your customers, your markets, and your company. Look at these across the 6Cs. Follow the lead of Steve Jobs, Sam Walton, and Jeff Bezos by thinking about your customers first. Most of the time, we must market and sell to people who are not like us. They do not think, feel, or act the way we do. History's greatest CEOs have invariably displayed an ability to feel their customer's pain and to address it, to share their customers' vision of desired benefits and to deliver them. Peter Drucker's twin-focus on innovation and marketing is even more imperative today than it was in 1954 when he formulated it, telling us that all business success comes down to synergizing innovation and marketing. Put another way, here is the prime directive in business: Make innovation. Then sell it.

In my consulting work, I use Big Data—or what I prefer to think of as *smarter* data. Everyone uses Big Data. It is today's marketing table stakes. I believe in using it and in stepping beyond it—from quantitative to qualitative research. I want to learn about customer pain and about the benefits to which customers aspire. This is the future, into which we are all headed. It is Wayne Gretzky's winning vision of *where the puck* will *be.*

Deep qualitative research includes, for example, in-depth consumer interviews and focus groups. *0*s and *1*s just don't cut it when it comes to capturing human behavior. See the behavior, hear it, and feel it for yourself. "People will forget what you said," Maya Angelou wrote, "people will forget what you did, but people will never forget how you made them *FEEL.*" Extraordinary leaders and breakthrough innovators must focus on how their customers act by discovering how they think and, above all, feel. This means lasering-in on how *you* make them feel.

To learn about your customers, learn all about their pain points. What ticks them off about a category? What compensations or compromises must they make because of the way this category presents its user experience?

Consumer pain is the fuel of innovation. Bill Gates once said he placed no value on marketing. Like Jobs, he believed that sales were all about the product. The thing is, developing a winning product requires an understanding of consumer pain. This is the best product and best marketing of all. Gates himself developed the Usability Labs at Microsoft to gain an understanding of customer's pain in everyday business and home tasks. He was looking to answer two questions: *How can we make it better?* and *How can we make it easier?*

CONTROL RULES

A big part of successfully applying the 6Cs is understanding how your customers decide. This is especially important in today's markets, which provide more choice and more confusion than ever before. For this reason, you need to probe the context of your *customer's* decision. The very first imperative behind any decision is gaining a sense of Control. For consumers, this may be Control over their personal security, their family's economic well-being, their health, or their personal satisfaction. Whatever form it takes, Control rules.

More Choice means more Control for consumers. Change in the marketplace means more Choice and more Control. Customization obviously gives consumers a greater feeling of Control. By contrast, being forced to accept the one-size-fits-all options of the incumbent and obsolescent mass-market marketplace makes consumers feel they have lost Control. They feel as if they have surrendered.

Today, an especially important aspect of Control is Connection. Consumers want to connect with people like them, people they like, and people they'd like to be like. Add to this Convenience, which often trumps all other factors. We cannot always control such commodities as bandwidth and patience, both of which are needed to handle complexity. So, we often opt for Convenience.

To drive innovation, you must lead customers to what *they* want. This means synching up *your* decision with insight into *your customers'* decision-making processes. For example, learn how your customers decide on repurchase. Big incumbent businesses cleave to tried-and-true formulas that have been tried and tried but are no longer true. This puts them into direct opposition against today's consumers, who increasingly have the self-confidence to try new ideas. *Free* is, understandably, a powerful concept. But for more and more consumers in today's markets, *new* is even more powerful than *free*. Today, the size of the early-adopter segment—those consumers who get their social currency from being first to try new ideas and lead others to them—is growing with the growth of customer confidence in all markets. This means that winning an initial trial or purchase is not nearly as hard as it used to be. Moreover, winning it is also not nearly as hard as winning the second or third purchase—and, of course, it is sustained repurchase that drives all companies to success and keeps the cost of acquisition low enough to generate profit.

Innovative companies with innovative products must sometimes *buy* their first "easy" sales. After this, however, it gets more and more expensive to continue to attract new customers or to attract repurchase with price discounts and promotions. So, successful innovators must continually try on their customer's shoes.

If you listen very hard to your customers, they will undoubtedly make you understand that *they* don't see the market the way *you* do. Deciding to lead innovation requires the courage to let yourself and your enterprise be led by your customers' needs and wants. You may think of your competition as those who line up against you in your category or sub-category. But this is not how your customers see it. Stop fixating on your competitors. Instead, consider share-of-mind, share-of-wallet, share-of-refrigerator, or share-of-stomach. Do so, and your competitive battlefield changes shape.

RENOVATE WHILE YOU INNOVATE

Client, partner, mentor, and friend Sergio Zyman is one of the most revolutionary thinkers when it comes to implementing Peter Drucker's edict on innovation and marketing. Throughout the 1980s and 1990s, CEO Roberto Goizueta, CMO Sergio Zyman, and others took The Coca-Cola Company to new heights of market success, including launching and then un-launching "New Coke." Next, Sergio built and sold companies and wrote four books, one of the most prescient being *Renovate Before You Innovate: Why Doing the New*

Thing Might Not Be the Right Thing.[68] It is a modern variation on Drucker's 1954 advice. Drucker wrote that innovation is not a panacea, is difficult to create, nurture, and activate, and must be synergized with marketing to make a real difference in business. Zyman warned us not to depend on revolutionary, deductive invention. Do not try to be Albert Einstein. Instead, focus on step-by-step, inductive innovation, or even go back to basics and "renovate." In other words, channel your inner Thomas Edison.

Renovation, according to Zyman, is not so much about inventing something new as it is about making the old new again. In fact, in all the crisis recovery and corporate turnaround projects I have helped to lead over thirty years—from Nike to Verizon to Coke to McDonald's to Microsoft—most have a strong "back to basics" dimension at the center of their recovery story. The strategy is always about finding the old that made you great and making the old new again.

Zyman's renovation-is-innovation framework is based on the difference between what he calls a company's "core competency"—what a company knows how to do—and its "core essence"—what a company really stands for as a brand. Put another way, your brand is an integral part of your innovation; marketing is part of innovation; therefore, if you try to innovate without renovating your marketing, you will fail. Bear in mind that Zyman's book and the program it espouses were written before the digital transformation, especially the exponential, platform-driven innovation that created such companies as Facebook, Google, Alibaba, Airbnb, Uber, and Bitcoin. Nevertheless, it is still a highly relevant strategic call to action and a reminder to be willing to go back to basics to advance an Edison-like agenda of inductive innovation. Most of all, in the spirit of Drucker, Zyman's book is a call to synergize innovation with marketing. For example, Zyman takes a leaf out of Steve Jobs's "start-with-the-customer" book and argues that companies get in trouble by thinking *"Let's start with what we can build and let's see where we can sell it"* versus *"Let's find out what we can sell and then we'll figure out whether we can make it."* The first approach ignores your brand and marketing and passes the ball to your engineers, whose point of view then runs your innovation and development pipelines. By contrast, the second and more powerful view begins from a customer-centric point of view, starting with customer pain and customer perceptions of future benefits.

Zyman's renovation-is-innovation argument goes on to make more five general points that are even more relevant today than when they were introduced in 2004:

- First, renovate the way you think—because thinking like an insurgent change leader is your only chance.
- Second, begin innovation with your destination clearly in mind—imagining where you are going and how you want your future customers to think, feel, and act.
- Third, map your competitive battlefield—to anticipate dangers and exploit opportunities.
- Fourth, debrief where your customers are and are heading—using behavior, demographics, psychographics, and segmentation.
- Fifth, control the dialogue with your customers—including all aspects of their experience with your brand, product, or service.

This, then, is exactly where you must go to lead innovation, especially in terms of positioning and building your insurgent brand to communicate customer benefits and point the way to your company's future.

BRANDING CUSTOMER BENEFITS

An innovator as iconic as Thomas Edison understood the power of brand. Celebrated as a technologist, the Wizard of Menlo Park was also brilliant at branding. He succeeded in linking himself personally to everything he innovated and marketed. His trademark *was* his name and unique signature. This combination was recognized worldwide, and it was the Edison brand that provided the juice to sell his innovations. Great innovation and marketing is a story with an intertwined plot that never ends. As Peter Drucker reminds us, "The aim of marketing is to know and understand the customer so well the product or service fits him and sells itself."

Telling the story—about your innovation and how it addresses customer pain by delivering customer benefits—comes down to building a brand that surrounds and leverages your innovation. Building a brand is not ancillary to innovation, it is foundational to innovation. Think of brand-building in terms of the following five dimensions. This a strategic and tactical checklist:

1. Activated Presence
2. Relevant Benefits
3. Competitive Differentiation
4. Brand Credibility
5. Change Imagery

Activated Presence is another term for traditional brand awareness among consumers, for the accessibility and acceptability of a brand in its markets. In today's digital environment, activated presence is above all about being *in my sight* and *in the conversation.* And successfully branding your innovation requires an active presence with key stakeholder groups, especially with early adopters and your best customers. Your innovation will fail commercially unless consumers encounter its presence in a marketplace. The in-the-center incumbents dominate by the force of their mass. Insurgents, out in the periphery, gain awareness and acceptability in a very different way—by creating an *activated presence*, by demonstrating usage of their product by early adopters, word of mouth, and other forms of viral communications. These create all-important momentum.

Relevant Benefits answer this question: How does a brand meet *my needs*, *my wants*, and solve *my problems*? The total experience of the customer with a brand is what determines the value of its relevant benefits. Every successful brand provides benefits relevant to its target audiences, to its early adopters and customers. The brand and the innovation it leverages and represents must solve problems, remove pain, fulfill desires, and help realize aspirations. The more personal the relevance for any consumer or consumer group, the better.

One advantage today's insurgent innovators have is that the incumbent marketplace leaders probably have been playing at table stakes levels for some time. It is therefore critical for insurgent innovators to understand customer needs better than the incumbents do, and to use their superior understanding to define the benefits of their innovation. Because, inherently, incumbents are reluctance to change, insurgents enjoy a natural opening, a market gap, which they can fill with clearer and better customized benefits.

Competitive Differentiation is based on the value created by marketplace scarcity. Differentiating your brand from the competitive options is the surest way to create market value for your innovation or innovative company. Value is created by scarcity, not sameness. Relevant differentiation, solving a marketplace problem in a unique way, is the key to the enduring value of Starbucks, Google, Porsche, and Sam Adams, to name a few prominent brands. It can be the key for you, too.

Being the same is not good enough. Today, most markets are dominated by undifferentiated "Me too!" brand positioning. Most companies are content to accept the category-defined benefits of usage. As an insurgent, however, you must differentiate to disrupt your market's status with a clear and compelling alternative.

Brand Credibility is how you can ensure that an innovation or brand fulfills its promises and delivers on the expectations you define. In working with Microsoft, my company developed a very simple customer satisfaction formula based on the successful model of Southwest Airlines, which has very often been the leading US airline for creating customer satisfaction. It is D+O+C=S.

- *D = Define expectations in advance.* All customers judge satisfaction subjectively, so it is important to focus the relationship from the beginning by clearly defining the expectations of both sides. Only *defined* expectations can be met or exceeded.

- *O = Over-deliver on these expectations.* Obviously, over-delivering on customer expectations leads to satisfaction and the recommendation of your brand. Often, the perception of over-delivery is achieved by defining expectations in the beginning and in such a way that you know you can over-deliver on key elements bound to create satisfaction. This has produced Southwest Airlines' strong customer satisfaction scores. The airline defines expectations they know they can over-deliver on with superior customer service.

- *C = Claim.* It is terrific to be relentless in over-delivery, but it is also important to constantly find ways to remind the client you have over-delivered and to benchmark the achievement. The formula is incomplete without making the claim.
- *S = Success/Satisfaction.* The result is self-explanatory.

Follow the Southwest paradigm by setting expectations clearly and modestly. Unlike its competitors, Southwest Airlines does not provide reserved seats, first-class, or upgrades. The airline does not even attempt to offer edible meals or fine wines. What they do, however, is promise a terrific service attitude without the ridiculous fees and boarding-gate battles that drag down other major airlines. Southwest over-delivers on a highly relevant attribute, delivering an unmatched service attitude, which they relentlessly contrast with the competitive big three airlines: Delta, American, and United. It is a comparison that seems almost unfair. Burdened by their promises, the other airlines are busy arguing with passengers over upgrades, changing seat assignments, or assessing baggage fees. Southwest, by contrast, focuses its passengers on just one relevant factor—service attitude—which just happens to be the one in which the airline is unquestionably superior to the rest.

Early in its corporate life, Southwest developed a reputation for cheap fares to business destinations. Southwest's fares are no longer cheap, let alone cheapest, but they still look good relative to the big three, especially when seen in the glaring, migraine-inducing bare-bulb light of the majors' strategy of grafting add-on costs to what should be included services. So, the lesson remains: build a Define, Over-Deliver, and Claim discipline into all your innovation and marketing, so that you deliver more than you promise. Then, remind customers that you did so.

Change Imagery is important to both an innovation and a brand. You must decide what images, ideas, individuals, and other brands should rub shoulders with yours. You need to determine the emotions your brand should evoke among your stakeholder targets. You must decide how your brand will communicate the essence of the change and innovation you are driving forward.

Every brand has a set of images and symbols associated with it. Yours should represent change and refreshment: *new*. Create a new look and represent customer breakthrough by breaking marketplace rules. Customer usage experience both shapes and trumps all other imagery. No fancy packaging or funny advertisement can overcome an unhappy usage experience.

IT'S THE BENEFITS, STUPID!

As you leverage innovation, build your brand, and drive marketing forward, resolve not to miss these two steps:

- First, walk around in your customer's shoes. Discover their pain and their future sense of benefits. Begin by answering the ten questions that follow.
- Second, develop a strategy that aims absolutely everything toward the answers you receive from the following ten questions. This will focus you directly on your customer's perception of benefits.

1. *What surrounds your customers' world?* In what context do they live? What are the most critical dynamics, forces, changes, products, services, and brands that touch these customers every day? How do they perceive the world these create?

2. *How do they see the future?* Is it headed in the right or the wrong direction? Remember to ask your customers the equivalent of the classic question Ronald Reagan asked in 1980: "Are you better off than you were four years ago?" What future do customers expect from your company or brand? What future do they expect from your competitors?

3. *What do they dream about?* What is the customer's ideal product, service, or offering in your category? Since 1984, I have developed with partner Scott Miller and political pollster Pat Caddell a groundbreaking "Candidate Smith" research approach, which asks voters to react not to existing candidates but to construct their own ideal candidate for president. Similarly, once you understand your customers' ideal innovation, their ideal product or service, you can probe ways to fill the gaps between their dreams and reality.

4. *What's in their hearts?* What emotional drivers are most important to your customers? Because more decisions are being made impulsively, more of marketing is driven by emotion. In politics, one of the most telling measurements of any campaign is the degree to which people believe that a candidate "cares about people like me." Behind this question is a combination of curiosity and cynicism. "Can this person understand my life? And can I understand this person and the way she or he makes decisions?" In innovation and business, customers want to know much the same thing. They want to be confident about how a company will make them *feel*.

5. *Where is their pain?* What are your customers missing that they most need? What keeps them

awake at night? During the internet gold rush of the late 1990s and the recession of the late 2000s, too many companies were funded without having articulated what marketplace "pain" their offering uniquely addressed. Chances are these companies' stock certificates are today about as valuable as used wallpaper. Find your customer's pain. It is the target for your next round of innovation.

6. *What's relevant and different?* Value is created by relevant differentiation: the benefits *you* provide to targeted customers and the way *you* provide them uniquely among all market choices. To achieve this degree of relevance, you must know what matters most to your customers. And you must know what attributes communicate and prove differentiation *for them*. To acquire this knowledge, consider using a laddering technique. Ask customers to rate a product or service in terms of its most important attributes, listed in order of importance *to them*. If you learn only one thing from market research, it should be how your target consumers define *relevance* and *differentiation* in terms of innovation and its benefits.

7. *Are they movable?* What are your customers' attitudes toward your product, service, or innovation? As we explore in chapter 8, you must segment your customers in terms of "Hard Opposition," "Soft Opposition," "Undecided," "Soft Support," and "Hard Support." This last segment consists of your loyalists. Ask each of your customers to tell you if *they* should be a prioritized marketing target. Get them to help you order your innovation and targeting priorities. Waste no time

or resources on trying to move the unmovable with misdirected innovation.

8. *How can you over-deliver on their expectations?* Based on today's market choices, what are your customers' current expectations? What will constitute an over-delivery on these expectations? When and how should you claim this success? How can you clearly define expectations in line with their perceptions, over-deliver on them, and then remind customers of your success at delighting them?

9. *How can you best define yourself?* In the end, how must your customers see you? What must you stand for? And how can you define your competition most advantageously? With an innovative company today, people are interested not only in *what* the company decides to do, but in *how* it decides to do it. This tells customers what they can expect from the company in the future.

10. *How can you control the dialogue in your favor?* You must understand and evaluate the effect of your competitors' claims in the marketplace. If the competition consists of the incumbent market leaders, chances are they have control of the market dialogue. If so, how can you take it away from them? What perceptual opportunities must you seize to turn customers' attention to you? What core messages and themes will help up the ante in your marketplace?

Develop a strategy that aims *everything* toward the answers you receive from the ten questions. Scott Miller and I developed a simple, two-word, noun-verb, philosophy: *Everything communicates.*[69]

In marketing innovation, every detail either adds to or subtracts from value. The tiniest details make all the difference. If they are not working for you, they are working against you. Here are the fundamentals:

- *Everything Markets.* Marketing is a part of everything you do, especially innovation.
- *Brand is Everything.* Brands are the sum of everything you do, especially innovation.
- *Brand is Everybody.* Everyone is part of your brand's meaning, especially your innovators.
- *It is not enough to pay attention to details,* you must make the details mean something. Form them around a single core communications strategy.

Everything communicates. All that you say and do is important to defining the value of your brand, the success of your innovation, and the success of your company. Despite all the logo design, packaging development, advertising, and PR releases, what really defines you in the marketplace? Running through the Pittsburgh airport, I once saw a sign at a US Airways counter: "Closed for your convenience." Nothing has ever better summarized the major airline service attitude. Those words, accidental or not, did an awful lot of communicating—with the emphasis on *awful.*

There are four ways to put the focus on the communicative details:

FIRST, SHAPE DETAILS AROUND INNOVATION AND STRATEGY

If you ever had to herd ducks—and who hasn't?—the first rule is never to lose your sense of direction as you try to keep them waddling along. Like ducks, details need direction. It is not enough to tell your people to care about the little things.

You must repeatedly add the *what.* Explain precisely *what* the details should be communicating. The most effective way to create a discipline for controlling the details of your company or brand or innovation is to form everything around one core communications strategy. Ask: "What is our core message to our customers? How are we communicating it? And how can we communicate it even better?" Check out chapter 8 for advice on what to do with the answers.

SECOND, DO AN "EVERYTHING COMMUNICATES" AUDIT

Your company's core communications strategy should connect to every other strategy in a hub-and-spoke relationship. Drill down to the tiniest details. Think about the customer's experience with your brand or with the innovation you have just launched. Define it down to the smallest detail. For example, former client Home Depot lists the hundreds of "customer touch points" for every one of their stores.

How do you compile such a list? Do an "everything communicates" audit of your company and your brand. This is about everything, so include everything that your customer might interact with: every action, expression, communication, sight, smell, and sound.

THIRD, ENSURE INNOVATION IS MARKETING

The textbook definition of marketing is "a process that adds value to transactions." True enough—but, then, what does your company do that is *not* intended to add value to transactions?

Every aspect of innovation, operation, administration, and communication should be adding value, or it should not be happening. Product innovation and manufacture are designed to add value, right? Recruiting, hiring, and managing talent should add value, right? Coffee breaks should add value, right? The answer, of course, is yes—across the board.

Everything should add value; therefore, everything is marketing. This is the reason the "Everything Communicates" audit is so important. McDonald's, for example, knows what a dirty bathroom implies about the kitchen. Toshifumi Suzuki of Ito-Yokado, the former owner of Southland's 7-Eleven, roused and marshaled his organization to the issue of dusty product on the shelf. Starbucks realized that drinking a $4 cup of coffee had better be a unique experience, so it created an experience to surround and envelop its customers. This includes everything from overstuffed easy chairs to comfort food snacks to soft lighting to earth colors to wonderful roasting smells to its own line of background music—everything that helps make Starbucks much more than what is in the cup. The experience is so memorable that it travels in the patrons' senses, far beyond the store.

Starbucks: it does virtually no advertising. Instead, it uses distribution and discipline to provide quality products and an "everything communicates" attention to communicating its brand meaning in everything it does and everybody who does it. While other quick-service food concepts have seen their brand-value diminished by the attitude and aptitude of their employees, Starbucks has trained workers to create meaningful differentiation. What is more, by providing employee benefits like health insurance and profit sharing, the company has attracted and held more talented and committed personnel.

A brand is a bucket into which all customer impressions and interactions are poured. Brand is a key element of marketing. Marketing is critical to leveraging innovation.

FINALLY, BUILD A BRAND STRATEGY

Once you accept the idea that everything is brand, you must develop a strategy and a tactical discipline to leverage your innovation to commercial success, expressing the brand in everything your company does and says.

Create a core communications strategy. Answer the question *"What do we do?"* in terms of relevant benefits, which are differentiated from those of the competition.

- *Define market targets.* Think in terms of a political campaign. Ask: Who must you recruit to win the election? What are the gaps the competition provides? Who are the priority targets for your innovation?

- *Create innovation around the target consumer's wants and needs.* Don't just create a product, focus on a product experience, relieving customers' pain, and delivering future benefit.

- *Define what your product experience means to your best customers.* Use the ten key questions earlier in this chapter as your guide. Your loyal voters—your hard supporters—understand and can best express your product experience. They can, in fact, tell you how to innovate and how to communicate their own rewarding and satisfying product experience to your "softer support" customers.

- *Describe how you will communicate active presence (usage by satisfied users), relevance (benefits of usage), differentiation, credibility (fulfilling the implicit brand promise), and imagery in everything you do and say.* In other words, work through the five key brand dimensions presented earlier in this chapter.

- *Define how you will communicate a relevant and different (therefore, valuable) product experience in everything you do and say.* Define customer "touch points," as Home Depot does. Create an enveloping experience around your product, even if all you have is a box or bottle or can on a shelf.

- *As above, do a thorough "everything communicates" audit.* Get all of your people to define how they are going to drive the details. Put everything you do and say—*everything*—through this strategic filter.

- *Think from the product experience outward, toward every expression, every piece of material, every meeting and show.* Think virally. The flow of day-to-day details and interactions is critical in communicating, marketing, and building brand today.

"If you don't know where you're going, any road will take you there," says the Buddhist proverb. Strategy is your roadmap. These days, it must be drawn down to the grainiest of granular details, because the details make or break brands, which make or break innovation, which makes or breaks value.

CHAPTER SEVEN

SAIL WEST TO FIND EAST

It's as if the first astronaut skipped the moon and went right to Mars!

—Unknown Sports Writer

He barely qualifies to stand here. The day before, he had overstepped the takeoff board—twice!—then remeasured his steps and took a careful, safe third and final jump from behind the board to squeeze into the 1968 Olympic long jump final in the razor-thin air of lofty Mexico City and amid the racial and social protests of the era.

This is the Olympic Final. He watches the first three men over-run the takeoff board and foul, just as he had done in the qualifying round. Now, at last, it's his turn. In an agony of nerves, he waits an eternal twenty seconds before galloping down the runway.

Later, he remembered: "I could not feel my legs under me I was floating." [70]

It feels good. His foot hits the board perfectly, and he is up, forward, and in motion. Now, with little control over his own destiny, he floats for a full six seconds, rising and hitch kicking his way along the rarified 7,350-foot Mexico City air. He extends his feet to land as far forward as possible and immediately feels he might have gone even farther, because he falls mistakenly backwards, losing some precious inches that can make the difference between a gold medal and nothing. He bounds out of the sand pit—bouncing and bouncing up and down like a Kangaroo.

It feels good. And the big crowd seems to agree, reacting immediately as if they can sense something special has just happened. But he has no real idea. He can only wait with everyone else. He thought, he hoped, he might win a medal—but maybe, maybe this will be something more.

Five minutes pass. Ten. Then fifteen minutes.

What is going on? What is taking so long?

He is told that the new electronic system cannot measure this leap, but, eventually someone rummages through a bag and produces a good-old-fashioned measuring tape.

He waits.

Finally, it hits the scoreboard: 8.90 meters.

But he did not learn meters at Jamaica High School, Queens, New York, where my friend, Larry Ellis, discovered this talented athlete. So, he's still in the dark, unaware of what he's done.

Then the announcer, tremendously excited, shouts out in English: "Ladies and gentlemen, Bob Beamon has just crushed the world record…." And they announce his jump, in feet now, twenty-nine feet and two and a half inches.

It's still difficult to comprehend—not just for this long jumper, but for the crowd. Bob Beamon has just broken the world record by twenty-one and three-quarter inches. It is a world record that had been broken before this only twelve times since 1901, by an average increment of only two and a half inches. It's no wonder, Beamon's long jump is an Olympic record still today, fifty years later. It is a jump that redefines not just Beamon's own sport, but athletic achievement itself.

The physiologist Ernst Jokl has a word for what happens next: "cataplexy," by which the emotional shock of something takes not just your breath away but steals your ability to stand or even move your body. So, Bob Beamon, the man who has just redefined athletic achievement itself in the accidentally perfect jump of the century cannot rise to his own feet.[71]

Mistakes are the portals of discovery.

—James Joyce

Her real life was not all that different from the 1943 movie starring Greer Garson and Walter Pidgeon. She was born on November 7, 1867, in Warsaw, Poland, then part of the Russian Empire, as Maria Salomea Sklodowska. After moving to Paris, enrolling in the Sorbonne in 1891, marrying fellow scientist Pierre Curie in 1895, she became Marie Curie or, as she was even more widely known, Madame Curie. She was the first woman to win the Nobel Prize, the first person and only woman to win it twice, and the only person to win a Nobel in two different sciences—for physics in 1903 *and* for chemistry in 1911. Her family ultimately won a total of five Nobel Prizes.

This was an extraordinary record of achievement, and the first of the prizes was awarded for her greatest discovery, which came through accident—more than one, and not all hers.

One day, in 1895, the German physicist Wilhelm Röntgen plays with a cathode ray device. Switching on the cathode tube and watching it glow, he accidentally passes his hand between it and a screen painted with a fluorescent pigment. To his astonishment, he sees a shadow cast on the screen. It is a shadow of his hand—or, more precisely, a shadow of the bones in his hand.

These rays, capable of seeing through soft tissue to bone, what *are* they? Röntgen has no idea, so he calls them X-rays—*X* being the universal mathematical symbol for the unknown.

A year after Röntgen's happy accident, in 1896, the French physicist Antoine Henri Becquerel wraps a photographic plate in heavy paper to prevent it from being fogged by exposure to light. He puts the wrapped plate in a drawer, and stores on top of it a crystal of uranium ore. When he later develops the plate, he is startled to find the piece of uranium has fogged the plate, creating on the negative its own shape. Becquerel had earlier experimented with phosphorescent uranium crystal on a wrapped photographic plate exposed to the sun. He had seen a similar image and concluded the sunlight caused the uranium to phosphoresce. But the environment inside the drawer is totally dark. Becquerel concludes that the energy came not from the sun or any other external source, but from the uranium itself.

Pierre and Marie Curie follow up on this conclusion and theorize that the energy comes from an element, not from a conventional chemical reaction among molecules in the ore. That is, the atoms within the ore spontaneously emitted the energy that fogged the plate. This insight implies a profound conclusion: the atom consists of particles, which, in breaking away from the atom, release energy. Up to this point—in fact, since the pre-Socratic philosopher Democritus (ca. 460-ca. 370 BC) formulated the atomic theory of the universe—atoms were believed to be the basic and indivisible building blocks of all matter. Becquerel's accident, which followed Röntgen's accident, shows the Curies that Democritus and everyone after him, for some 2,300 years, had been wrong about atoms.

Using a device they called the "electrometer," capable of measuring very small electrical charges, Madame Curie goes on to explore more energy-emitting—that is, "radioactive"—substances. In 1898, she and Pierre Curie discover two new radioactive elements, Polonium (which Marie names after her native Poland) and Radium (Latin for "ray"). As pure science, the discoveries are epoch-making. As applied science, they show early promise for treating cancer, since the energy they emit tends to kill fast-growing tumor cells while causing no harm to surrounding tissue. Later, of course, high-energy radioactive emissions will also be revealed as capable of causing cancer. Röntgen, Madame Curie, and her daughter, the physicist Irène Curie all eventually succumb to cancers. Pierre shows signs of illness as well, but dies in 1906, at the age of forty-six, the victim of a carriage accident on the streets of Paris. Later still, "atomic energy" generates electric power and propels ships and submarines—but first, it is used to create the most destructive weapons in the history of humankind.

ON THE SHOULDERS OF ACCIDENTAL DISCOVERY

In science and business alike, accidental invention and innovation happen more than you might imagine:[72]

- *Charles Goodyear* accidentally spills a mixture of rubber and sulfur on a hot stove in 1844. He has labored for years to find a way to commercialize rubber. Now, accidentally, the heat causes the rubber to react with the sulfur, resulting in the "invention" of what Goodyear calls the *vulcanization* process, which makes natural rubber unnaturally durable and is used to manufacture rubber tires. Born from this happy accident is the Goodyear Tire and Rubber Company and an entire industry.

- *John Pemberton* is addicted to morphine and desperately wants to cure his headaches in 1892. By profession a pharmacist, Pemberton plays with two ingredients, coca leaves and cola nuts, hoping these will provide relief. His assistant accidentally mixes the two in carbonated water. With this, *Coca-Cola* is born. Pemberton sets into motion the reinvention of what we drink, the way we drink, and how our beverages are marketed.

- *Alexander Fleming,* British physician and microbiologist, thoughtlessly leaves a petri dish dirty in 1928. Returning from vacation, he notices this dish—originally filled with Staph bacteria—has now produced a mold that has killed the pre-vacation Staph. Born from this dirty dish is *penicillin*, the first antibiotic.

- *Roy Plunkeet*, working for DuPont in 1938, searches for alternatives to the hazardous ammonia-based refrigerants used in refrigerators throughout American homes. One substance he experiments leaves an odd, slippery resin in the container in which it was stored. Intrigued, Plunkeet plays with it and discovers that it is resistant to extreme heat, cold, and solvent chemicals. In the 1940s, this slippery and durable new material finds a use in the Manhattan Project. In the 1950s, the auto industry, always eager to reduce friction, applies it. In the 1960s, it finally gets a name, *Teflon*, and transforms, among other processes, the art of cooking.

- *Georges De Mestral,* a Swiss engineer enjoying a hiking trip in 1941, notices plant burrs clinging to his pants and to the fur of his dog. Instead of picking them off and discarding them as the nuisance they are, he takes a closer look. The bristles of the burrs have hooks that attach to anything loop-shaped—the twill weave of hiking pants, the curly coat of a dog. The accidental discovery of one of nature's marvels gets Mestral thinking. Could a combination of "velvet" and "crochet" surfaces be recreated by manufacturing to make a new way to join fabrics together? The answer is *Velcro*, which makes astronauts more secure in zero-G space and transforms clothing fashion and function.

- *Percy Lebaron Spencer*, an engineer for Raytheon Corporation working on radar in 1945, is designing "magnetrons" to more efficiently radiate microwave signals. One day, he notices that his proximity to these devices has melted some candy in his pocket. Doubtless, he was looking forward to eating that candy—especially in an era of wartime sugar rationing. Instead of getting angry, he builds a box to contain the generated microwave radiation and melts the candy inside it. Working to improve radar, he invents the *microwave oven.* The first commercially produced model is called the Radar Range.
- *Andrew Ball, David Brown, and Nicholas Terrett*, Pfizer scientists looking in 1991 for ways to stop chest pain and prevent spasms in the heart's coronary arteries, lead a team in producing a pill designated UK92480. The medication dilates blood vessels and thus relieves chest pain, but it has a most interesting side effect: it helps treat erectile dysfunction (ED). As a result, UK92480 is never marketed as a blood pressure and cardiac drug, but becomes *Viagra*, one of the world's bestselling medications.

Christopher Columbus knows the world isn't flat. He's been sailing over vast stretches of it for decades and never fell off the edge. Widely read but self-taught in mathematics, astronomy, cartography, and navigation, in 1492 he persuades the Queen and King of Spain to finance an experimental voyage. He proposes to sail west along the watery surface of the globe that is planet earth to reach the east. This will reduce the distance and time required in the highly profitable "Oriental" trade. Whatever nation pioneers this route, he tells Isabella and Ferdinand, will grow immeasurably rich and powerful.

Columbus miscalculates the distance between Europe and the so-called "Indies" (the general name by which Europeans designate the Far East) and ends up landing in the Caribbean. He has discovered what the cartographer and explorer Amerigo Vespucci will soon call the "New World."

Today, the expression "*sail west to find the east*" describes taking a radically different, even perverse, approach to innovation. The phrase describes a kind of deliberate error, an effort to purposely create the kind of happy accident that has so often led to remarkable innovation. Call it serendipity, mistake, accident—sometimes we just get lucky—and sometimes we purposely set off the wrong way to get to the right place.

FIXING SERENDIPITY

As we argue in chapter 6, innovation is often born not from a single laser-like focus, but by bolstering creative peripheral vision. This allows you to stumble upon the happy accident, the unexpected insight, to cross an idea from one discipline into another, and to innovate a solution to a problem even before the existence of a problem has been identified.

Isaac Asimov reputedly once quipped, "The most exciting phrase to hear in science, the one that heralds new discoveries, is not 'Eureka!' But '*That's funny.*' " In athletics, this is Bob Beamon's *twenty-nine-foot-and-two-and-a-half-inch* jump. The totally unexpected combination of Mexico City's thin air, extensive preparation, athletic talent, and hitting the takeoff board at exactly the right place, angle, and velocity produced a jump that transformed Olympic history.

In science, sport, philosophy, the arts, entertainment, politics—*and* business—"*That's funny*" is central to innovation breakthrough. Innovation often advances by serendipity, which is not the same as random chance. It is a meeting of the unexpected with a mind that, at some levels, *expects* the unexpected. Serendipity is an eloquent argument for a prepared mind wide open.

A wide-open mind loads the dice of discovery. We can take steps to rig the game of serendipity even more in our favor. We cannot create happy accidents, but we can encourage them, invite them, purposely sail the wrong way to get to the right destination—perhaps an unexpected one.

Biochemist and social scientist Ohid Yaqub is working to find ways of fixing serendipity in favor of innovation. He is cited in a 2018 editorial in the prestigious scientific journal *Nature* concerning a major European Research Council study. Yaqub believes he has found a way to unpack serendipity:

> First, he defines serendipity in a way that goes beyond happy accidents, by classifying it into four basic types.[73] The first type is where research in one domain leads to a discovery in another—such as when 1943 investigations into the cause of a mustard-gas explosion led to the idea of using chemotherapy to treat cancer. Another is a completely open hunt that brings about a discovery, such as with Röntgen's X-rays. Then there are the discoveries made when a sought-for solution is reached by an unexpected path, as with the accidental discovery of how to vulcanize rubber. And some discoveries find a solution to a problem that only later emerges: shatterproof glass for car windscreens was first observed in a dropped laboratory flask.[74]

So, there it is, a happy accident framework. Cross-discipline yourself and your innovation, consider "open-hunting" your quest for solution, keep an eye out for the unexpected path, and persist in innovating and workshopping because the solution you find today might solve the problem of tomorrow.

Yaqub goes on to further detail mechanisms by which serendipity happens: Astute observations, errors plus "controlled sloppiness," and collaborative action of networks of people. All are means by which we might more reliably load the dice of discovery to produce more happy accidents. Most recently, Yaqub has focused his fixing on biomedicine, but he plans to expand to other disciplines. The key to unlocking it all is open-mindedness. If you wish to lead a business toward greater innovation, give curious minds free rein to innovate beyond the confines of the current quarter.

THE BUSINESS OF HAPPY ACCIDENTS

Consider these business breakthroughs made possible because those involved were not busy looking where the light is better, but dared to grope in the dark, where happy accidents are most often found.

WHAT COULD POSSIBLY GO WRONG?

Enzo was born in 1898, in Modena, Italy, the son of an owner of a metal-working business.[75] At ten, Enzo watches car races in the 1908 Circuit di Bologna and knows immediately he will become a race car driver. At eighteen, out of school and two years after losing both his father and brother to influenza, Enzo, the family business having collapsed, applies for a job at Fiat. Initially spurned, he finds work as a test driver for a tiny car company called CMN. This leads to racetrack competition. He finishes ninth in his first race, in 1919, but soon learns enough to get hired by Alfa Romeo. By 1920, he wins as a racer, beginning to enjoy success in the passion he foresaw at age ten, racing.

Back during the Great War, in 1918, Italy's top aerial ace, Count Francesco Baracca, is shot down after 34 dogfight victories. Baracca's valor is legendary, symbolized by a personal emblem painted on the fuselage of his aircraft. It harks back to his years as a cavalry officer and features a rearing Persano horse, an animal of the noble breed used by the regiments of the House of Savoy. At the end of the war, Baracca's parents offer Enzo the right to use the symbol. He takes advantage of this serendipitous opportunity and begins using the logo for his "*scuderia*," his small "stable"—that is the meaning of the word—of racecars and drivers. The Baracca family arms features the rearing horse on a shield below three stars. Enzo colors the shield yellow in honor of his hometown, Modena, and replaces the stars with the Italian tricolor. It is painted on all the cars he races. Later—again, by chance—the International Automobile Federation assigns Enzo's cars the color red, a color the company he founds in 1939 will make famous with every extraordinary car it produces.

By 1926, amid the rising fascism of what is becoming Benito Mussolini's Italy, Enzo has an emotional breakdown. He stops racing and turns to fixing and modifying cars. In 1929, he starts Scuderia Ferrari, a team of race drivers and mechanics working for Alfa Romeo. Soon, he attracts similar deals with Bosch, Pirelli, and Shell, and his new car racing team begins earning attention with eight victories in twenty-two competitive races. Enzo collects fifty full- and part-time drivers. The future looks magnificent. Thanks in large part to the quality of his *scuderia*, automobile racing gains popularity in Europe—and Enzo has discovered that he is better at and happier managing a *scuderia* than racing cars.

What possibly can go wrong? It is 1938.

The clouds of a new world war gather—and yet the coming horrors of World War II, destined to hit Italy very hard, become the happy accident of Enzo Ferrari's business.

As Fascism grips Italy, Mussolini's government assumes control over Alfa Romeo. Ferrari's team is ordered to shift from racing to making tools and airplane parts for Italy's war effort. But, secretly, in 1939, they also build a new kind of car. Designed exclusively for racing, it cannot be introduced until the war ends. No matter, Enzo uses the roll of history's dice to his advantage. Turning out war materiel to satisfy Il Duce, he perfects his racers. Nevertheless, as the war nears its end, Enzo realizes that racing will not pay the rent. "Why don't we sell cars to the public?" he asks himself. "And why don't we put everything we've been developing throughout the war and aim it toward customers worldwide?"

The catastrophe of world war in Italy is the happy accident that results in the creation of a company synonymous with the rise of the supercar. *That's funny.*

WHY NOT SELL THOSE?

In the early 1980s, Michael Dell works in his garage and then in his University of Texas dorm room. The two locales are familiar breeding grounds for recent historic innovation. His peripheral business is buying mainstream PCs and customizing them, making them faster and better. What will become one of the world's biggest computer companies, a company that has sold over 650 million computers, gets started before the term "startup" is even in common usage.

Michael Dell comes of age just as companies like Texas Instrument and Compaq are laying the hardware foundation for the information revolution. He later speaks of being "pulled" toward these new things called computers. As a teen, he takes them apart, examines how they work, and thinks about how they might be made to work better. By good luck, a Radio Shack store is along Dell's bike route to and from school. He can buy parts whenever he feels the need, and, in this way, try the newest components.

At sixteen, Dell is good at math. Using math, he understands opportunity. It is this—a computer that retails for $3,000 costs $600 in parts. So, why does it sell for so much more? Dell ponders the still-nascent industry and concludes that it is riddled with inefficiency while refusing to address the many points of customer pain. Somehow, the industry manages to avoid giving customers what they seem to want.

Dell decides that computers can be made better in every way, and that *he* will make them better. He starts with existing computers, which he modifies and resells directly to the public, not as completely assembled units, but as kits, to be fully assembled by the end user. It is a nice little homegrown business. He is a shade-tree computer mechanic—until college, when a happy accident becomes the tipping point that creates Dell Computer Company.

Word of mouth gets him a growing customer base. Dell begins taking more and more computers apart. He can tear down a computer and add the necessary kit parts in about 45 minutes per machine. At eighteen, Michael Dell is making $50,000 to $80,000—each month. He moves off-campus.

Then comes a day when a customer orders 150 of Dell's souped-up computer kits. Prior to making the buy final, he insists on visiting Austin to tour the "plant." Dell prepares by cleaning up his off-campus dorm-like room. As Dell shows the prospective customer around, pointing out his kits, the man points to a group of fully assembled computers.

"What are those?" he asks. "Why not sell those?"[76]

That's funny, Dell thinks. His business model has been tearing down existing machines, gathering parts to make them better, and then bundling the result as kits. He has never thought of selling fully assembled computers. In 1984, Dell produces its first complete and completed computer, the "Turbo PC," for $795 with an Intel 8088-compatable processor running at 8MHz. By the end of the decade, Dell offers a range of PCs, all presented in a slick color catalog that includes text intended to help buyers decide which turnkey machine is right for them. The new business model preserves the best of the kit era—innovation that makes computers better and better suited to the needs of the customer—but without the hassle of self-assembly. Today, Dell is a technology company with more than 100,000 employees and $60 billion in revenues. It got there by accident.

CAN HE HELP PEOPLE CONNECT?

It is 1995, and Craig Newmark wants to send an email to a few friends. Newmark enjoys sending digital missives, a bug he caught in high school, where he was, in his own words, "a full-on nerd."[77] (Only recently he brags: "I have since learned social skills and I can simulate them for short periods…."[78])

In 1975, Newmark graduates from Case Western Reserve University, from which he also earns a Master of Science in 1977. He is intrigued by something called the Arpanet, a government-sponsored precursor of the internet. When he goes to work for IBM, the nerdy Newmark's job is to improve the technology of this new thing called a personal computer. Working in Boca Raton, then Detroit, and then Pittsburgh, he ascends IBM's PC ladder, from programing to sales, hoping to elevate his still unimpressive social skills. The enterprising Newmark even takes yoga and ballet classes, ostensibly to up his social game, but mostly to meet girls.

In 1993, after seventeen years at Big Blue, Newmark quits—today admitting he should have done so earlier. At forty, he goes to work for the Charles Schwab investment bank in San Francisco. His new job is analyzing computer security and includes methodically watching how people use the internet. Noting that many use the new World Wide Web to help others, he wonders if he might be able to do the same. Can he help people connect and do good on the internet?

"Happy accident" is the very phrase Newmark uses to describe what comes next.[79] In early 1995, he begins emailing mostly friends and fellow workers about interesting area events and places to see art. His first emails focus on two events: Joe's Digital Dinner, where patrons use multimedia technology and eat spaghetti and meatballs around a large table, and a party called "Anon Salon," which is devoted to a combination of technology and theater. The recipients of his emails start asking questions, unrelated to the subjects he writes about. "Do you have any leads on apartments?" They ask. "Any ideas on job openings?" "Bakeries you recommend?"

His email contact list grows. *That's funny.*

Newmark is having fun. He encourages the population of his list, now more than 200 people, to contribute their *own* information input. They do, and Craig Newmark's list grows. When it becomes too large to manage with email tools, he creates a listserv, so that he can contact everyone with a single email.

Soon, it is called Craigslist.[80] He quits his corporate job and sets up as an independent consultant, his listserv growing exponentially. After it gets to one million page views, people start asking him to run banner ads. They also offer to help Newmark run the website on a volunteer basis.

Soon, the happy accident of listserv demands Newmark's fulltime attention, and the rest is internet history: Seeing his resume posted on Craigslist, Newmark hires Jim Buckmaster to expand and professionalize operations. Buckmaster will eventually become CEO and manage all operations, with the now less socially awkward Newmark focusing on customer service. Craigslist continues to grow at an accelerating pace, first in the US and eventually across 70 countries, serving more than 20 billion monthly page views, with more than 80 million new classified advertisements each month.[81]

In 2004, eBay purchases a 28.4 percent stake in Craigslist from a former employee, whereupon, slowly but surely, financial, ownership, and legal tensions ensue. In 2015, just before spinning off PayPal, eBay announces that it will divest its stock back to Craigslist for an undisclosed sum and settle all litigation. Today, along with a robust philanthropic operation, the highly profitable Craigslist earns over $700 million in annual revenues with 50 employees focused intently on helping people connect and do good on the internet.

PREPARING FOR LUCK

Luck is not a strategy. In business and innovation, waiting around for luck is not a good idea. The proverbial "I find the harder I work, the luckier I get" is attributed variously to at least three great innovators: Thomas Jefferson, Thomas Edison, and Samuel Goldwyn. Doubtless, more innovators have said it, too. Golf's great Gary Player pointed out, "The harder I practice, the luckier I get." At the very least, an American founding father, our favorite inductive innovator, a motion picture mogul, and a champion golfer are all associated with this sentiment, which has the added advantage of being true.

There is a saying of much earlier vintage—*Audentes Fortuna juvat,* which appeared slightly altered in Virgil's *Aeneid* (Book X, line 344) as *Audentis Fortuna juvat.* It is typically translated as "Fortune favors the brave" or "Fortune favors the bold," and it has been adopted as the motto for any number of military organizations—those that tend to be *winning* military organizations. The message is a variation on the correlation between hard work and luck. Being brave or bold enables you to take advantage of luck, which breeds more and more of the happy accidents that allow innovation, business, and military success. As a business and political consultant, I always advise cultivating a bias for action. It is certainly possible to *do* stupid things. This, however, is far less likely to get you in trouble than failing to do anything while waiting for your luck to change. In both business and innovation, playing offense brings more success than meekly and reactively playing defense.[82]

The utility of the *Audentes Fortuna juvat* approach is that it can be combined with thoughtful preparation. Indeed, there is yet another variation on the Latin proverb, which we alluded to earlier. In 1854, Louis Pasteur remarked in a lecture at the University of Lille, "*Dans les champs de l'observation le hasard ne favorise que les esprits préparés*"—"In the fields of observation, chance favors only the prepared mind." English translations usually pare this down to: "Fortune favors the prepared mind." Pasteur, we know, was speaking in the context of experimentation, but what he said applies to any innovator, since innovation, like science, favors the prepared mind.

LEARNING BY LUCK

From Röntgen to Curie to Goodyear to Pemberton to Fleming to Plunkeet to Mestral to Spencer to Ball, Brown, and Terrett, many happy accidents turn on learning something. Take one of history's greatest investors, Ray Dalio, who admits that the 1982 crash of Mexico's currency nearly ruined his business and life. He came to understand that he made every mistake possible, buying gold when he should not have, betting on treasury bill futures when he should not have, buying when he should have been selling and selling when he should have been buying.[83] Over and over, he was dead wrong and ended up nearly bankrupt. Over eighteen years of bull markets, Dalio's market-short position looked worse than stupid. And it was not helpful that his mistakes were all very public. At one point, Dalio became his company's only employee.

He hit rock bottom, but kept coming back to the advice of one of his heroes, the brilliant investor and trader Bernard Baruch: "If you are ready to give up everything else and study the whole history and background of the market and all principal companies whose stocks are on the board as carefully as a medical student studies anatomy—if you can do all that and in addition you have the cool nerves of a gambler, the sixth sense of a clairvoyant and the courage of a lion, you have a ghost of a chance."[84]

Like Steve Jobs learning how to become a better CEO after getting fired from Apple, Dalio took advantage of his bad luck to learn and, with greater knowledge, make some good luck. He learned lucky lessons about guarding against over-confidence and emotion-based decision-making, to be humble when you think you understand all there is to understand about things like debt, denomination, currency, restructuring, banking, and government, and to stop trying to do the impossible and time the markets. Dalio went a step further and developed a checklist of business (and life) principles founded in his own mistake and misfortune:

- Seek out the smartest people who disagree with you, so you can try to understand *their* reasoning.

- Know when *not* to have an opinion.
- Develop, test, and systematize *timeless* and *universal* principles.
- Balance risks in ways that *keep* the big upside while *reducing* the downside.

What is striking about these four principles is how they apply to much more than investing. They are invaluable to innovating, to business, to leadership, and to life in general. At a time when social media and cable news pulls us back into our own prejudices and narrow points of view, Dalio's principles are a checklist for innovation, for fixing your business, and for fixing the nation.

EXPLOITING LUCK

"Guard against results," Thomas Edison once warned one of his principal model and instrument makers, John Ott. Edison meant: guard against the critical mistake of narrowing your vision and focusing so intently on anticipated results that you ignore the unexpected, the happy accidents that often point to innovation. Indeed, Edison invited distractions. He put his faith in *planned* spontaneity. He often freely sketched ideas for innovation on scraps of paper and pushed his employees to do the same, placing notebooks and pencils on every workbench in the workshop. He created an environment capable of exploiting any luck that might come his way.

Perhaps the best-known example of the limits of Edison's "accidental" vision is the so-called Edison Effect. While he was working on the incandescent electric lamp, Edison tried improving the device by introducing a charged metal plate near the filament. What he discovered is that, in a vacuum, electrons flow from the heated filament to the cooler charged metal plate, producing a glow between the filament and the plate. Looking only to improve his lamp, Edison saw no practical value in this phenomenon, but, hedging against some future brainstorm, he nevertheless took out a patent on the Edison Effect. Years later, the British physicist John Fleming used the Edison Effect to create the vacuum tube, a "valve" that converts alternating current into direct current and can use a small current to control a larger one. This launched the field of electronics, and, until the invention of the transistor, all electronics depended on vacuum tubes. Built in 1946, ENIAC, one of the world's first all-electronic computers, required 20,000 of them.

Intellectually, Edison was wide open to surprise. The limitations of his vision did not typically concern technology, but marketing. This is important, because innovation breakthrough often comes down to an ability to imagine not a new product but a new market. Consider what happens to thirty-year-old Bill Gates as he leads the company he has only recently formed. His rotary-dial desk phone rings, he picks it up. The man on the line is from a company in Albuquerque and says he is working on something called a "personal computer," or PC.

"They've got the hardware almost ready," he tells the young Gates. "But to run it, now they need the 'basic software'—they are calling it an *operating system*." The man explains that they need this because nothing like it exists. Gates himself, listening to the man, has never really thought about an "operating system." Why not? Because there has never been a need for one.

But that does not matter to Gates. He needs customers, and here is a potential customer on the phone. Perhaps Gates is thinking *"That's funny,"* when he confidently tells the caller, "Yes. Yes, of course we can create your operating system." And then he doubles down on exploiting luck: "We can deliver it in a matter of weeks."

The rest, as they say, is history. Looking forward from this rotary-dial call, Gates imagines that his small company—not quite yet called Microsoft—will build what he decides to call a Disk Operating System, or DOS. And, of course, more than this one wildly successful innovation is born of the phone call and Gates's response to it. DOS drives the exponential success of the PC. Propelled by this success, Gates goes on to make Microsoft far more wildly successful by imagining an even larger mission for the company.

In Las Vegas, in the late 1990s, I listened to Gates, leading Microsoft at its zenith, deliver a speech without once mentioning the name of his own company. He talked instead about the future and invited the audience to imagine with him what this future could bring. It was a future founded on the company motto born of the rotary-dial call: "A computer on every desk and in every home."

Exploit luck. Be ready for the happy business accidents born of unrealized markets.

EXPLOITING CRISIS

One of the best ways to exploit luck is to exploit crisis. During three decades of advising clients and companies in various forms of crisis, I have found that a key truth emerges. The most effective leaders want to do more than merely survive. They want to exploit a crisis as an opportunity. Take my company's client, the late Roberto Goizueta, who helmed The Coca-Cola Company from 1981 to 1997. CEO and chairman of one of the world's most iconic brands, Goizueta was nevertheless an insurgent and change leader ready to exploit luck and crisis. In 1981, when he took over the top spot, he told his company's employees that he would hold no cow sacred. Everything was subject to change.

In 1984, it looked like change was becoming urgently necessary. For many decades, Coca-Cola's closest competitor had been Pepsi-Cola. Over the years, "closest" had been a relative term, because Pepsi's second-place showing was always comfortably distant. But, by 1984, the competitor was catching up—fast. By 1984, Coke's lead over Pepsi had narrowed to a frightening 5 percent, maybe less.

At the time, Pepsi was taking an insurgent leaf from the playbook that served the auto rental company Avis so well. Avis exploited its identity as number-two in rental cars, behind industry giant Hertz. "We're No. 2!" and "We try harder" became one of the most famous and successful slogans in advertising history. Inspired, Pepsi launched its "Pepsi Challenge," cordially inviting—and double-dog daring—loyal consumers of the number one product to try number two. Not only did this challenge stimulate Pepsi sales, it demonstrated that, in blind taste tests, most drinkers preferred the sweeter, lighter Pepsi to the meatier Coke.

With a Coke crisis impending, Goizueta commissioned a top-secret initiative dubbed "Project Kansas," directed by his marketing vice president Sergio Zyman and Coca-Cola USA president Brian Dyson. Their brief was to butcher the most sacred of cows by formulating, testing, and perfecting a new, sweeter flavor for Coca-Cola. While some in the company, those senior enough to have been read-in on the top-secret Project Kansas, believed this innovation was necessary and overdue, others condemned it as a heresy that, in the days of the Inquisition, would have merited burning at the stake. It was analogous to a loss of religious faith.

In this context of deep controversy, Zyman and Dyson's marketing team ventured into the field, testing an array of new sample tastes. The results seemed unambiguous. A new formula with high fructose corn syrup consistently beat not only regular

Coke, but Pepsi, too. A substantial majority of test participants reported that they would buy the newly formulated drink if it were Coca-Cola, although almost all conceded that it might take "some getting used to."

Expanding on my point in chapter 1, for Coke, this caveat was too important to ignore. But it was ignored, and, farther down in the research findings was another nagging result, made difficult to surface amid the secrecy surrounding this product launch. Even under careful test conditions, 10 to 12 percent of tasters reported feeling "angry" and "alienated"—those were the remarkable adjectives they used—at the mere thought of a reformulated Coca-Cola. How might they act on these feelings? They might well stop drinking Coke.

It was a disturbing finding, but it seemed to be overwhelmingly countered by the fact that anywhere from 88 to 90 percent of tasters felt positive about a new formula. Numbers, they say, don't lie. But, in marketing, the significance of a minority opinion can go well beyond the numbers. Following each test, the angry 10 to 12 percent were so angry that their very presence in focus groups skewed results toward the negative. That is, after a test, the disaffected minority forced some of the more complacent majority to change from a positive to a negative response—their own taste buds notwithstanding.

Despite the passionate minority, Goizueta and his senior management team, with Pepsi nipping at their heels, were persuaded that they had to proceed with the rollout of a new formula. They took the gamble, and the initial consumer response was gratifying, as Coca-Cola sales rose 8 percent over the short term. As any marketer will tell you, the only advertising concept more compelling than the word *free* is the word *new*. In 1984, as now, consumers loved change. In this case, the love was fleeting.

Directly reflecting the pre-launch taste test results, a vocal minority of consumers emerged, found their voices, and spoke up. They did not merely criticize the "New Coke," as The Coca-Cola Company called it, but reviled it. When ads for New Coke lit up the scoreboard at the Houston Astrodome, they were greeted by raucous boos. In Atlanta, Coke's hometown, company switchboard operators fielded thousands of heated calls. The company's public affairs department plowed through tens of thousands of irate letters. Calls also flooded the company hotline, 1-800-GET-COKE, coming in such volume and with such vehemence that Coca-Cola hired a psychiatrist to monitor them. He reported that many callers sounded genuinely grieved, as if they were talking about a death in the family. An activist group calling itself the "Old Cola Drinkers of America" filed a class action lawsuit against The Coca-Cola Company. More serious was a revolt among bottlers, some of whom were already engaged in ongoing litigation with the company.

Goizueta moved fast to both confront and exploit bad luck and crisis. On July 10, 1984, just three months after the launch of New Coke, he announced the return of the original formula, alongside the "New Coke." At least one television network, ABC, interrupted regular programming to broadcast the bulletin of the announcement, and one US senator, David Pryor, Democrat of Arkansas, noted it on the floor of the US Senate as "a meaningful moment in US history."

Business pundits, brimming with Schadenfreude, lambasted what they called the worst marketing disaster since the Edsel. But, thanks to Goizueta's determination to exploit crisis, the episode brought new and unprecedented attention to the old brand. True, Pepsi very briefly stole the lead from Coca-Cola, but, by the end of 1985, Coke Classic was outselling both New Coke and Pepsi.

In today's turbulent business environment, expect crisis to visit you on a regular basis. Goizueta knew how to exploit crisis, but even he did not foresee the marketing bonanza hidden in the New Coke catastrophe. The most important thing to understand is that a crisis is no longer an unusual event. It is just another problem to be solved, and it is best solved by exploiting it. Ignoring a crisis is bad, but "managing" it is worse, because it keeps the crisis going as a separate event in the life of a company. Solve crisis by looking for ways to use it to accelerate needed change and pursue unrealized opportunity.

If crisis can be a boon, why be afraid to sail west to go east? Innovation is about seeing an opportunity and exploiting it. Innovation is about preparing for, learning from, and exploiting your luck, good or bad. Most important of all, innovation requires more than leadership. It demands change leadership.

CHAPTER EIGHT

BE A CHANGE LEADER, NOT A BUSINESS LEADER

Just because they say it's impossible doesn't mean you can't do it.

—Roger Bannister

Forty years after he did the impossible, it's the early 1990s and we're walking together across historic Franklin Field during the Penn Relays, with 40,000 fans yelling as runners circle the track.

"What did it feel like, to break the barrier?" I ask.

"It felt important, like I was leading something, something historic," he replied.

Fourteen years before Bob Beamon's long jump leap into history, it's 6:00 p.m., May 6, 1954. In front of 1,200 spectators, a twenty-five year-old London medical student is preparing on a wet, blustery early evening at Oxford's singularly unimpressive Iffley Road track. He is preparing to make history.

His opponent is a mystical barrier, as much psychological as physiological. The challenger is a tall, blonde, lanky athlete, with a forceful stride that makes his head bob along as if floating above the agony that comes along with this territory.

The relentless wind makes him think about calling it off to save energy for another try in ten days, but just before the race, the winds die down, and the challenger decides this is the moment. He has, after all, been preparing for six months, and this is his first contest in eight months. He's ready.

The starter's gun cracks the air. In this race, teammates Christopher Chataway and Chris Brasher are here only to help the challenger in his assault. Right away, Brasher sets the early pace, allowing the challenger to tuck in behind and rest his body and mind. The challenger comes through the first quarter mile in 57.5, the second in 1:58, and then it is Chataway's turn to help the challenger rest and ready his own attack. The time at three-quarters is 3:00.7—almost, almost on pace. It's time to change the game.

"The decision to 'break away' results from a mixture of confidence and lack of it. The 'breaker' is confident to the extent that he suddenly decides the speed has become slower than he can himself sustain

to the finish. Hence he can accelerate suddenly and maintain his new speed to the tape. But he also lacks confidence, feeling that unless he makes a move now, everyone else will do so and he will be left standing."[85]

Time to break away. Body and mind know this. The challenger passes his two friends with 300 yards to go. And the final yards and the final seconds are "never-ending"—until: "I leaped for the tape like a man taking his last spring to save himself from the chasm that threatens to engulf him."

The Oxford announcer bides his time after the finish, saying nothing as 1,200 spectators wait without knowing whether they've just witnessed history or nothing, change or status quo.

Finally, "Ladies and gentlemen," crackles over the PA, "here is the result of Event No. 9, the one mile." The announcer takes a beat, building to…something. "First, No. 41, R. G. Bannister, Amateur Athletic Association and formerly of Exeter and Merton Colleges, Oxford, with a time that is a new meeting and track record and which, subject to ratification, will be a new English native, British national, British all-comers, European, British Empire and world's record. The time was 3…"[86]

The crowd erupts, so that almost no one can hear the rest of the announcement. "…minutes, 59 and 4-tenths of a second."

This is change. This is history. This is the future.

But the challengers and leaders of change do not run in place. It had been nine long years since a new world record in the mile, the day Roger Bannister broke the 4-minute barrier on May 6, 1954. After this, however, change flowed like a spring freshet. Just weeks later, John Landy, whom Bannister will later defeat in a famous head-to-head battle, breaks Bannister's record by running 3:58. The following year, three more runners break the 4-minute barrier, all in the same race. Within two and a half years, 10 athletes run under 4 minutes, and within four years, Herb Elliot drops the world record all the way down to 3:54.5.[87] *In 1975, the 3:50-minute-barrier is broken by John Walker, and the current world record, set in 1999 by Hicham El Guerrouj, is 3:43.13—running at a pace more than 100 yards ahead of Roger Bannister. Change begets change.*

No problem can be solved from the same level of consciousness that created it.

—Albert Einstein

Einstein is a historic model of the power of exponential thinking. I encourage all readers to think exponentially. But, of course, Einstein is, let's face it, hard to imitate. His deductive invention is breathtaking, whereas Thomas Edison's inductive innovation is far more pragmatic and gives us hope of channeling its lessons. Make Edison your innovation model and Einstein your innovation inspiration.

Often, scientific breakthroughs come from scientists who manage to break the linear logic trail. Linear thought—*a* to *b* to *c* and so on—is comfortable. Innovation is often uncomfortable, requiring strenuous effort, exponential effort. Imagination is the catalyst that converts linear to exponential thought. As Archimedes is said to have proclaimed: "Give me a lever and a place to stand and I will move the earth." His proposition makes a perfect metaphor for the exponential power of imagination, even as the lever is the product of this exponential power. The lever is both metaphor and product.

In science, imagination powers the exponential thinking necessary for breakthroughs of insight. For example, in his *Einstein's Cosmos: How Einstein's Vision Transformed Our Understanding of Space and Time*, physicist Michio Kaku lists five reasons Einstein could think exponentially:

- First, Einstein was not an *experimental* physicist—he was a *theoretical* physicist. He lived inside thought.
- Second, Einstein spent up to ten years working on a single *"thought experiment."*

- Third, Einstein was a *rebel*, a bohemian—in my terms, an insurgent.
- Fourth, *Newton's* physical world was just then crumbling, so Einstein lived at the right time to make his difference matter.
- And, finally, he was *Einstein*....

If Billy Joel can't be Mozart, we certainly can't all be Einstein. Nevertheless, studying Einstein on innovation provides important lessons. For example, late in life, he was asked about how schools in the U.S should teach history. Einstein's advice: "there should be extensive discussion of personalities who benefited mankind through *independence of character and judgement.*"[88]

This concept is central to my argument about how to move innovation forward. Think like a status quo incumbent and innovation invariably dies. Think like an insurgent change leader and innovation flourishes. Independence of character and judgement is at the heart of Einstein's genius. He had trouble with rote learning, with recitation. Like Roger Bannister, Einstein broke barriers by the independence of his character and judgement, by the strength of his imagination.

Imagination is the lifeblood of change leaders. For years, Bannister imagined what breaking the four-minute barrier would feel like. Einstein spent years visualizing how equations are reflected in nature. He saw in his mind's eye how James Clerk Maxwell's electromagnetic field equations could be imagined as a boy riding alongside a light beam.

"Imagination is more important than knowledge," Einstein proclaimed. It allowed him to see things differently and to reject the status quo prejudices of his times. Einstein's powerful combination of independence and imagination separated him from his peers, positioning him to discover new scientific theory while others could not. Kip Thorne, a physicist who was Einstein's contemporary, noted Einstein's "conviction that the universe loves simplification and beauty, and his willingness to be guided by this conviction, even if it meant destroying the foundations of Newtonian physics." Together, these "led him, with a clarity of thought that others could not match, to his new description of space and time."[89]

Of course, in Einstein, the potent mixture of independence and imagination, which are inspirational, were leveraged by a faculty he shared with all great change leaders. He was an extraordinary *communicator*. Few could turn a phrase as well as Einstein, and he was obsessed with "translating" his theory of relativity into a comprehensible language that everyday people might grasp. Often, he read parts of his book, *Relativity: The Special and the General Theory*, to his wife, Elsa, checking that each section was simple and descriptive enough for most readers to understand.

While he complained about fame, Einstein also exploited it. In 1921, when he was representing the world Zionist movement, Einstein toured America and quickly became accustomed to the cameras and his role in communicating memorable messages to all who flocked around him, including reporters. His schedule was a roadshow that would exhaust the likes of Roger Bannister. There were meetings with reporter after reporter and with President Warren Harding; and there were numerous rallies and dinners, where he delivered lectures and speeches. In his media interviews, Einstein used simple metaphors to help reporters understand—and thereby explain to readers—his theory of relativity.

A final point about the great genius. I argued earlier that if we must select a spot along the conceptual continuum between Thomas Edison's inductive innovation and Albert

Einstein's deductive invention, the pragmatic choice is to model Edison's step-by-step *innovation* approach. Then, we can follow with Einstein's exponential breakthroughs as inspiration for our own *invention*.

Interestingly, during Einstein's 1921 American tour, Edison and Einstein "met," but only via a series of questions. The practical Edison, then a cranky seventy-four-year-old, criticized American universities as too theoretical in approach, an affliction, he believed, Einstein shared. Edison devised a test to screen job applicants. It consisted of 150 factually rooted questions, all stressing the practical over the theoretical, the inductive over the deductive: "How is leather made?" "What country consumes the most tea?" "What was Gutenberg's type made of?"[90]

It was called the "Edison questionnaire" and, predictably, reporters aimed it directly at the visiting Einstein, asking him if he knew what the speed of sound was?

Arguably, Einstein knew more about sound and sound waves than anyone who had ever lived. Yet he did not know the answer to this question. I don't "carry such information in my mind since it is readily available in books," he admitted. Then he counterpunched by observing that the "value of a college education is not the learning of many facts but the training of the mind to think."

THINK LIKE A CHANGE LEADER

Change leaders are the ones who break barriers, like Roger Bannister, or transform science, like Albert Einstein. Today, change leadership is also front and center in politics. Most candidates who are winning campaigns, including some we have advised, are change leaders, disruptors. From Brexit to Bernie Sanders to Rodrigo Duterte to Donald Trump to

Emmanuel Macron to Moon Jae In to Mahathir Mohamad to the League and the Five Star Movement Italian electoral victory in 2018, the change leader, or insurgent candidate, holds greater advantage today than ever before. Google searches for the word "populism" are today four times what they have been over the last decade, and a recent thirty-six nation survey found most respondents are dissatisfied with their political system, and 70 percent agree that institutions in society ignore their individual goals.[91] People want change.

In this context, the only leaders who succeed in passing their agendas these days are those who act like insurgents rather than incumbents. A few years ago, in *Fortune* magazine's "World's Most Admired Leaders" issue, one person garnered more votes than anyone else: Pope Francis. It is difficult to argue against his being a change leader.

What is true in contemporary politics is true in contemporary business. Only the insurgents, the change leaders, succeed in transforming their companies, their products, their services, and their markets. Today, if you are in business, you are in the business of change. You need to think and act less like a business leader and more like a change leader. There is no time to delay the transformation. The Sony Walkman took years to be absorbed by its consumers, but Apple's iPod was ubiquitous in a matter of months. Your favorite app? It takes control in a matter of days. You must run faster and think more exponentially to stay ahead and succeed.

As Ron Adner argues in his book *The Wide Lens: A New Strategy for Innovation*, you must be ready to change the game itself.[92] This comes down to reconfiguring the ecosystem to work for you, putting in place five levers of change by asking five critically important questions:

- *What can be separated?* Is there an opportunity to decouple elements that are currently bundled in a way that can create new value and move the value proposition forward?
- *What can be combined?* Is there an opportunity to bundle elements that are currently uncoupled in a way that can create new value and move the value proposition forward?
- *What can be relocated?* Is there an opportunity to shift existing elements to new positions in the ecosystem in a way that can create new value and move the value proposition forward?
- *What can be added?* Are there elements that are currently absent, but whose introduction to the ecosystem can create new value and move the value proposition forward?
- *What can be subtracted?* Are there existing elements whose elimination from the ecosystem could be accommodated in a way that would allow for the creation of new value and move the value proposition forward?"

This is a vital checklist for a change leader's strategic planning. Separating, combining, relocating, adding, or subtracting are ways to drive change not as a business leader but as a change leader. The business of business is no longer business. It is change.

CHANGE LEADER FRAMEWORK

The insurgent change leader today operates in the context of remarkable change, which escalates the importance of playing offense and using communications to control the dialogue. Research shows as much as 49 percent of a company's brand and reputation comes down to one thing: its leader.[93] What the CEO says and does not say, the way they look or do not look, the confidence they imbue in employees and in investor analysts, the discipline of their communications—absolutely everything.

We also know that as much as 70 percent of all our success in business and life comes down simply to our ability to communicate. Jobs, Gates, Murdoch, Milken, Goizueta, Iger—all great communicators. One reason Roger Bannister is so widely remembered for breaking the 4-minute-mile barrier is his ability to articulate what it felt like to break it and what it means for us. Albert Einstein's enduring fame as a "brand" does not entirely rest on an equation but also on his talent as a communicator. He told his story in the context of the larger story of scientific change.

It is officially the worst time in history for incumbents. That makes it the best time for insurgents and change leaders. Incumbents, people who think like business leaders, and insurgents, people who think like change leaders, view reality differently from one another. They approach strategy differently, and they are on opposite sides in a war between "Bigness" and "Change." Let me expand on the argument made in chapter 5:

Incumbent "business" or "bigness" leaders…

- Believe deep in their bones in the power of size and scope—the power of "number one-ness."
- Take comfort in bureaucracy, hierarchical decision-making, and the passive promise of "What was, will be."

- Are formal in organization and operations—and therefore often highly ritualistic and superstitious.
- Are heritage-driven, embracing in the present the strategies by which they have succeeded and dominated in the past.
- Almost uniformly hate and resist change; after all, when you are number one, why do you want to change? Change is your enemy, and not your friend.

Insurgent "change" leaders...

- Value speed and mobility over size and scope.
- Use surprise as a key tactic. (And incumbents are unfailingly surprised.)
- Hate bureaucracy and instead believe flat is fast. They instinctively use the military principle of "driving power to the edge"—to speed market feedback and market decision-making.
- Are informal to the point of irreverence.
- Create strategy based on a future vision that assumes a changed reality.
- Love change because change means opportunity. They recognize that change is constant and that change is not their enemy, but their friend.

What I learned in working with Steve Jobs is that insurgents play by a different set of rules than incumbents. In the current turbulent, instant, surround-sound information environment, insurgents have the advantage. When an incumbent business misses its innovation or marketing objectives, the go-to response is to "refine" its strategy, "reset" its goals, and "renew" its efforts so that "We'll do better next quarter…." The assumption is that "Election Day" can be moved back—over and over. For politicians, of course, Election Day is carved in stone. It happens. It's done. I counsel my business clients to formulate their goals and to consider these goals as life-or-death, as final and absolute as the count from the ballot box. Create an Election Day and, on that Election Day either win at least 50.1 percent or go home.

Incumbents can find consultants who will present Election Day victory as just one possible viable scenario. A strategy of "managed decline" for a product, a brand, or a whole company is another option. Insurgents reject this. Come out ahead on Election Day or go home. They follow seven principles:

1. Define Success

Mark out a clear finish line, the kind Bannister drove himself across in 1954. In politics, the finish line comes readymade. It is Election Day. In business, elevating the idea of a "business objective" to an "Election Day" amplifies its urgency to a matter of life or death. "*We should*" becomes "*We must.*"

Creating an Election Day requires clearly understanding what winning means, what you want to accomplish. As we detail in chapter 2, this is "destination planning." It answers three questions: *Where will we be in two or three years, if we do everything right? What will be the metrics of this success? How will our stakeholders think, feel, and act differently because of our win?*

Microsoft's Bill Gates was famous—or infamous—for his annual "Bet the Company" speech. He convinced himself and his employees that coming up short on "Election Day" meant the end of Microsoft.

Change leaders must create a vision of a changed world, as Bill Gates did with his "A computer on every desk and in every home" corporate mantra. They use destination planning to define the result of the company's success. They define the future toward which they want to lead others. Without this definition of the future, why should anyone follow them?

2. Move Faster

Moving faster is the change leader mandate. Speed wins. Discipline enables speed. Change leaders must build the flattest decision-making structure possible, one that is as close as possible to the battlefield or the marketplace. Incumbent business leaders vie for the corner office. Insurgent change leaders worry about being too far away from the heart of the market or the problem they are trying to solve. Not that physical distance is the real issue. Mutual trust, shared values, and commonly understood objectives within your organization are the effective means of dramatically compressing the distance between you and your market or problem. If you cannot trust the information and execution at the edge of your organization, you will not know what is happening in the next cubicle, let alone the next country.

Remember the Boyd Loop from chapter 4? The faster the fighter pilot or the change leader moves through the key elements of the OODA loop (*Observation, Orientation, Decision,* and *Action*) the more likely he or she is not only to survive, but to shoot down the other guy. The key to an effective, fast, agile organization is not found on the organizational chart, but in the emotional bonds that hold the organization together. Microsoft CEO Satya Nadella's desire to build a "culture of empathy" is not an idle corporate group hug but an urgent necessity for the company's recent and continuing rise in the world.

3. Build Momentum

In sports, business, politics, and warfare, momentum is magical and self-sustaining, constant and unrelenting. Think about it in football terms, four yards and four yards and four yards more versus the Hail Mary. Momentum is based on the immutable law of football that is true in all human pursuits: "Take what they give you." If the defense allows a quick hit off-tackle, or a quick out pass, take it—and take it again, until your opponent changes its defense to take it away. And, because they have changed their defense, they have inevitably created a new opening. Find it. Do whatever it takes to "move the sticks." There is no more powerful sound in sports than the silence of a home stadium in which the visiting team has created momentum.

There are two principles in building momentum: First, *"Do the Doable."* This is premised on the fact that the insurgent begins with insufficient resources and must therefore marshal them carefully. So, never take on impossible or even long-reach goals. Chances are you will only demoralize your team and invigorate the opposition. Instead, go for the small-yard gain. Pick up the fruit on the ground, even before you reach for the low-hanging fruit on the branches. Do whatever it takes to create an internal sense of momentum, because momentum is magical and ripples throughout any organization.

Second, *"Move the Movable."* Focus on moving only the "votes" and "voters" you need to gain momentum toward your destination. Think in terms of attitudinal segmentation. Consumers may be segmented into *Hard Opposition* (they hate you, and work actively against you); *Soft Opposition* (they prefer another brand but are not activists); *Undecided* (they make very uninvolved decisions); *Soft Support* (they may like your brand, but not enough); *hard support* (your activist-loyalists). An attitudinal map of an electorate, a market, or any group looks like this:

HO SO UNDECIDED SS HS

HO = HARD OPPOSITION: They actively oppose your company or brand. They may be competitors or activists against your industry or company. They are immovable; and while you must never waste resources in trying to win their favor, you must always understand their effect on other groups.

SO = SOFT OPPOSITION: They prefer a competitor or have had a negative experience with your company or brand. They are prohibitively expensive to win over, but you nevertheless want to monitor their attitudes to make sure they are not joining the Hard Opposition.

UNDECIDED: This segment is unaligned. We find they are most often undecided by character or circumstance. Either they refuse to align with one brand or company, or they are forced to decide based on price or availability. While their "votes" can be won, holding them is very expensive—a matter of repeatedly buying them.

SS = SOFT SUPPORT: They prefer your company or brand, but they are not your most loyal or profitable customers. They are relatively weak on performance and profitability. And they require more reasons to purchase more often and to pay more.

HS = HARD SUPPORT: These are your most loyal customers—and the most profitable. Importantly, they provide the most powerful, compelling, and credible form of viral advertising for any brand or candidate: word of mouth.

This model applies to voter franchises worldwide and to internal and external brand franchises in every kind of business. Most attitudinal distributions have the fewest people in the extreme categories—Hard Opposition and Hard Support—and the most in the "Undecided" middle. The distribution across all industries is in the range of 5–8 percent Hard Opposition, 12–18 percent Soft Opposition, 40–50 percent Undecided, 12-18 percent Soft Support, and 5–8 percent Hard Support.

The Holy Grail of B2B and B2C marketing is getting more people to come back more often to buy more…and sometimes to be willing to pay more. The key is to move more soft support to hard support. This increase in loyalty will preserve and even increase customer satisfaction, making all communications and marketing more efficient and effective. Above all, this means nailing down the hard support, moving soft support to hard support, dividing or disrupting the soft and hard opposition—and deprioritizing the undecided. Focus on your loyalists and moving soft support to hard support and creating the momentum of change leadership.

4. Use Change to Control the Dialogue

Remember, the information revolution has brought an increased demand among consumers for control. This is a result of knowing too much, too often. Consumers have become accustomed to increased choice and frequent change, along with customization, which gives them a greater perception of control. They want control, they expect choice and change, and they want customization. They are much less driven by habit, and even less so by traditional mass marketing tactics. This means that the obvious move for an insurgent change leader is to take on the *status quo* in most markets.

Like consumers everywhere, Americans love change. In politics, nothing unites American voters more today than dissatisfaction with politics-as-usual, with the existing political establishment, and the practices of the political elites. Now is the time to promise choice, change, and customization. In any contest, change helps gain or regain control. In the market dialogue of competitive products or in a political campaign, change creates the opportunity for reshuffling the status quo. Like voters, consumers are tuned to this change.

5. Make Everything Matter

Everything you say and do, what you say on camera and off, what you wear, who you're with, where you are, often what you *fail* to say or do communicates. Details communicate. Not one of them is neutral. A successful change leader makes every detail important to their team. Each little thing either adds to or subtracts from value. Align all details of communication with your brand to create an engaging and consistent total brand experience.

6. Communicate Inside-Out

An insurgent organization is essentially a communications machine. By communicating inside-out, you amplify the brand's messages as they move out from leader, to team members, to suppliers, to market partners, to HS and SS customers, to the friendlies among press, regulators, legislators, and influencers. This is called "getting buy-in," but it costs nothing. In fact, it pays for itself.

To communicate inside-out, you, the change leader, must transfer ownership of your strategies outwardly. Give everyone ownership of these strategies. Think Bill Gates and his annual "Bet the Company" speech. The farther out you can transfer your themes and messages, the better. When your employees, suppliers, partners, friends, best customers, and even your competitors' customers know your brand's value proposition, you are doing this right.

7. Never Play Defense

Insurgents do not need goading. They are by nature aggressive. Nevertheless, playing offense is not just shoving forward with your head down. It is driving an offensive strategy *all the time*, never departing from the change leader's strategy, constantly forcing the competition to react to *your* change, even in challenging market situations or in crises that tempt you to hunker down in a defensive crouch. Insurgents never play defense.

When you make a mistake, admit it quickly. Be proactive when you see a problem for your customers or voters. Do all you can and must to make up for it. Remember, when your customers think you are wrong, you are wrong.

DECIDE TO LEAD CHANGE

Leading change requires, first, the *decision* to lead change. Driving innovation and marketing to new levels of success means that you must learn to love change and to lead by change. All markets are transforming today. Most companies are either transforming or need immediately to start. This makes the rule of today simple: Lead change or *be* changed. Getting behind change means losing. Leading change means winning.

If you are not transforming the markets you are in, someone else is doing it. Soon, you will be playing by *their* rules. In most markets, a rising insurgent brand is doing the disrupting; therefore, the new leadership coming of age is change leadership.

To lead change, you must lead a group, a team, a company, or a corporate enterprise. Gallup does monthly polls measuring "employee engagement," and, lately, the engagement number is in the low 30 percent range. That means some 70 percent of employees come to work, check Facebook, snooze and doodle through a couple of meetings, play Candy Crush, eat, complain, and go home.

You must urgently communicate the meaning of the work and the destination of each project. When Ronald Reagan was president, the press often characterized him as "The Great Communicator." As a change leader in today's information environment, you must be a great communicator, period. You can be a genius innovator, but if you cannot communicate effectively and compellingly, you are out of luck. If you are going to lead change, you must excite people about the possibilities of change.

Insurgent brands and insurgent leaders are on the rise, disrupting every marketplace, every industry, every political campaign, and every part of our society. Yet, stunningly, managers of incumbent organizations continue to tell their people to "act like a leader," by which they mean "act like an incumbent." They might as well just say "act like a loser."

Even mega-corporations like AT&T learn to transform culture from incumbent to insurgent. That is the law of survival today. Still, numerous companies persist in following the incumbent market leaders. This does nothing but reinforce *the incumbent's* advantage, which depends precisely on competitors acting predictably.

Unfortunately for both incumbents and their followers, acting predictably is the very last thing insurgents do. Lead your organization to where the market will be, not where it is. Little wonder that Steve Jobs disdained consumer research. "The people can't tell you what they want next," he scoffed. "You have to show it to them."

Incumbent business leaders scramble to protect the status quo, defending the market of yesterday rather than anticipating the market of tomorrow. If incumbent business leaders find themselves under attack, it is because the market status quo is under attack. Eventually, all incumbent leaders fall prey to the insurgents coming up from behind, helmed by change leaders who empower both employees and customers by defining the future of innovation and business.

CHAPTER NINE

EMPOWER, DON'T MANAGE

Power can be taken, but not given. The process of taking is empowerment itself.

—Gloria Steinem

In the middle of Tom Wolfe's Bonfire of the Vanities New York *of the late 1980s, I meet her walking along Park Avenue, recognizable even in classic sunglasses, and so I say hello and offer immediately that I like her writings. She, of course, asks which ones? In the moment, my very best answer is "Articles," and she smiles, instantly understanding that I have not read a single one of her books, which include such bestsellers as* My Life on the Road, Revolution from Within: A Book of Self-Esteem, Outrageous Acts and Everyday Rebellions, Moving Beyond Words, Marilyn: Norma Jean, *and* As If Women Matter.

Gloria Marie Steinem, who would later go on to become a renowned writer, lecturer, political activist, and feminist organizer, is born on March 25, 1934 in Toledo, Ohio. Her family lives and travels in a trailer that serves as a moving antique shop for her father, Leo, the son of Jewish emigrants. Her mother, Ruth, a Presbyterian, suffers a nervous breakdown at age thirty-four, before Gloria is born, becoming an invalid trapped in delusions that send her in and out of sanatoriums.[94]

When Gloria is ten, her parents separate and divorce. The entire experience, including her mother's inability to hold a job and the apathy of some of her doctors, fuels a passion for social and political equality.

Graduating from Smith College in 1956, Steinem inaugurates a lifelong passion for travel, spending two years in India as a Chester Bowles Asian Fellow. While there, she is influenced by the activist teachings of Mahatma Gandhi.

This begins her life's work. Steinem initially becomes a journalist—for example, in 1963, working as a Playboy Bunny at the New York Playboy Club while writing an article for Huntington Hartford's Show Magazine. *Everyone growing up in the 1960s remembers the black-and-white photo of Steinem in her Bunny uniform. Some even remember the piercing quality of her prose about how women are treated at institutions like Playboy. Steinem merges her magna cum laude brain with the fact that she is an ex-dancer and beauty queen. She begins to write history and write it brilliantly.*

Driven by a hunger for social justice and armed with the teachings of Gandhi, Steinem begins empowering more than one generation of the disadvantaged, including, of course, women. From her co-founding of Ms. *magazine in 1972, Steinem goes on to help launch or lead the Women's Action Alliance, the National Women's Political Caucus, the Women's Media Center, Voters for Choice, Choice USA, the Beyond Racism Initiative, Equality Now, Donor Direct Action, and Direct Impact Africa. Culminating a long string of the most important awards for leadership and giving, she receives in 2013 the Presidential Medal of Freedom, the nation's highest civilian honor.*[95]

Today, the woman from Toledo continues to set in motion change around the world, empowering millions upon millions of change agents. She works to define the future of social and political equality.

Never tell people how to do things. Tell them what to do and they will surprise you with their ingenuity.

—George S. Patton Jr.

He is controversial, but incredibly effective. George S. Patton grows up in a non-military family with a rich military heritage. Suffering from a learning disability, he enrolls in VMI for a year to prepare for West Point, in which poor grades force him to repeat his plebe year. He graduates in 1909, 46 out of a class of 103, is commissioned, and competes in the Pentathlon in the 1912 Olympics. Though he does not win a medal, he excels in fencing, writes the US Army's saber manual, is named the army's first-ever Master of the Sword, and even designs a new saber for the service. Unlike the cavalry's traditional curved saber, intended for defensive slashing, Patton creates a straight-bladed weapon meant for offensive thrusting. The "Patton Sword" is adopted by the army as the M1913.

In 1916, Patton serves with Major General John J. Pershing in the Punitive Expedition to capture Pancho Villa. Leading a patrol consisting of three Dodge Model 30-35 Touring cars—making this the first mechanized combat attack in US Army history—Patton personally shoots one of Villa's top lieutenants, Julio Cárdenas, and two of his guards. When the US enters World War I in April 1917, Patton is in the first contingent of troops shipped to France, serving as Pershing's aide-de-camp. He then trains the US Army's first tank soldiers and leads the US Army's First Tank Brigade in the service's first two armored combat missions. Between the world wars, he develops the army's mobile warfare doctrine, bucking the conservatism of senior commanders, who are convinced that World War II will be just like World War I on the Western

Front: static combat fought from trenches with little need for tanks or other vehicles.

In 1942, after training the first-generation of US Army desert fighters in the California training facility he himself designs, Patton commands American troops in the Mediterranean Theater.[96]

Throughout his one-of-a-kind military career, Patton applies the lessons of the military history he has ravenously ingested throughout his youth and young manhood. In North Africa, up against Erwin Rommel's vaunted Afrika Korps, he quickly rehabilitates the demoralized troops of II Corps after a humiliating defeat at Kasserine Pass (February 19–24, 1943).

Rehabilitated? They are transformed, empowered, becoming victorious. Most famously, beginning in July 1944, Patton leads the Third US Army in France, Belgium, Germany, and Czechoslovakia in the months following the Allied Invasion of Normandy.[97] He leads his army in a campaign that liberates more villages, towns, and cities and kills or captures more of the enemy than any other unit on the Western Front. His army moves faster and farther than any Allied ground force in World War II.

Flash back to II Corps after Kasserine. The unconventional—insurgent—Patton, unannounced, arrives at HQ and immediately sizes up the unit's problem as one of leadership—or, rather, lack thereof. The troops are slovenly, uninspired, a rabble more than an army. In the maiden battle of the US Army against the most celebrated German unit led by its most iconic general, these soldiers are governed by a mixture of their own fear and apathy.

A change leader if there ever was one, Patton acts immediately, decreeing an uncompromising regime aimed at achieving perfect discipline. ("The only discipline is perfect discipline," he writes.) He begins by enforcing the regulations governing uniforms, including what will become infamous in army lore as the "Necktie Order," which requires all soldiers, all the time, including frontline soldiers, to wear leggings, helmets, *and* properly knotted neckties. As General Omar N. Bradley later observes, "Each time a soldier knotted his necktie, threaded his leggings, and buckled on his heavy steel helmet, he was forcibly reminded that Patton had come to command the II Corps, that the pre-Kasserine days had ended, and that a tough new era had begun." At first outraged by the new regime, the soldiers of II Corps soon proudly brand themselves as "Patton's men."

Patton understands that when it comes to leadership *everything* matters. All the small details of how you lead must empower those you lead to themselves lead. Witness his infamous speeches to the US Third Army, in 1944, prior to the Allied invasion of France, empowering and motivating the inexperienced Third Army for the battles to come. In remarkable and sometimes profane oratory, Patton exhorts his soldiers to move beyond personal fear and, above all, move constantly to the offense. He points out the truth that to dig in defensively is to dig your own grave. A forward-moving soldier is less of a target than a motionless man cowering in a foxhole.

Patton also understands that nearly 80 percent of a leader's mission is to lift the morale of his men. He understands the power of transforming himself into a symbol, often appearing on the front line in person. "Soldiers should see that a general can get shot at," he writes.

EMPOWERMENT FUNDAMENTALS

One thing is clear: Steinem and Patton are not managers. They are leaders.

Managers *manage*. They use traditional business thinking. They are logical, require proof, lean on precedents, and assume there is a right or a wrong, a black or a white. They hate ambiguity. They want results. They think a lot about process. By contrast, change leaders *empower*. They think different. They are innovative, intuitive. They constantly ask: "What if?" They do not lean on the past, but spend more time imagining the future, always looking for a better way as opposed to a "we do it this way" approach. They embrace ambiguity. They want change. They think a lot about breakthrough.

Change leaders are vital to innovation. You cannot drive innovation if you cannot lead change. As the philosopher Heraclitus wrote: "The only constant is change," and over 2,500 years later, that is not only true but truer. Change itself continues to change and continues to do so with more speed, volatility, and unpredictability than ever before. As Chase LeBlanc, a leadership expert and the founder and CEO of Leadagers, LLC, writes: "Management is how well it runs when you are there; leadership is how well it runs when you are not."

The threat to traditional businesses is that traditional business managers typically fail to be change leaders. They are managers who focus on keeping things under control. Change leaders focus on disrupting things. Managers drive budgets and fill quotas. Change leaders inspire and mobilize a broad base of people. Often, managers focus on personal success, while change leaders want to change the way people perform. Managers delegate. Change leaders leverage.

This chapter unpacks the difference between managing and empowering, between managers and change leaders. Steinem and Patton never met and would not have enjoyed the same dinner party conversation, but they share a commonality of change leader approaches proved by history: an ability to focus, to align, and to engage.

A business will always encounter a ceiling that represents the limits of its leader's psychological and change abilities. In *Mastering Leadership*, Bill Adams and Bob Anderson find the highest-functioning businesses in the top 10 percent score 80 percent on their scale of leadership effectiveness. By contrast, the lowest-functioning businesses in the bottom 10 percent score only 30 percent on their leadership effectiveness scale. A company cannot rise above the leadership effectiveness of its own leader. *This* is the ceiling of their success.[98]

Recall from chapter 8 that driving change leadership and positive empowerment means positioning you and your organization as a hungry insurgent, not a fat-and-happy incumbent. It means never playing defense. It means embracing change but riding ahead of it. Change leaders must always think, plan, and act like a come-from-behind insurgent. And they must motivate every employee to do likewise. Playing offense, even when favorable results tempt you to a conservative defense, is the new way to win.

Change leaders make strategy the boss. A successful change leader's strategic discipline must drive everything he or she does and does not do. The strategy must be based on the intersection of what key constituents—such as customers and shareholders—want and what the company can and must do to deliver long-term value. Your strategy must round up the thousands of nitty-gritty tactical decisions that are made every day. It must aggregate and focus every one of your employees and constituents in the same direction and toward the same objectives. Making strategy boss is fundamental to victory.

Finally, successful change leaders like Steinem and Patton redefine the role of communication to empower their supporters. The rules of leadership, business, and communications have changed dramatically. Today's consumers (think in terms of consumers of information, who may be customers, employees, investors, or voters) are empowered with instant and ubiquitous information produced by an interconnected network of sources. These consumers have infinitely more choices, brands have infinitely more competition, and all of us are engulfed in a tsunami of data, the crassly trivial and the critically important swirling together in a crushing, relentless wave. Communication is the change leader's tool to focus, align, and engage. It is their secret weapon of empowerment.

SHAPE SUCCESS

Ray Dalio might refer to Steinem and Patton as "shapers." That is his word for change leaders who develop and build unique and valuable visions, often fighting opposition, doubt, and naysayers. Dalio's shapers are change leaders who include the likes of Jobs, Musk, Bezos, Netflix's Reed Hastings, and the Gates Foundation's Bill Gates. They are also change leaders found in many wider fields: Nobel laureate microcredit pioneer Muhammad Yunus, Winston Churchill, Martin Luther King Jr., Singapore's founding father Lee Kuan Yew, China's Deng Xiaoping, Andrew Carnegie, Sigmund Freud, Charles Darwin, Isaac Newton, and, of course, Thomas Edison and Albert Einstein—not to mention such religious shapers as Christ, Muhammad, and the Buddha.

Shapers are typically rebellious thinkers who drive relentlessly for innovation. By the sheer force of their passion, they "market" their innovation to everyone who will listen. They yearn to tell the story and define how they will "put a dent in the universe." Dalio is fascinated by the common denominators of shaper-change leaders. Applying his own one-hour personality assessment tool to those he knows personally—Bill Gates, Elon Musk, Reed Hastings, Muhammad Yunus, Geoffrey Canada (Harlem Children's Zone), Jack Dorsey (Twitter), David Kelly (IDEO), and others, he concludes:

> It turns out they have a lot in common. They are all independent thinkers who do not let anything, or anyone, stand in the way of achieving their audacious goals. They have very strong mental maps of how things should be done, and at the same time a willingness to test those mental maps in the world of reality and change the ways they do thing to make them work better. They are extremely resilient, because their need to achieve what they envision is stronger than the pain they experience as they struggle to achieve. Perhaps most interesting, they have a wider range of vision than most people, either because they have that vision themselves or because they know how to get it from others who can see what they can't.... Above all, they are passionate about what they are doing....[99]

There is one more common denominator. By some combination of instinct, passion, and talent, shapers deliberately define themselves, their values, and what is at stake in their version of change. They define what the future will look like once their vision of change takes hold.

DEFINE, DEFINE, DEFINE

My company has worked with one the great shapers, Disney's Bob Iger. Taking over from Michael Eisner in 2005, Iger was selected as the company's new CEO—but now it was time to be "elected." This meant running an insurgent campaign to empower change leadership. Scott Miller and I called it our "CEO as Candidate" campaign. It begins by defining yourself and defining change—that is, defining the stakes in the "election." Above all, it is about defining the future you will lead.

Driven by a sense of urgency, Iger differentiated himself from his predecessor. Whereas Eisner had firmly believed that only *he* understood the "Disney magic," Iger convened his top managers in his corner suite at Team Disney Burbank, the building architect Michael Graves had adorned with a Seven Dwarves façade. Facing his management team, he pointed to himself: "The magic is not in here. It's not in this building. It's not in Burbank." He purposely met the eyes of each executive. "The magic is out *there*. Our job is to find it."

From that moment and through his tenure today, Bob Iger consistently defined himself as a leader who leads good people to do their best. And at the center of this "CEO as Candidate" campaign was a "stump speech" based on a simple "3 x 5 card" message we worked on together. A 3 x 5 card format is an essential element of campaign and empowerment strategy. Iger's card is a strong example. It was titled: "The Magic Is Out There," and it positioned the quest as "ours," not "mine." It consisted of just six key sentences, which fit comfortably into the 3 x 5 format:

- Our job is to find the magic, wherever it is in the world.
- We must restore our relationship with young families and especially young moms.
- We must stand for family fun.
- We must restore our relevance for and relationship with teens.
- We must be agnostic about how our customers consume our information/entertainment.
- We must restore the quality of the Disney brand.

Notice the pronoun—first person plural "*We*," never first person singular. This basic linguistic element spoke volumes about inclusion, in contrast to Eisner's exclusionary *I*. It delivered a message that enabled Iger to control definitions of his change leadership and empower everyone within earshot. Via his direct reports, he spread his personal version of this six-sentence message to the rest of the sprawling Disney conglomerate. Sometimes, he introduced the first sentence on this by explicitly disclaiming exclusive ownership of the Disney Magic. Often, he went much further, declaring that the Disney Magic was nowhere to be found in Burbank, either. It was, he said, "out there." And then he delivered the opening 3 x 5 sentence: *Our job is to find the magic, wherever it is in the world.*

Iger made strategy the boss across these six key messages. He set about rebuilding the many bridges his predecessor had burned. He won over key board members Stanley Gold and Roy E. Disney. He won over the Disney family. He won over Steve Jobs, at the time running Pixar. Far more important, he began winning over the moms and the young families, the teens and tweens, and more. Most of all, he allowed the incredibly talented people of The Walt Disney Company to do their jobs, and he never, ever claimed credit for any idea, no matter how successful.

The stakeholders of The Walt Disney Company discovered that they had elected a change leader. Chances are that *your* customers are voting for change by considering and choosing new innovations, products, and services across more and more usage occasions. Chances are that *your* partners, employees, and constituents are voting for change, too. Arms folded across their chests, they wait for you to inspire them into action.

Just about every great change leader we have worked with immediately gets the Jobs-inspired metaphor of a political campaign, with its urgent and absolute "Election Day." They understand that they truly are the equivalent of the political candidate. They must move voters and win the hearts and minds of their constituents. They must apply the focus, discipline, and tempo of a winning political campaign. This requires creating and controlling definitions—a task best accomplished by applying "3 x 5 card discipline."

These are the basic principles of how to emulate Iger:

- *Define yourself.* Over the three decades I have been creating strategy, I have seen no global political campaign win with a candidate who is predominately on the defensive. To be on the defensive is to relinquish control of your own self-definition. In politics, as in business, successful leaders define their own character, personality, and values. Fail to do so, and others will define these attributes for you. And you can bet *their* definition will *not* be to your advantage.
- *Define change.* Falling behind the forces of change puts both organization and leader in reactive mode—permanently on the defensive. As the 1932 Roosevelt presidential campaign, the 1980 Reagan presidential campaign, and the 2008 Obama presidential campaign demonstrate, there is only one consistently effective competitive strategy: to lead change. In business, this has never been more urgently the case.
- *Define the future.* In politics, the candidate who best defined the future for voters has won nearly every free and fair election in history. Successful change leaders must define the future of their own industry and business in compelling and credible ways. Articulate your vision and define your brand as both different and better than the others. By this,

empower your employees, partners, and constituents to join in and leverage the change you are leading.

AN EMPOWERMENT CAMPAIGN

We are living the ancient Chinese curse of "interesting times." Up is down. Down is up. Change is the constant, and it comes at us faster and faster. It is a reset environment, in which everything is different. There is infinitely greater competition for share-of-mind, stomach, wallet, and market. Consumers and voters alike are more savvy and cynical than ever before. They are also more open to the next new thing.

New challenges and opportunities surround us, but most businesses persist in the same old approaches. Good! This leaves open vital territory for the change leader to seize. Sameness is death. So, "Think different."

Run a campaign to control definitions and empower your constituents. This allows you, the change leader, to deliver the products and services Steve Jobs once described as "Bicycles for the mind." Here's how to emulate Jobs in adopting an insurgent campaign format:

- *Embrace the campaign model* to focus on delivering the win, the whole win, and nothing but the win.
- *Define your win and define success* in simple and clear terms and proclaim an "Election Day" by which you must achieve that win.
- *Set achievable goals* on the way to the big win. Nothing is as important to the insurgent campaign as momentum. Do the doable first. Get some first downs. Get some easy things done.

- *Cultivate a bias for action* by attacking the status quo and defining and driving change in the marketplace.
- *Plan and drive across a campaign framework.* Follow the steps Scott Miller and I write about in our book, *The Leadership Campaign: 10 Political Strategies to Win at Your Career and Propel your Business to Victory*[100]:
    - *Decide to run.* Make the existential choice to be and become a change leader and commit to a campaign to get this done.
    - *Think, plan, and act like an insurgent.* Reject the incumbent mindset. Embrace the mindset of the insurgent change leader. Don't manage. Empower. Model this success formula.
    - *Build your kitchen cabinet.* Surround yourself with what we call a trusted and tell-you-the-truth "Core Strategy Group." Drive your change leadership from within this group.
    - *Prepare your campaign inside-out.* You must win the election from within before you win a campaign from without.
    - *Announce your candidacy.* Take control of the dialogue and model other great change leaders by defining yourself, your "Election Day," the change you will bring, and the future.
    - *Define everything.* Everything communicates, and everything matters. So, running a campaign means making strategy boss and driving even the tiniest details in the direction of this strategy.

- *Control the dialogue.* For a change leader, communications must be two-way, never one-way. Listen, align, and engage all key audiences, from employees to customers.
- *Gain momentum.* Model great leadership examples who "Do the Doable" and "Move the Movable." Nothing is as magically viral as getting some things *done* and then using this to create word of mouth that empowers your supporters.
- *Exploit crises.* They are as inevitable as rain or snow; therefore, anticipate, prevent, train for, and get ready to take advantage of every small and large crisis to pivot to a future of change.
- *Run a leadership campaign.* Commit to the insurgent campaign, with its focus and discipline. Keep running it as if your change leadership life depends on it, because it does.

EMPOWER INSIDE-OUT

Running a change leadership campaign begins inside-out. It is fueled by example and empowerment. Go back to Thomas Edison and this 1879 scene featuring the Wizard of Menlo Park at his innovation workshop as described by the *New York Herald*:

> At six o'clock in the evening the machinists and electricians assemble in the laboratory. Edison is already present, attired in a suit of blue flannel, with hair uncombed and straggling over his eyes, a silk handkerchief around his neck, his hands and face

> somewhat begrimed and the whole air that of a man with a purpose and indifferent to everything save that purpose.
>
> Carelessly attired, somewhat grimy, Edison appeared to be just another workman in the shop. As the "hum of machinery drowns all other sounds and each man is at his particular post," Edison himself "flits about, first to one bench, then to another, examining here, instructing there; at one place drawing out new fancied designs, at another earnestly watching the progress of some experiment."[101]

Edison led change inside-out. He hired craftsmen he trusted, directed, and empowered. He allocated the various aspects of a project as if he were running a series of campaigns aimed at winning a series of Election Days. The culture of focused craftsmanship that Edison built and exemplified was among his most powerful inventions. His change leadership and inside-out culture of craftsmanship empowered creative innovation through 80-hour work weeks that produced invention after invention. He encouraged hard work, along with plenty of play.

Edison did not model conventional rules or time zones. His schedule was fluid. Like the general Napoleon and the magician David Copperfield, the inventor Edison cultivated a habit of catnapping, getting a few minutes of sleep whenever possible, day or night, in a chair, lying on a work table, anywhere—including the crawl space under the stairs of his workshop. Edison created a workshop and a workday to empower ideas and make change happen.

Leading change inside-out is what *Built to Last, Good to Great,* and *Great by Choice* author Jim Collins identified as one of Steve Jobs's most powerful leadership lessons. Speaking to one of Collins's Stanford University classes a few years after he was fired from Apple, Jobs most impressed Collins with his ability to redirect his passion away from the company that had fired him and toward the company he had *just* founded, Pixar. As Collins listened, he formulated a key lesson. Having been ousted, Jobs learned that it was not enough to be a creative genius. A change leader had to create a creative genius *culture* destined to survive him. Jobs realized: "It's not about me, it's about the company and it's about the cause. It's not about everything being dependent on me. I have to build a culture, I have to think about a successor, I have to think about setting this thing up to do well over time. And in the end, what matters is, I want Apple to be an enduring great company and prove it didn't need me."[102]

As Amazon CEO Jeff Bezos concluded in his recent annual letter to shareholders, corporate culture is key: "For better or for worse, [corporate cultures] are enduring, stable, hard to change."

Companies led by change leaders like Jobs and Bezos come down to two things: culture and people. They succeed by the health of their inside-out leadership. They empower, focus on people, guard against meetings for the sake of meetings, define their vision, and engaging with people rather than judge them. For you, the change leader, your most important customer is your *internal* customer. You sell your employees before you sell anyone else. You move your internal "soft supporters" to "hard support," because it is their empowerment that translates into the empowerment of your external customers.

Revolutions are built from the inside out. In business, fomenting revolution calls for focusing on three groups: Employees, your most valuable resource ahead of your brand and capital; Partners, your internal system of stakeholders; and Friends & Family, your external loyalists. Each of these groups must be empowered and mobilized.

I have helped developed "Friends & Family" programs for companies like Nike, Verizon, and The Coca-Cola Company and campaigns such as Vicente Fox in Mexico, Kim Dae Jung in Korea, and Barack Obama in the US. These programs centered on inspiring soft support and hard support to self-select into the club. They themselves sign up to get updates, breaking information, and detailed briefings. They *want* to be more loyal. In the case of companies, most Friends & Family want to be future change leaders. It is the wise change leader who recruits, arms, and empowers the activists of the future.

Above all, building a "Friends and Family" program is about listening, understanding perceptions, creating a dialogue with your allies, and moving your soft support to hard support, increasing loyalty, and empowering word of mouth.[103]

WIN HEARTS AND MINDS

Both inside and outside the company, recruit evangelists. They will not merely be sold by you, they will sell *for* you. Here is a Nike ad from the late 1990s, when the company was a client of ours. It could have been written by Gloria Steinem:

> A woman is often measured by the things she cannot control. She is measured by the way her body curves or doesn't curve. By where she is flat or straight or round. She is measured by 36-24-36 and inches and ages and numbers. By all the outside things that don't ever add up to who she is on the inside.
>
> And so, if a woman is to be measured, let her be measured by the things she can control. By who she is and who she is trying to become because as every woman knows, measurements are only statistics, and statistics lie.[104]

Empowering inside-out means capturing the hearts and minds of your internal and external audiences. It is a question of real belief, something you cannot achieve by spin, announcements, or press releases. Working with the Walt Disney Company, Scott Miller and I developed a definition of what creates a truly healthy and productive change culture. Change leadership must engage an entire company and the company's system. From our work with Disney, we developed a definition of such a change culture. It is one in which employees say and believe three things:

I am a part of something great.

My individual effort can make a difference.

Somebody recognizes my difference.

Driving cultural change into every corner of your organization starts in *the* corner office. *You*, the change leader, must be willing to change your own approach, to be more open, inclusive, and invariably, fundamentally truthful. Fail in these three aspects, and you will become isolated from the reality of the marketplace, the reality of your corporate culture, and the reality of a world in which the deck is heavily stacked in favor of the insurgent.

DRIVE CHANGE FROM THE CORE

Some individuals rise to the top of an organization on their own talent and energy, but sustained change leadership depends on building a solid team. We call it your core strategy group, and it is the engine of transformation for the entire organization. Like the presidential campaign's "War Room," your core strategy group must be focused, disciplined, and robust. It must represent the breadth of your business. It should drive *the* central strategy. In clear language and with impeccable logic, this core strategy defines how you will perform your mission as a company. Your mission is your destination. Your core strategy is the road map that gets you there.

Pull your core strategy group together from among the 8 percent of your most loyal *and* most productive people. If they are loyal without being particularly productive, they are disqualified. And the same goes for those who are productive without being particularly loyal. The core strategy group should consist of your most talented people. They should not be chosen simply by rank or title. You want diversity of background and viewpoint, which is a prerequisite for establishing a culture of innovation. You also want to establish a working process that is open to collaboration. So, all corporate titles are checked at the door. Core group members must be unafraid to express their opinions, even as they are prepared to listen to the frank opinions of others.

It is essential that your core strategy group is driven by data and facts, informed by creative peripheral insights, committed to openness, dedicated to aligning strategy with execution, and biased to create change in your markets and to drive innovation forward.

PREPARE FROM WITHIN

Your leadership brand begins with you. Become your own brand leader in the brand campaign of *you*. Control the definitions that flow from your leadership brand by defining yourself, defining change, defining the Election Day, and defining the future. Get and keep control of the stakeholder dialogue about you. If you do not build your own leadership brand and campaign, someone else, likely your competitor, will do it for you and, naturally, against you.

As the saying on Broadway goes, "Talent needs direction!" You cannot coach yourself any more than the 2018

World Champion Philadelphia Eagles coached themselves. Outside, objective, trusted, strategic, honest, and experienced perspective has no substitute. Even the most talented of future change leaders needs to reach out for this perspective via an executive coach or the trusted inner circle of advisors we think of as a kitchen cabinet.

Don't overlook the coach of coaches—Tony Robbins. I'm not referring to the Tony Robbins of the old infomercial days, a "motivational speaker" who was selling you cassette tapes about finding the power within. He has evolved to become perhaps history's finest "CEO coach." His approach is both simple and complex, culminating in his hosting a super-sized 5-day, 15-hour-a-day life-planning and deep-immersion event called "Date with Destiny." We recommend all Robbins's products, writings, and business mastery events, but the core of his philosophy is this: *Take control of your own destiny, your own change leadership, your own insurgency.* This means controlling what you focus on, the meaning you give to life's events, and your own physiological state. Fortunately, there's a lot of free Tony Robbins to be had on YouTube. Watch him apply these principles along with his "six fundamental human needs" to one successful intervention after another. Robbins drives his own special process of change leadership across seven steps:[105]

- Connect, understand, and appreciate "their" world—what's really going on?
- Connect and get leverage—find out what makes change a must.
- Interrupt and annihilate the limiting pattern(s)—focus, meaning, and physiology.
- Define the problem in solvable terms.

- Access the empowerment resources and make the change real—find an empowering alternative.
- Condition the change—until it becomes a habit.
- Test and check for ecology—link to a higher purpose and empowering environment.

Robbins's change strategies apply to people and to companies, organizations, and campaigns. Each step mirrors the process of change great change leaders drive from within their organizations. Each step can be put in organizational terms to drive enduring change of the kind that fuels lasting empowerment. It all begins from the inner concentric circle of the change leader himself or herself. The change leader must begin the change from within.

Cutting-edge behavioral assessment surveys and frameworks can be powerful in helping to drive this kind of change. Our friend and change leader John Hopkins is a former PricewaterhouseCoopers partner. He is founder and CEO of Inspirit Growth, a company that provides commonsense coaching for business leaders and their teams. He focuses on making strategy happen, on driving execution, and on aligning a change leader's business goals with his or her life goals. To this process, Hopkins brings science-based evaluative tools designed to understand how individuals and teams are wired. One tool, the Predictive Index (PI)[106] is a framework that goes back all the way to World War II. Arnold Daniels was a bombardier on an Eighth US Air Force B-17 flight crew when he began learning about personality and talent assessments. He noticed that the individuals and jobs on the B-17 were quite different from each other. The pilot was different from the navigator in personality and wiring, the co-pilot was different from the bombardier, and so on. Nevertheless, every one of these differently wired individuals needed a common language to survive, let alone accomplish their assigned missions.

Working with a psychologist, Daniels began focusing on why bombing missions succeed or fail. He soon discovered that assessment tools and statistical modeling can improve communications and teamwork. The war ended, but Daniels's interest in assessment did not, and, as a result of spending time at Harvard Business School, he continued to work on them. In 1955, he founded PI Worldwide, which is now the Predictive Index. Since Daniels's death in 1998, The PI has expanded to include cognitive and skills measurements as well as behavioral assessments. Today, more than 25 million PI assessments have been taken in over 70 languages in 140 counties. More than 10,000 people train in PI workshops annually. Talk about empowerment.

Hopkins is a master of PI, which he uses in his own framework designed to drive, align, and balance change leadership and execution.[107] He sees today's newest iteration of behavioral assessment tools as important weapons in your battle for change. Be aware of them. Make use of them. Science-based personality, aptitude, and behavioral assessments give you a new lens through which to evaluate people, performance, and business results. Research shows the PI becomes something like a fingerprint or DNA. It is the same from birth to death. Your wiring is your wiring—and knowing how you and others in your organization are wired will help you to focus, balance, and leverage your human assets.

Imagine the future possibilities. You can better maximize your own leadership performance and balance and synergize your innovation team, your core strategy group. Think of this in the *Moneyball* context of sports and Big Data. Today, for example, consider the number of general managers in professional baseball with Ivy League degrees, and note some teams have as many as nine professionals working on the analytics of potential recruits, trades, and roosters.

INNOVATION NEEDS A DEADLINE

Just as a campaign needs an Election Day, innovation needs a deadline. One of the great deficits in today's business world is a failure of urgency. If there is a single thing that most clearly differentiates an insurgent culture from an incumbent culture, it is a sense of urgency. In the insurgent culture, everything matters. In the incumbent culture, nothing really matters. Why so? A little startup with five people sweating in a loft thinks it can change the world or, at the least, the marketplace. But thousands and thousands of people in the air-conditioned nightmare of a giant, market-leading corporation come to feel that nothing they do really makes much difference. They think nothing much of being told that the corporation will operate more efficiently if it lays off another 2,000 people—and gives the CEO a $7 million bonus.

By contrast, change leaders know what the hurry is all about. Why? Because they are out to change things. Like, *now*. Everything they do—or fail to do—matters. Every detail is important. But so is acting on every detail. Satchel Paige, the insurgent right-handed pitching legend of the old Negro Leagues, had very good advice for fellow outliers: "Don't look back. Something might be gaining on you."

CREATE A CHANGE CULTURE

Revolutions do not come with user manuals, but the leaders of successful revolutions build on the same essential principles. Combine the wisdom of Southwest Airlines Herb Kelleher—his discipline of "Defining, Over-Delivering, and Claiming" everything his company does—Jack Welch's extremely effective "Honest Dialogue" and workout sessions, and Bill Gates's remarkable ability to "Re-Recruit" his best people at Microsoft and the Gates Foundation. Together, the framework of these three change leaders is a checklist for insurgency—five steps that can empower your people and drive innovation forward:

- *First, structure every innovation challenge as a political campaign.* Set an Election Day, an urgent deadline, and drive an insurgent campaign with focus, strategy, and discipline. Work with a core strategy group to develop your strategic destination. Find "Do the Doable" actions that will build early momentum. Identify the "Move the Movable" targets that you need to win. Above all, never play defense. Use strategy to play more offense. Transfer ownership of this strategy to your employees, so that it is not *your* strategy, but *their* strategy.
- *Second, define change and control the dialogue.* Use internal and external research to understand, anticipate, and monitor perceptions. As a change leader, define yourself, the must-win change or Election Day(s), and the future of your industry. Take control of your own leadership brand.
- *Third, develop "3 x 5 card" discipline:* Summarizing your three to four core messages and a longer-form stump speech that can be delivered anywhere, anytime, to any group. Specifically, the 3 x 5 Card should be repeated over and over. It should consist of a headline or campaign objective and four to five key bullet points: e.g., relevant benefits for stakeholders, competitive differentiation, and your definition of a better future.

- *Fourth, monitor inside-out perceptions and attitudes and stand for change.* Use research to plan and track your inside-out change leadership campaign. Focus first on understanding your hard support and what motivates them. Focus second on moving soft support to hard support; use an internal "Future Leaders" or "Friends & Family" program. Finally, ignore or fire the Hard Opposition, and when you are feeling especially courageous trim some of the Soft Opposition as well. They will not change, and they are a sinking anchor on your change leadership. Know the votes you need to win.
- *Fifth, symbolize, leverage, and empower change.* Do not be afraid to change the rules and violate corporate rituals. Disrupt rather than be disrupted. Confront the embedded fear of change. Run right at it. Moreover, reward taking the initiative and playing offense. Model our favorite Tom Peters' PowerPoint slide: "*Reward Excellent Failure, Punish Mediocre Success.*"[108]

CHAPTER TEN

RELEASE EARLY AND OFTEN

Do something. If it works, do more of it. If it doesn't, do something else.

—Franklin D. Roosevelt

Still in the throes of the Great Depression, he rises confidently to begin what will become a larger and historic rising of an entire nation. Holding tightly to the podium on the stage of Atlanta's Fox Theatre, he has minutes ago accepted an honorary degree on this night of May 22, 1932, from Oglethorpe University. The university's president, Thornwell Jacobs, has handed him his honorary degree. He had given or will later give similar degrees to William Randolph Hearst, Bernard Baruch, Walter Lippmann, Amelia Earhart, and David Sarnoff.[109]

Picture this: A nation brought to its knees by economic crisis is waiting to be inspired by a man unable to walk, currently the governor of New York, and fighting hard for his party's nomination against the more conservative Al Smith. A month before, Roosevelt began disrupting the usual political dialogue with an Albany radio address about the "forgotten man." He lambasted the idea of "trickle down" economic proposals that fail to build recovery "from the bottom up." This is a popular position. But his nation still wants more, and the disabled man senses that he needs to give them more.

Ironically, the draft emanates from those charged with writing about it: the press. Days before, Roosevelt is picnicking in Warm Springs, Georgia, with three members of the press—it is a different era from ours—who tease him about the cautious campaign speeches that have followed his provocatively inspiring "forgotten man" address. Teasing back, Roosevelt playfully challenges the writers: "Well, if you boys don't like my speeches, why don't you take a hand at drafting one yourselves?"

They do.

Reporters Ernest Lindly, Walter Brown, and Louis Ruppel produce a draft. Following his political instinct, the candidate likes it and uses it.

Now it is 7:45 p.m., and the disabled man, standing with difficulty at the podium, has delivered the customary salutations and is busy challenging boldly the established order, the status quo, the state of affairs that has delivered and deepens the Great Depression. He is just warming up. Near the end of the speech, the New York governor lifts his head high above the podium, as if speaking to someone not actually in attendance, and so begins the singing cadence that will become as famous as it is inspirational:

> "This country needs, and unless I mistake its temper, the country demands bold persistent experimentation. It is common sense to take a method and try it. If it fails, admit it frankly and try another. But above all, try something."[110]

I'd like to die on Mars—just not on impact."

—Elon Musk

I remember my dad getting choked up when he spoke about a 1.25-million-pound Union Pacific "Big Boy" articulated 4-8-8-4 steam locomotive as it began its mighty thrust forward, breaking the technological barriers of its day. He grew up seeing and feeling this remarkable paradigm shift. He was seeing the magic of innovation.

Imagine my dad watching the television screen on February 12, 2018. Anyone who dreams of going to Mars or beyond understands the technological landmark that is the "reusable booster rocket." Such boosters change the game, because they transform the economics of experimentation and execution, just as the steam locomotive, whose technological apogee was reached in 1941 with the American Locomotive Company's Big Boy, changed the game by becoming safer, cheaper, and better than the economic alternatives of riding horses or bicycling or walking.

About the time of Jesus, Hero of Alexandria described the Aeolipile, a simple, bladeless radial steam turbine. Some 1,700 years later, in 1698, Thomas Savery, in England, invented the first modern steam engine. Nearly two centuries later, they continued to drive the Industrial Revolution at a time when my dad watched them change everything, only to be replaced by engines of greater efficiency and power.

It is something to see the magnificent fire and fury of a modern rocket launch. In 1998, a friend experienced this in person, witnessing my former boss, Senator John Glenn, launch again into space at age seventy-seven. My friend described the rocket launch as like "seeing God."

Yes, it is one thing to see this mechanical god go up. But it is quite another to see it come down—under control, in one piece, landing upright and with perfection.

On February 12, 2018, the SpaceX Falcon Heavy carrying a payload called Zuma stands on the very same Cape Canaveral launch pad from which, forty-nine years earlier, Neil Armstrong, Buzz Aldrin, and Mike Collins began their journey to the moon in Apollo 11. Now, as then, there is a cheering crowd. But this day it numbers tens of thousands—the most since the launch of the final Space Shuttle—you remember the Space Shuttle—and they hear and join the count-down: 7, 6, 5, 4, 3, 2…1… Lift Off!

Up it climbs with the combined force of 18 Boeing 747s—the Jumbo Jet that debuted as a technological marvel in 1969 and was, in 2018, in the late stages of phase-out for general passenger service. Thirty-seven miles above the earth's surface, two booster rockets split away. They are now on their own mission, not up, but down, heading back to earth. At 56 miles up, the core booster turns as if it is not ready to go any farther and heads back down, too, to a drone barge awaiting it in the Atlantic Ocean. On this day, the core booster will miss its rendezvous, burned up beyond ash as it re-enters earth's molecule-dense atmosphere.

But the two booster rockets are still coming down. If they make it, returning safely, this will be a leap forward in reusable booster rockets and a breakthrough in the prospects of space travel to Mars and beyond. What happens is recorded on video. It looks like rocket launch footage run backwards. Two giant but slender-looking booster rockets simultaneously lower themselves, thrusters first, onto a landing pad. The crowd, miles away, goes crazy. They are seeing the magic of innovation. They come to rest, like something out of 1950s sci-fi space travel fantasy, coming safely to rest, upright, on their home planet earth.

"Falcons have landed!" an announcer proclaims, and MSNBC's Ari Velshi, off-camera, becomes audibly emotional. I flash back to the reaction of CBS's Walter Cronkite as Apollo 11 lands man on moon for the first time on July 20, 1969. Cronkite took off his heavy-framed glasses, wiped his eyes, and uttered the most eloquent "Whew… Boy…" in history.[111] Another commentator reporting the 2018 event summed it up less emotionally but no less truly. The landing "opens the door to a future of many other things we can and will do in space.[112]"

SpaceX is not a public but a private model of bold, persistent experimentation. It was founded by Elon Musk, an American immigrant from South Africa, an American citizen since 2002, and an American innovation legend working hard on his day job, which is the breakthrough all-electric car and solar-energy company Tesla. At this writing, Musk has resigned as Tesla's chairman to settle fraud charges brought by the US Securities and Exchange Commission over public claims he made about taking Tesla private; but Musk still remains the company's CEO and continues, often controversially, to drive innovation speeding forward.

Born on June 28, 1971, in Pretoria, Musk is in some ways today's Edison. In addition to founding Tesla and SpaceX, he is cofounder of Neuralink, a company focused on innovating brain-computer linkages, not to mention the founder of SolarCity, a solar energy services company, OpenAI, a nonprofit aimed at producing "friendly" artificial intelligence, and the Boring Company, which is working to advance infrastructure and construction through lots of bold, persistent experimentation.

Since he turned twelve, the self-taught computer programmer has been turning out software. He is a graduate of my alma mater, the Wharton School at the University of Pennsylvania, and he also earned a degree in physics from Penn's College of Arts and Science. While at Penn and Wharton, Musk found time to rent, with a classmate, a 10-bedroom fraternity house, which they transformed into an "unofficial" nightclub.[113] In 1995, he entered the PhD program in applied physics and material sciences at Stanford University—dropping out after just two days to begin changing the world of science and business.[114]

Musk's first companies, Zip2 and X.com, merged to become PayPal, which was purchased by eBay in 2002 for $1.2 billion. By 2018, Musk's net worth was $20.8 billion, according to *Forbes*.[115] That was quite a hefty sum of capital to fuel more innovation.

He launched SpaceX in 2002, inspired by science fiction author Isaac Asimov's *Foundation Series*.[116] Musk's founding vision is what he calls "Mars Oasis," a project to land an experimental greenhouse on Mars to contain and grow food crops as a prelude to an eventual colonization enterprise. He speaks of reducing the "risk of human extinction" by establishing a colony on Mars. As Musk was inspired by Asimov, his own vision inspires Ridley Scott and his 2015 science fiction movie *The Martian* (based on Andy Weir's 2011 self-published novel of the same name, which was rereleased by Crown Publishing in 2014) as well as a 2016 National Geographic television series, *Mars*.[117] As for the SpaceX rockets of today, they are the products of Musk's realization that it is better to build affordable rockets than to buy them readymade at outrageous retail prices. He calculates that the materials for a rocket represent only 3 percent of its sale price—and concludes that by applying vertical integration and the modular approach he has learned as a software engineer SpaceX can slash rocket launch prices by a factor of ten.

AGILE SOFTWARE DEVELOPMENT

The thirty-second president of the United States, who won four presidential elections, led his nation out of the Great Depression, through the New Deal, and toward victory in World War II, is, like the inventor of SpaceX, Telsa, Inc., Neuralink, SolarCity, OpenAI, and the Boring Company, a remarkable example of releasing innovation early and often. Both FDR and Musk are bold persistent experimenters. Consider: While FDR was dead long before the Digital Revolution and while Elon Musk is a product of and practitioner in it, their approaches to innovation remind us of the principles of so-called Agile software development.

Digital technology has both created and accelerated the need for rapid and continuous iterations of software products. The rigidly linear stepwise models that governed product production in the pre-digital world are simply too slow to serve the demands of digital productivity. Analog systems are stolid and stately. Digital systems are swift and agile. It is the digital model that best symbolizes our argument for innovation driven by bold persistent experimentation—enabling the release of innovative products and services as early and as often as possible. Today, change leaders must spur urgency deep into innovation and the marketing of innovation, because today's companies have no choice but to dramatically compress development and sales cycles. They must innovate and market faster. Or just drop dead—death being the ultimate absence of urgency.

I am in Hangzhou, China, near Alibaba headquarters, attending a meeting of 600 executives of Asia's largest auto companies as I prepare a keynote speech for my client, Xingda, China's largest manufacturer of steel cord, which is used in tires, timing belts, and other automotive components. One presentation surprises me. Today, the average development cycle for an automobile has contracted from four years to six *months*—and soon, the argument goes, it will likely shrink to *one* or *two* months.

This exponential contraction in development drives home the urgent need for exponential speed and agility in business. Agile software development, with attendant concepts of continuous development and continuous security, represents a powerful model and metaphor for the level and speed of innovation demanded today.

Let's dig deeper. Agile software development is an approach in which innovation requirements and solutions rapidly evolve through collaboration and self-organization[118]; it draws on powerful concepts such as adaptive experimentation and open innovation. Driven by such companies as SourceClear, iTechArt, Orases, Spire Digital, DevMynd, along with the Big Four accounting firms—Deloitte, PwC, EY, and KPMG—large consultancies, and many others, Agile is all about adaptive planning, evolutionary development, inductive innovation, early delivery, continuous improvement, and rapid and flexible response to change. It is the speed and agility FDR talked about in 1932 and Elon Musk embodied in SpaceX.

In 2002, when Musk was both becoming a US citizen and inventing SpaceX, 17 software developers met in Utah to develop an operating framework to drive software development faster, with more agility, and with stronger results. Their work culminated in a Manifesto that has evolved over time and helped guide much of software development and IT management during the last fifteen years. The Manifesto offers 12 grounding principles for managing the extraordinary challenges and opportunities at today's intersection of technology and business[119]:

- Deliver customer satisfaction by *early and continuous* delivery of valuable software.
- *Welcome changing requirements* even in late development.
- Ensure working software is *delivered frequently*—in weeks rather than months.
- Foster *close and daily cooperation* between business people and developers.
- Build projects around *motivated and trusted* individuals.
- Use *face-to-face conversation* as the best form of communication.
- Remember *working software* is the primary measure of progress.
- Drive *sustainable development* to maintain a constant pace.
- Afford *continuous attention* to technical excellence and good design.
- Remember *simplicity*—the art of maximizing the amount of work *not* done—is essential.
- Ensure best architectures, requirements, and designs emerge from *self-organizing* teams.
- Reflect regularly on how the team can become *more effective* and adjust accordingly.[120]

Notice the overlaps here with Kelly Johnson's 14 Skunk Works principles in chapter 5. And notice, too, the commonsense elements these 12 principles represent for driving innovation earlier and more often: early and continuous development, welcoming change, delivering frequently, working face-to-face in self-organized teams, continuously focusing on the measurable challenge, stripping-away complexity, and regularly reflecting and adjusting. These principles help explain the experimentation of Roosevelt and Musk, and they ground the two apparently disparate case studies that follow, telling us a great deal about the power of releasing innovation early and often.

CLARENCE BIRDSEYE: INVENTING FROZEN FOOD

We experience the legacy of the early twentieth-century entrepreneur and inventor Clarence Birdseye every time we buy a frozen pizza—or a frozen anything—at the supermarket. Strawberries in winter, peaches off-season, pineapples whenever. We can buy Maine lobster in Kansas, Alaska king crab legs in Tennessee, or Naples pizza in New Jersey. What is more, our frozen broccoli or carrots contain most of the vitamins and minerals we might get if we marched into our own gardens and yanked them out of the ground ourselves. That is, if we all had vegetable gardens and the season was right.

We owe all of this to the rough-and-ready frontiersman Clarence Birdseye—even if our local supermarkets do not stock some of Birdseye's own favorite dishes, such as porcupine, skunk, and rattlesnake. As a boy, Birdseye read and reread *Redskin and Cowboy: A Tale of the Western Plans*, an 1891 novel by the British writer G. A. Henty. At age ten, driven by a frontier imagination, he began trapping and selling live muskrats to earn enough to buy a shotgun. Later, attending Amherst College, he moved on to live rats and frogs to sell to the Biology Department.

After dropping out of college, Birdseye went to work for the US Biological Survey in Arizona and New Mexico. He developed a taste for living on the land and eating indigenous foods—including his favorite, fried rattlesnake. In 1910, Birdseye was sent to Montana's Bitterroot Valley to research the causes of Rocky Mountain spotted fever, so that ways to control the disease might be developed. At the time, spotted fever was killing 72 percent of those who contracted it, and Birdseye and his team risked their lives in the field to discover how the disease spreads and how it might be controlled. Later, in 1912, Birdseye's moved his adventures north and east to remote Labrador. Sparsely inhabited, disconnected, poor, and freezing, Labrador was far from paradise. Here, Birdseye worked with a medical missionary, Wilfred Grenfell, to aid in the survival and welfare of residents. One of Grenfell's projects especially intrigued Birdseye—a fox-farming experiment intended to provide income for impoverished residents.

Unquestionably, foxes were a step up from muskrats, rats, and frogs. So, borrowing $750, Birdseye moved to bone-chilling Labrador to set up his own fox farm. He quickly discovered that farming foxes does not work. They are either exorbitantly expensive or downright impossible to trap, and the fox pups have a discouraging tendency to die. Still, Birdseye persisted in experimenting, traveling by dogsled across the tundra in 40-below weather, searching for…something.

One thing he positively relished was the Labrador tradition of extreme frontier eating: fried rabbit livers, fresh and salt fish, seal meat, partridge, ducklings, wild goose, snipe, porcupine, beaver, otter, skunk, lynx, hawk, owl, and—perhaps his favorite—"fish and brewis," a combination of salt cod, hardtack, and salt pork baked together and served with lumps of fat. Less appetizing, even for Birdseye, are what he designated as his "emergency rations": stewed chipmunk and seagull gravy.

Then something struck Clarence Birdseye. The native Inuit use traditional ice fishing to find food, but in midwinter, the minus 40 temperatures freeze their catch in mere seconds, even as they haul the fish up through the hole in the ice. Astoundingly, Birdseye discovers, these fast-frozen fish taste fresh when they are finally defrosted and cooked. He further observes that fish caught and frozen in the warmer weather of spring and fall, are of much poorer quality when thawed and cooked.

Breakthrough! Food frozen right away retains its taste, texture, and nutritional characteristics, whereas fish that is slowly frozen becomes tasteless, mushy, and, in fact, less nutritional—if you can even compel yourself to eat the unpalatable meal.

But breakthrough is not execution. Birdseye's frontier epiphany is only the beginning of years of bold persistent experimentation. And it takes him time to get started. In 1920, having returned to the United States, Birdseye begins working with the US Fisheries Association, a group lobbying on behalf of commercial fishermen. He becomes increasingly concerned about the problem of getting fresh fish to market in an edible condition—concerned enough that, in 1923, he quits the association and founds his own company, General Seafoods.

His focus is finding a solution to the "quality-to-market" shipping problem by designing a special container to keep fish fresher. It is progress, yes, but proves to be only a partial answer. Falling short in this first attempt at a solution, Birdseye finally connects the dots, recalling his Labrador epiphany. In his own kitchen, he embarks on endless experiments with quick freezing. After many attempts, he succeeds in "flash-freezing" small amounts of food. Good! But scaling up the process will not be cheap. In need of funding, Birdseye and his wife sell their house and their life insurance policy. They move to Gloucester, Massachusetts, determined either to make it in the frozen seafood business or go down trying.

Gloucester offers two enormous advantages. The cost of living here is far lower than in New York, and all the fish he can ever want are right at hand. His first attempt at scaling up involves passing foods through two metal plates cooled by the hazardous ammonia-based refrigeration process of the day. It works, but he needs something on an industrial scale. Little more than a decade earlier, Henry Ford introduced the moving assembly line to automobile production. Birdseye replaces the stationary refrigerated plates with a pair of conveyer belts that are cooled with a continuous spray of calcium chloride solution. This way, large amounts of food can be continuously, quickly, and effectively flash-frozen.

But how to get the frozen product to market?

Birdseye innovates new forms of packaging to keep frozen food frozen en route to the grocery store. After many tries, he finally persuades DuPont to make a waterproof cellophane that is not damaged by contact with frozen food. Wonderful! But he is left with two problems. First, there is no supply chain for frozen food. Grocery stores of the 1920s have no freezers, and the refrigerator cars the railroads offer are both hard to find and inadequate in function. They cannot maintain the necessary freezing air temperature. Second, even if the supply chain can be created, how will Birdseye persuade people to buy and eat frozen food? After all, everybody knows that frozen food tastes awful—and frozen fish is simply not worth eating. How to overcome a bad rep that dates from an early and infamous attempt to freeze food? In 1861, Thomas Sutcliffe Mort built a large ice plant in Sydney, Australia. Seven years later, he sent his first shipment of frozen meat to England. It was edible but unpalatable—and therefore cheap, fit for the poor. But only the poor. Some years later, in 1882, New Zealand farmers began shipping tons of frozen lamb and mutton to London. It came to be called "colonial meat" and found consumers in London's Southwark and Spitalfields slums, but would never be served upon Queen Victoria's table or to diners at Wiltons in St. James's.

In the United States, freezing is used to preserve fish, but at the cost of texture and taste. As formidable as the technological problems have been, the marketplace stigma seems insuperable.

Then comes another breakthrough. In the spring of 1929, just before the Stock Market Crash that ushers in the Great Depression, Birdseye sells his company and patents to the Postum Cereal Corporation. The firm is soon renamed General Foods Corporation, and Birdseye's products are renamed along with it. They are now called "Birds Eye Frosted Foods." Mmmm. *Frosted?* This was a much more pleasant image and concept than *frozen!*

Although he sells his company, Birdseye retains a financial interest and an executive position. He has new allies in his weakest areas of business—finance, marketing, and supply chain management. Soon, he becomes a millionaire driving a Packard in the depths of the Depression, a lovely time to be rich. He could kick back and revel in the good life. Instead, he spends most of his time in laboratories, developing an inexpensive freezer that General Foods rents to grocery stores, and, between 1932 and 1934, he invents more than 100 new types of frozen foods.

In fact, Clarence Birdseye invents not merely a product or set of products or even a company. He invents an entire *frozen food industry*. It is nothing short of a revolution in the way foods are manufactured and marketed—foods that taste fresh, are quickly prepared, and available anytime and anywhere people want them.

JAMES DYSON: DRIVEN BY BETTER

James Dyson always wanted to change something. After losing his classics instructor father at age nine, Dyson receives a free education at the boarding school where his father taught,

Gresham's School in Holt, Norfolk, UK. To survive there, he must toughen-up, rely on himself, prove something, and above all learn the power of persistence. A long-distance runner, he applies the persistence this sport demands, and he learns lessons that will re-enter his life at key times.

As Thomas Edison did not invent but improved electric lighting, James Dyson did not invent the vacuum cleaner—he *improved* it. In 1979, when he began innovating this invention, the electric vacuum cleaner is already more than eighty years old and dominated by two big and in-the-center incumbents, Hoover and Electrolux. Between them, these two companies own the market and control the status quo.

Dyson has an insurgent idea. What if he can make the vacuum cleaner better by increasing suction and getting rid of the bag? What if he can reinvent this eighty-year-old invention? His impetus is frustration. Dyson notices his own vacuum works efficiently only after a new bag is inserted. After several uses with the new bag, the vacuum fills and clogs with hair and dirt, which constrict airflow and suction.

Like Edison, Dyson believes in the power of prototypes. And it takes him exactly 5,127 prototypes, many constructed in his backyard shed, before he reaches success. The sustained effort pulls his family into debt. He bets his house on a future innovation. But at the end of a long and anxious road he develops a better vacuum cleaner.

Dyson's first prototype is a crude combination of cardboard and scotch tape, all hooked up to a Hoover. But it shows signs of working. His theory is that "cyclone technology" will out-perform conventional vacuum cleaners with their quickly clogging bags. After proving the concept, he must advance his innovation, again like Edison, one prototype at a time. There is no revolutionary breakthrough, only evolutionary progress. It is inductive innovation.

How does he do it?

A crucial career pivot comes when his early boss and mentor, Jeremy Fry—much like Kelly Johnson's early boss, Hall Hibbard—makes a mission of hiring young and fresh-thinking workers. He also has an innovation project going on the side, designing what he calls a Sea Truck, a fast-landing water craft. From Fry's mentorship, Dyson learns an important lesson: "You don't think about doing something—you do it!"[121]

So, how does Dyson do it?

He begins to do it. He starts by innovating a new kind of wheelbarrow that uses a spherical wheel. He calls it a "BallBarrow." From here, Dyson performs a series of bold persistent experiments through a life of innovation. He visits sawmills and cement factories to study the large cyclone device they use to suck dust from their factory floor. Once, he even climbs a high fence to study the 30-foot-high cone that spins dust out of the air by centrifugal force to expel waste. He sketches and prototypes his way to a version of this that is the size of a standard vacuum cleaner for the home.

Over these years, Dyson studies Thomas Edison, and he consciously applies to his work the Wizard of Menlo Park's approach to innovation. He works across prototype after prototype, convinced that he can bring the principle of cyclonic separation to home vacuum cleaners. Proclaiming to his first group of investors that he has solved the problem of the vacuum cleaner, they respond by kicking him out of the very company he helped to found.

Dyson takes his firing as good news. Circling back to his mentor, Dyson asks Fry to borrow money on his behalf and help him continue pushing ahead. More prototypes emerge from his backyard shed. Steadily, the machines get better and better.

Debt, rejection, and setback drive more and more boldness. More persistence. More experimentation.

Eventually, Dyson begins selling his vacuums through a Japanese company, Apex, for the ridiculous price in today's currency of $6,000 per model, far beyond anything the marketplace is likely to bear. So, he drives on to even more experimentation—all focused on a single idea: "Say goodbye to the bag." He develops a model with trademarked Dual Cyclone technology, the DC01, to the point at which it is a premium-priced, but not ridiculously priced, product, and it becomes the number one vacuum in the UK. Within two years of its introduction there, it earns $100 million in annual revenues.

Dyson makes his next market move into the vast US presence, first via Best Buy. That large chain's purchase is triggered after one worker takes the model home and immediately swears that it does everything as promised. As the Dyson catches on, the tireless inventor applies to it his wheelbarrow-transforming Ball™ technology. He goes on to create a cordless vacuum, a robot vacuum, and a hand-held vacuum.

Bear in mind that he is not making a pure technology play or creating some exponential digital platform. His is a series of innovations upon an old-fashioned and familiar product in almost all our homes. "What attracted me [to vacuum cleaners] was that they were an unloved object," he recounts in 2014. "Manufacturers made them. They didn't really care what they are making. They were just copying each other. It had become a commodity. I got really excited about that."

You should get excited, too. When a product devolves into a mere commodity, consumers are deprived of choices. Since consumers—especially today's consumers—crave control, they demand choices, and the first provider of credible choices will likely get their attention, premium price and all.

How far can this be taken?

Today, the Dyson 360 Eye™ robot vacuum offers "twice the suction of any other robot vacuum." It has Dyson's innovative V2 motor and eight cyclones for suction. It is called the 360 Eye because it uses a live-vision camera on the top that scans the room using Simultaneous Localization and Mapping (SLAM) technology. The camera's shutter speed is 30 frames per second, precisely matching the speed of the vacuum and making its position accurate to within 2 inches. Moreover, the technology can be paired with an app and remotely controlled by the touch of a finger or the command of a voice. The app can be used to schedule start times, and it will download software updates as they are distributed. Today, Dyson continues to change-lead innovation with products such as the Airblade hand dryer, the Air Multiplier fan, and the Dyson Supersonic hair dryer.

"50 percent of everything I do is wrong," Dyson recently admitted. So what? Persistence gets him the other 50 percent, much as what passed for Edison's genius was 99 percent perspiration. "I was a long-distance runner at school," Dyson recalls. "And when you feel tired you should accelerate—that's when you start winning. I've learned this with development of new technology. When you feel like giving up, it is at precisely this point that everyone else gives up—and that's when you should put in extra effort. You do that, and success is lying just around the corner."

FIRST: EARLY AND OFTEN MEANS FASTER

I was attending an elite business mastery seminar in Palm Springs with a hundred hard-charging CEO types. We were being asked to do something strange. Broken up into groups of eight around tables, we were given an array of stuff—

junk, really—and told to build the highest structure possible in eight minutes.

I flashed back to the scene from Ron Howard's *Apollo 13* (1995). NASA engineers must save the three astronauts after a major malfunction. The most immediate crisis is a failure of the spacecraft's CO_2 "scrubber," which removes carbon dioxide from the cabin. The buildup of this gas is killing the astronauts. The engineers know that they can cannibalize parts from the scrubber in the main capsule to repair the scrubber in the Lunar Excursion Module (LEM), which is serving as the astronauts' "lifeboat." The problem is that the scrubber in the LEM has a square hole and the one in the main capsule is round. It is a classic jury-rigging problem: how to fit a square peg in a round hole.

The NASA engineers are gathered in a war room. Several of them dump four boxes filled with the same stuff the three trapped astronauts have in their LEM up in space. "Ok people, listen up. The people upstairs handed us this one, and we gotta' come through. We gotta' find a way to make this"—the engineer holds up a square scrubber filter—"fit into this hole"—round—"for this"—the LEM scrubber—"using nothing but that." The speaker indicates the pile of miscellaneous crap on the table.[122]

Our task in Palm Beach was not actually life-or-death. But in a room full of hyper-competitive hot-shot leaders, it sure felt that way. The eight of us at our table dived into the jury-rigging, organizing, and plotting. How to build a strong foundation? How to delegate phases of this eight-minute job? How to get folks working together as a team? And then noticing that a team at a nearby table was already building something now twice as high as ours.

We try to work faster. But another table wins. The winners, we are told, are not Silicon Valley software engineers or a gaggle of MIT graduates. They are not even in the room with us. They are children, aged six to ten, who won because they approached the task by just getting to work. They started by starting to do something. There was no time spent on figuring out who is in charge, reading organizational politics, or creating a checklist of who does what. The kids just started playing, creating, following their instincts.

They possessed, naturally, the power of speed and urgency of FDR's "do something" exhortation and Elon Musk's answer to this question:

> Q: How did you learn about rockets?
> A: I read books.[123]

Musk began by reading books. Clarence Birdseye dogsledded across Labrador when it was 40 below. James Dyson declared, "You don't think about doing something—you do it!"

"Anything which tends to slow work down is waste," Thomas Edison wrote in 1926. Right. If urgency is an essential missing element in much innovation today, then speed must be the game changer.

Build urgency and speed into the heart of your culture. Do something. Never leave a meeting or conversation without a "by when?" answer to who will do what by when. Set an Election Day or Election Days, so that you treat innovation as a deadline. This also means shifting from *should* to *must*, and from *hope* to *do-or-die*. It means *Doing the Doable* to create magical momentum and *Moving the Movable* to move only the votes or consumers you need to win. It means beating back the lack of urgency inside big incumbent companies and yanking up the remarkably low 8 percent of all corporate projects that, in fact, ever reach their stated goals.[124]

SECOND: CHANNEL YOUR OWN VERSION OF AGILE DEVELOPMENT

There is an axiom in show business: The performers who perform the most are the best. They have the most experience. They have seen and done and felt everything—what can go right, what can go wrong—and they know how to be in the moment and handle any challenge and any opportunity with agility. It is the same with pilots, surgeons, and consultants. The man or women with the most hours logged, the most experience in the heat of the battle, the pilot who has flown in every kind of weather, the surgeon who has faced every kind of "unpredictable" medical complication, the consultant who has seen every kind of crisis or meltdown—hire *them*. Hire experience. As Malcolm Gladwell wrote in his 2008 *Outliers: The Story of Success,* doing something hard for 10,000 hours carries one beyond "expert" to "phenom."

It is the same with the Agile software development. This approach, once a radical idea and now a Silicon Valley best practice, gets better with experience. It gains speed, agility, clarity, and success the more it is used and the more data and knowledge and experience it gains. The 12 principles that ground Agile software development shine through in the examples of Birdseye and Dyson: early and continuous development, welcoming change, delivering frequently, working face-to-face in self-organized teams, continuously focusing on the measurable challenge, stripping-away complexity, and regularly reflecting and adjusting.

All 12 Agile principles apply as much to marketing as they do to innovation. Business partner Scott Miller and I learned the power of this in the 1990s with something Scott called "Momentum Marketing." Working with the chairman of one of the top beer companies, we learned that their average product launch involved at minimum a $40 million investment. And most of the launches failed. Talk about an expensive, slow way to learn. Clearly, an alternative was needed. So, we built a new framework that resembles Agile software development. It allows us to launch, test, refine, and launch again the company's latest new products with maximum effect and minimum investment in both time and money.

Momentum Marketing prototypes marketing, as Edison prototyped innovation and Agile developers develop and release software iterations—never intending any one iteration to be final. For the beer producer, we always started small, in a discrete test market of local bars and with drinkers who represent Undecided consumers. We introduced a new elixir, often with an early version of its new packaging, and we looked for one thing: *momentum*. If the product created early interest and pull-through attraction, we began loading more and more resources into it—much as you might prototype a new light bulb, a new frozen food, a new form of customer service, or a new vacuum cleaner. Conversely, if the product stalled or was confusing or failed to gain traction, we ruthlessly pulled it and replaced it with another new product. It was all about momentum, which was all about agility and gaining speed.

Consider these three additional examples:

RED BULL

In 1987, Red Bull was confronted by one barrier after another to US marketplace entry. Like an Agile software developer, Red Bull and its founder, Dietrich Mateschitz, swarmed and probed and claimed ground wherever they could. First, they failed to get traditional distribution through Coke or Pepsi bottlers. So, they went to beer distributors. Next, they failed to get placement in supermarkets. So, they went into liquor stores.

Following this, after they failed to communicate adequate marketing differentiation, they presented Red Bull as an energy drink "mixer." And when they failed to get into restaurants, they gave away free samples to dance club bouncers and bartenders. Finally, when they failed to get a major sports sponsorship, they invented a sports category all their own: extreme street sports. *Agility* describes this *take-what-they-give-you* approach.

APPLE

In 1997, when founder Steve Jobs returned to begin the greatest corporate turnaround in modern business history, he moved fast. Very, very fast. First, Jobs unconsciously anticipated Agile software development's tenth principle—*simplicity*—the art of maximizing the amount of work *not* done. He whittled down Apple's clumsy strategic plan with its more than one hundred core elements to only three or four. Second, he anticipated Agile software development's fourth and fifth principles: Foster *close and daily cooperation* between business people and developers and build projects around *motivated and trusted* individuals. The iconic advertising campaign Jobs crafted with Chiat Day in 1997—"Think Different"—reminds Apple loyalists *and employees* what makes them special. Finally, Jobs did one more thing—and it was simple, and it was cheap. At a time when all computers were a dull beige, Jobs produced iMac computers in a choice of colors. Soon, mothers and grandmothers were asking husbands and grown-up kids for one of "those nice-looking Macintoshes."

CVS

In 2014, not only did our former client lead the entire retail pharmacy industry with its courageous decision to stop selling tobacco products (predicting an initial $2 billion hit to revenues), but today CVS has expanded from retail heath care to patient advocacy. Moving fast, with agility, CVS launches innovation early and often. For instance, the chain sells less expensive alternatives to the outrageously costly EpiPen; it pulls off its shelves sun screens with an SPF below 15; it stops selling products with parabens, phthalates, and similar substances; it stops selling food products containing trans fats. “We think about the customer first,” says Helena Foulkes, the CVS Pharmacy President.[125]

The reward? The retailer earned a 2.5 percent increase in overall sales and a 7 percent increase in food purchases—not to mention its pending (as of this writing) $68 billion acquisition of Aetna.

THIRD: SURGE

There is a precious window of opportunity for every innovation and marketing initiative. The stories of Birdseye and Dyson all display an inflection point, a pivot, a moment of truth at which the leader must ramp it all the way up to 200 on a scale of 100. What is done or not done at this point provides or fails to provide the all-critical first mover advantage—the thing that often makes or breaks a company.

Red Bull, Apple, CVS, each faced a critical Election Day or set of such days. Like Roger Bannister, each crossed the finish line. Election Day, finish line? Maybe it’s even more effective to think in such military terms as “D-Day” or “Surge.” In 1944, D-Day was the ultimate moment of truth, in which the allies’ bold and precise military planning bent history. Even so, at Omaha Beach, the Americans’ main landing beach, plans quickly prove flawed, and it is the agility of the commanders and soldiers on the ground that saves the day. Similarly, in 2007 General David Petraeus directs the “Surge,” a highly successful major shift in US Iraq War strategy, combining more troops and more aggressive tactics with a sincere effort to win the support of the local Iraqi Sunnis. Resources are piled on in a shorter timeframe, a compression that yields the first real military success for the US since the invasion of 2003. Leadership and planning are essential, but it is the agility of the troops on the ground that ensures the Surge is a success.

My advice is to apply the military metaphors of D-Day or Surge in ways more horizontal than vertical, so that you can lay on maximum agility, adjusting, refining, testing, and revising as necessary, in real time, while continuing to build all-critical momentum.

D-Day may be "launched," but you need to recognize the ongoing inflection points or moments of truth, which should be your triggers to "Surge." In innovation terms, this affords maximum focus and urgency. In marketing terms, it means preparing and launching a strategic Surge as the equivalent of the successful launch of a blockbuster movie. Working backwards from the premiere, which is the Election Day, movie studios devote as many resources as possible to a short pre-launch ramp-up. They pile trailers on top of ad campaigns, on top of product-placement deals and co-branding promotions, on top of interviews. It all happens fast and compact. The studio maximizes resources to load in every possible way the means of seizing attention, clustering and compacting advertising, media, celebrity interviews, and previews across a shorter time frame for a more powerful result. When you think of a marketing Surge, picture driving a spike through the heart of the marketplace.

Election Day, D-Day, Surge. Build your capacity to exploit the designated moments of inflection. Then deploy. Play offense, move to the attack, accelerate your strategic execution—and take time now to read the next and final chapter of this book. It will tell you how to punctuate your equilibrium, pulling everything you have into one point of focus that surges forward to the next new success.

CHAPTER ELEVEN

PUNCTATE YOUR EQUILIBRIUM

Never confuse motion with action.

—Benjamin Franklin

He was a bedraggled runaway who came from nothing. Author, inventor, scientist, diplomat, entrepreneur, American founding father. Older than the other American founding fathers, he provided wise counsel and spiritual energy. He leavened the imperial Washington, the cerebral Jefferson, and the bull-headed Adams. One dares speculate that, without Benjamin Franklin, the Declaration of Independence, the Treaty of Paris, and the US Constitution might never have come into being. Of all the founders, Franklin is the only signer of all three documents. So, let's go further. Without Franklin, the United States might never have come to birth or at least to a birth as extraordinary.

Franklin has a brand. He's often called "The First American" because of his passion for colonial unity and plans for creating a federal model of government for a nation that promises opportunity and, with remarkable consistency, delivers on that promise. Even now, we hear him through his words, letters, and Autobiography*. When we are at our best, we see a reflection of Franklin in ourselves. Most important, we who study him marvel at his ability to redefine himself, redefine a challenge, and ultimately redefine America.*

He was an indefatigable innovator—investigator of electricity; creator of bifocal glasses; founder of the Library Company of Philadelphia, the nation's oldest library; innovator and marketer of the Franklin stove, a breakthrough in heating efficiency; inventor of fire and life insurance; early advocate of inoculation; tireless searcher after cures for the common cold; printer; publisher; and creator of the celebrated Poor Richard's Almanac, *a periodical that served colonial America in much the same way that the social web serves the nation today. His curiosity was boundless. He was a student of demography, oceanography, and meteorology. He innovated theories of phenomena as diverse as light waves, temperature, and decision-making. In his eighty-four years, as his most recent biographer, Walter Isaacson, concludes, Franklin was America's foremost scientist, inventor, diplomat, writer, business strategist, and practical political thinker.*[126]

What he understood best was urgency. At the signing of the Declaration of Independence, he replied to John Hancock's admonition that the signatories must now all hang together. "Yes," Franklin quipped, "we must, indeed, all hang together, or most assuredly we shall all hang separately."[127] *It was not an idle joke. Franklin well knew that, if captured, all 56 signers would suffer execution. In fact, five were captured by the British and tortured before they died. A dozen had their homes ransacked and burned, two lost their sons to the British, one had two sons captured, and nine fought and died in the Revolution, either from wounds or the hardships of the campaign. For Benjamin Franklin, innovation was a deadly serious necessity.*

It's now or never.

—Elvis Presley

In his paradigm-shifting *On the Origin of Species* (1859), Charles Darwin described biological evolution as the product of natural selection, a process that occurs over a very long time as individual genetic variations result in certain biological adaptations that increase an organism's chances of surviving to reproductive maturity. In this way, survival-promoting genetic changes tend to proliferate through multiple generations, eventually creating new species. This happens over hundreds of thousands or even millions of years.

Now, relative to this cosmically glacial pace of evolution, individual mutations are sudden. Yet it has always been assumed that the evolution of a species invariably takes many millennia. This assumption is called "phyletic gradualism," and it is, to this day, the mainstream view among evolutionary scientists. In 1972, however, insurgent paleontologists—there are insurgents in every field—Niles Eldredge and Stephen Jay Gould published a paper on what they called "Punctuated Equilibrium." They presented an argument almost as heretical as evolution itself had been something over a hundred years earlier. The most significant evolutionary changes, they posited, those that create new species, occur rarely yet rapidly—at least relative to the very slow pace of geological time. These changes, by which species split into branches, some branches destined to survive and evolve further, others to die off, cannot be imagined by picturing a smooth curve of evolutionary change. Punctuated Equilibrium is more jaggedly incremental and might be charted as a stepped curve.

The concept of Punctuated Equilibrium remains controversial in evolutionary science, but various students of management have seized on it as an analog to illustrate how business organizations typically evolve slowly during periods of little change—but undergo dramatically disruptive rapid evolution in environments or periods of upheaval.[128] Others have been even more specific, citing *technological innovation* as a frequent trigger of instability, which prompts or necessitates the rapid evolution—the "disruption"—of business and market paradigms.[129]

Through most of geological time on earth, evolution moved slowly. Why? Because the planet was not usually a very disruptive environment. This changed, for example, some 66 million years ago when an eight-mile-wide asteroid created what is now the Gulf of Mexico. The asteroid's impact raised a cloud of debris so dense and widespread that it blocked out the sun, brought a period of lethal cold, created a famine, and rapidly sent the dinosaurs into extinction.

Our civilization has been pummeled by historical asteroids—wars, revolutionary ideas (Copernicus and Galileo come to mind), religious reformation, and so on. When steam-driven technology entered the scene early in the eighteenth century, the Industrial Revolution quickened the pace and volume of these figurative "asteroid" impacts. As technology grew, so did the tempo of incoming disruption. When the Industrial Revolution gave way to the Digital Revolution, in whose midst we find ourselves, our businesses, and our politics, civilization, and enterprise all accelerated under a veritable asteroid shower. In Darwinian *evolution,* disruption is the rare *but* highly significant exception. In the Digital Revolution, disruption is the common *and* highly significant rule.

Nature has a bias toward stability until it encounters a disruption of sufficient magnitude to be a "speciation event," a change that punctuates the prevailing equilibrium with a sudden evolutionary jump. Once the new species appears, it tends toward stability, slowing down evolutionary change for much of that species' history. This is called stasis, a biological metaphor of the status quo.

The key moment in Punctuated Equilibrium is called cladogenesis, the splitting of one species into a "clade"—a group of organisms with a common ancestor that forms a new branch on the tree of life. A speciation event does not prompt a species to transform itself, but to split into two distinct species. Cladogenesis is rare—but it is exponential when it occurs. Like Thomas Kuhn's paradigm shift, Punctuated Equilibrium is the opposite of phyletic gradualism. Evolutionary scientists including Ernst Mayr in 1954 and Eldredge and Gould in 1972 point out that the effect of the sudden jump is diluted in central and mainstream populations. The effects of cladogenesis tends to stabilize as the products of sudden evolution are diluted by the population's large size and by interbreeding among like creatures.

By contrast, however, smaller populations in the isolated periphery are decoupled from this general trend toward the stability of dilution. Because these isolated populations are separated geographically from the larger group, they undergo changes that create a survival advantage as they face a more brutal natural selection. As a result, they are less likely to interbreed and more likely to experience the rare sudden jumps of species evolution without "restoration" of the status quo. Viruses, some argue, are examples of this. They come into being away from the center of organic life and therefore evolve mainly through sudden jumps.[130]

Some scientists argue that Punctuated Equilibrium occurs more frequently at phylogenetic levels *above* the species. This view holds that evolution proceeds more rapidly in terms of new Classes, Orders, Families, or Genera of organisms—the four phylogenetic sets (in order of descending size) of which Species is a subset. As Darwin observed in the first edition of *On the Origin of Species*,[131] "Species of different genera and classes have not changed at the same rate, or in the same degree."[132] In short, species are generally stable and change little over millions of years, but this leisurely pace is "punctuated" by a rapid burst of change that results in a new species. Evolution of this kind occurs in bursts, or not at all. Significant change happens in these rare and sudden jumps forward.

PUNCTUATE YOUR EQUILIBRIUM

Does this excursion into evolutionary biology sound familiar in the context of business, innovation, and marketing? It is my final metaphor.

The theory of Punctuated Equilibrium echoes much of the argument carried on throughout this book. It implies change is not easy, but it is also not accidental. Change comes when we are challenged, when we get out—or are forced out—to the creative periphery, away from the bureaucratized center, when we decouple from stabilization, when we create a change leader culture around us, and when we do something. Change happens when we create momentum, move to the attack, and play offense.

My argument to you is that, if you would lead change, you must line up your own Punctuated Equilibrium. Today, the traditional approaches to R&D and innovation are broken, crushed by the asteroid of the Digital Revolution; therefore, innovation needs innovating. Fortunately, such innovation can be taught, and innovation itself thereby accelerated.

I have already summoned a wide array of global sources and examples. Reflect on them in the context of Punctuated

Equilibrium. My argument is that change and innovation and marketing happen and happen at their best out in the creative periphery, in the outer concentric circle of the organization, where disruption is born and flourishes.

I argue that creating your own Punctuated Equilibrium requires the hand of an insurgent change leader. To change, you must borrow and apply principles of insurgency, which have worked throughout history to build, among so many other organizations, the world's greatest companies, driving innovation breakthroughs across the ages.

The examples of such change leaders are numerous and varied—from Abraham Lincoln to Galileo Galilei and Thomas Kuhn; from Billy Joel and Thomas Edison to Richard Branson and the Wright brothers; from Bill Gates and Kelly Johnson to Steve Jobs and Jeff Bezos; from Bob Beamon and Madame Curie to Roger Bannister and Albert Einstein; and from Gloria Steinem and George S. Patton Jr. to Franklin Roosevelt, Elon Musk, and Benjamin Franklin.

I argue that innovation must, as Peter Drucker implored, be about marketing, about stealing the very best thinking from the very best marketers and then looking at it, admiring it, understanding it, and then using it to deliver perceived benefits to your customer. This success provides the leverage of every single step forward in your innovation. Innovation without marketing fails.

I argue for the power of channeling your own Agile software development framework aimed at your products and services *and* your business model: Early and continuous development, welcoming change, delivering frequently, working in self-organized teams, focusing on the measurable challenges, stripping-away complexity, and regularly reflecting and adjusting and then adjusting some more.

Finally, I argue for the practical. Over some three decades, I have seen this innovation and marketing movie before, so I offer as many spoilers as possible. Each strategic principle about innovation and marketing is followed by a tactical "how-to-do-it" step. Without action, there is no motion, no innovation, no change. Out of it all, I believe you find three large lessons to take to your innovation bank.

LESSON 1: CROSS YOUR DISCIPLINES

My previous book, *Creating Business Magic,* focused on translating the lessons of the world's greatest magicians to business.[133] Well, why not? There is astounding synergistic power in crossing disciplines. Above all else, it forces you to channel a change leader's curiosity.

Years ago, I worked with Walter Isaacson on several projects. There is no better biographer writing today. He connects a key thread between his biographies of Benjamin Franklin, Albert Einstein, Leonardo da Vinci, and Steve Jobs. All of his subjects display, he says, "almost childlike curiosities." Franklin crossed science with statesmanship to fuel brilliant innovating. Einstein, stuck on an equation, picked up his violin to play Mozart and thereby found his way out of the problem by reconnecting with the universe. Da Vinci borrowed from his work on anatomical drawings, including the dissection of lips, while struggling some fourteen years to paint the world's most famous smile on the face in history's most famous painting.[134]

As for Steve Jobs, he borrowed continually from his early visits to Japan, his study of calligraphy, and memories of a rebellious youth. On June 12, 2005, delivering one of history's most watched and re-watched commencement addresses, knowing he is very sick, Jobs offers one big piece of advice for the Stanford graduates who lean in, listening for the future meaning of their lives.[135]

Jobs recalls for his audience his youthful memories of the *Whole Earth Catalog*, a bible for his generation, assembled by Steward Brand using typewriter, scissors, and a Polaroid camera. The iconic catalog was about to cease publication when Jobs was 22, the same age as the Stanford graduates he now addresses. He talks of how he absorbed the headline from the final issue, printed beneath a photograph of an early morning country road, a road along which the twenty-two year old might hitchhike. It says, "Stay Hungry. Stay Foolish." Jobs tells his graduates: "And I have always wished that for myself. And now, as you graduate to begin anew, I wish that for you: Stay Hungry. Stay Foolish."[136]

The change leaders of this generation and the next must stay hungry and foolish.

LESSON 2: AWAKEN YOUR INNER INSURGENT

"I hold it that a little rebellion now and then is a good thing," Thomas Jefferson wrote to James Madison on January 30, 1787, "and as necessary in the political world as storms in the physical."[137] Today, this has become, if anything, truer than ever before.

Today, it is in the "little rebellion" of the upstarts and the startups that the inertia of change resides. Insurgents and change leaders have never had more advantage—strategically, tactically, and in terms of innovation and marketing—than they do right now.

I argue that it is the insurgent change leaders who hold the advantages in the current business environment. To begin with, they have a lot less to lose and, conversely, a lot more to gain. Consider the words Jeff Bezos wrote more than two decades ago in his annual letter to shareholders:

> To invent you have to experiment, and if you know in advance that it's going to work, it's not an experiment. Most large organizations embrace the idea of invention but are not willing to suffer the string of failed experiments necessary to get there. Outsized returns often come from betting against conventional wisdom, and conventional wisdom is usually right. Given a 10 percent chance of a 100 times payoff, you should take that bet every time. But you're still going to be wrong nine times out of ten. We all know that if you swing for the fences, you're going to strike out a lot, but you're also going to hit some home runs. The difference between baseball and business, however, is that baseball has a truncated outcome distribution. When you swing, no matter how well you connect with the ball, the most runs you can get is four. In business, every once in a while, when you step up to the plate, you can score 1,000 runs.[138]

To score 1,000 runs today, you must be a change leader. In innovation and marketing, you are either on the attack as an insurgent or on the defensive as an incumbent, a bigness leader. Change leaders awaken their inner insurgent. They take chances, reward risk, constantly re-evaluate, think informally, hate bureaucracy, define success, communicate inside-out, value speed, bolster vision, use surprise, build momentum, and love change. In innovation and marketing, never play defense. Always play offense.

LESSON 3: STRENGTHEN YOUR MINDSET

Innovation and change leadership begin with you and from within. Gazing into a cloudy crystal ball, we see remarkable economic and political turmoil, down markets, and unprecedented and unpredictable change, distraction, and stress all coming at us. In the future, the focus, strength, and resilience of the change leader will be more important than ever. Now is the time to focus, discipline, and bolster your inner change leader.

Winter is coming, as sure as the only two certainties Franklin asserted—death and taxes. Our best chance for survival and victory is focusing on what we ourselves can control. Bring to battle your inner gladiator. Carry into combat all the lessons of this book.

Channel as well your inner Edison by assuming the role of genius and driving inductive innovation. This means step-by-step progress, prototyping, workshopping, remembering that while Edison invented the incandescent electric lamp, the phonograph, and motion picture technology, his progress was more evolutionary than revolutionary. Like him, drive steady, relentless progress.

As our friend Tony Robbins advises, manage your physiology, manage what you focus on, and manage the meaning you ascribe to what comes at you. Work out and center yourself. Shed the distractions. Stay optimistic—if only because every single change leader modeled in these pages was or is at heart an optimist. White House staffers heard President Ronald Reagan tell this joke "a thousand times":

The joke concerns twin boys of five or six. Worried that the boys had developed extreme personalities—one was a total pessimist, the other a total optimist—their parents took them to a psychiatrist.

First the psychiatrist treated the pessimist. Trying to brighten his outlook, the psychiatrist took him to a room piled to the ceiling with brand-new toys. But instead of yelping with delight, the little boy burst into tears. "What's the matter?" the psychiatrist asked, baffled. "Don't you want to play with any of the toys?" "Yes," the little boy bawled, "but if I did I'd only break them."

Next the psychiatrist treated the optimist. Trying to dampen his outlook, the psychiatrist took him to a room piled to the ceiling with horse manure. But instead of wrinkling his nose in disgust, the optimist emitted just the yelp of delight the psychiatrist had been hoping to hear from his brother, the pessimist. Then he clambered to the top of the pile, dropped to his knees, and began gleefully digging out scoop after scoop with his bare hands. "What do you think you're doing?" the psychiatrist asked, just as baffled by the optimist as he had been by the pessimist. "With all this manure," the little boy replied, beaming, "there must be a pony in here somewhere!"[139]

The late Roberto Goizueta once declared: "You can't fight a war without an enemy."

True enough. But your enemy is not just the one or two market incumbents you must set your sights upon, or even the point of pain within your customer's lives. Often, your enemy is your own incumbent bigness and bureaucracy, or even your own inertia, your own pessimism. If you need to adrenalize, look in the mirror and focus on the one enemy you can always count on. Let the line *Pogo* cartoonist Walt Kelly made famous be your rallying cry toward your Election Day: "We have met the enemy and he is us."

Line up your own change leader campaign for *internal* change. Stay right there alongside Ronald Reagan's faith-pony and prepare to swing hard for the fences to make 1,000 runs.

Above all, practice curiosity. Like Franklin, Einstein, da Vinci, and Jobs, go back and find your best childlike wonder. Sketch out ideas, play with numbers, and imagine, share, empower, and prototype. Transform curiosity into action. As Theodore Roosevelt loved to say in preparation for jousting with Tammany Hall, Washington bureaucrats, and his own demons: *"Get action!"*

But before you can "get action," you must:

- *Define the Win.* Work through the destination planning exercises in chapter 2. Imagine what success looks like.
- *Understand "Why."* 80 percent of change leadership is psychological; and 20 percent consists of tools, tactics, and techniques. Write down the reasons why what you are doing is a *must.* Make those reasons irresistible. Return to them repeatedly when the going gets tough.
- *Check Alignment.* Ensure your emotions and beliefs are all lined up and aimed at your definition of the win. Check that neither the naysayers nor your own tired old baggage is holding you back. Aim straight for the heart of the win.

- *Model Success.* Success leaves clues. Identify two or three people you admire and who have done what you are trying to do. Borrow and channel their lessons and strategies.

DO SOMETHING

Get action. Begin immediately by doing the doable to load the magic of momentum onto your side. Go to www.playoffense.com for a checklist—an action list drawn from the pages of this book—of 57 ways to make bold persistent innovation happen.

LEAD CHANGE

In far too many companies, amid today's remarkable innovation of technology, science, medicine, information, and artificial intelligence, there is a paradoxical dearth of innovation success and breakthrough. While platform companies such as Apple, Google, Amazon, and Facebook have exponentially grown their business models, and while these and other companies have created the markets they now lead, most big and incumbent companies fail to innovate.

By the numbers, it is even worse. A failure ratio of 8:1 has been true for years. Eight out of ten startups and new products fail. Again, 50 percent of all businesses fail in their first year, 80 percent by their fifth, and 96 percent by their tenth. Of the remaining 4 percent of businesses still standing a decade from birth, just 5 percent ever reach $1 million in annual revenue, and a mere 6 out of 100,000 of these survivors achieve over $10 million in revenues.[140]

Such statistics might make even Charles Darwin nervous, but this book is an optimistic primer intended to restack the odds. It is a field manual to fix your own innovation, your own marketing, to "do something," to do it faster, fast enough to punctuate your own equilibrium. This means unleashing your imagination to drive creativity, innovation, and change leadership.

Imagination allows and prompts us to ask better questions. What is our customer's pain? What if we "think different"? What will make us unique, special, and better? What will revolutionize my marketplace?

Imagination spawns and nurtures these questions, and it fast-forwards our answers. Imagination is our ability to think, create, and innovate beyond what we can see, hear, feel, experience, and know. It elevates us above all other species, punctuating our equilibrium, thereby driving our creativity toward unique ends.

Creativity is our ability to harness a hyper-conscious and hyper-disciplined focus and to transform imagination into ideas, visions, models, products, services, and innovations. Creativity is the great arterial bridge that allows us to walk from imagination all the way across to innovation.

Steve Jobs's ungrammatical imperative, "Think different," is a phrase for this bridge. For Jobs, it was also a mantra and change leader platform, which, to this day, drives Apple's transformational enterprise. But it had a beginning, coming shortly after August 19, 1997, Jobs's first day back as Apple's CEO. He worked hands-on, head-on to craft a television ad with Lee Clow of TBWA/Chiat Day. Its purpose was to remind customers, and even more employees, of Apple's unique identity and change leadership DNA.

If you were around in 1997, you remember it.

The ad featured a stunning black-and-white montage of iconic change leaders: Albert Einstein, Bob Dylan, Martin

Luther King, John Lennon, Buckminster Fuller, Thomas Edison, Muhammad Ali, Ted Turner, Maria Callas, Mohandas Gandhi, Amelia Earhart, Alfred Hitchcock, Martha Graham, Jim Henson, Frank Lloyd Wright, and Pablo Picasso. The montage unfolded against a voiceover narration. Jobs himself recorded the narration. That version, with his voice, exists, but it was not broadcast. He decided against guiding viewers to think the piece was about him. He wanted it to be about Apple. But the Jobs version was used to guide actor Richard Dreyfus in crafting his voiceover. The ad was a triumph.

• • •

On a stunningly beautiful morning, the kind of morning that makes everyone long to live in Northern California, October 24, 2011, thousands of employees, friends, and family gathered for a memorial service on Apple's Cupertino Campus. Steve Jobs was gone at 56.

They are surrounded by gigantic black-and-white photos of a young and a mature Jobs. The audio of the "Think Different" ad, with Steve Jobs's own voice, pierces the air:[141]

> Here's to the crazy ones, the misfits, the rebels, the troublemakers, the round pegs in the square holes, the ones who see things differently. They're not fond of rules, and they have no respect for the status quo. They change things, they push the human race forward. While some may see them as the crazy ones, we see genius. Because the people who are crazy enough to think they can change the world, are the ones who do.[142]

"Think Different" transforms grammar itself. The conventional adverb, *differently,* would have focused us on the thinking. The quirky noun, *different,* forces us to the result, the product of *creative thought,* which is a synonym for imagination. My friend the renowned Broadway director Bob Fitch offers this observation: "Creativity comes from failure, which opens up new possibilities. So, there's no failure in this work, only discovery." The ever-quotable Albert Einstein concludes simply: "Creativity is intelligence having fun."

In military terms, at the outbreak of what seems a hopeless revolution in 1775, creativity allowed some 3,800 militia troops without a navy to defeat the greatest military power since the fall of the Roman Empire. Here began the leadership of change against the Britain of King George III, a nation of about seven million, a GDP of about $10.8 billion, with an army of some 120,000 men and a navy of 131 ships of the line and 139 ships of lesser classes.

Creativity is in the mind of President John Kennedy when he declared in 1962 that his nation will send a man to the moon and back by the end of the decade.

Creativity sends a satellite to Pluto, decodes the human genome, creates more cell phones on the planet than toothbrushes, changes the economics of energy, and pulls a billion people from poverty. By 2030, creativity will build a computer in some ways smarter than our human brains.

In business, creativity is the bridge to innovation. It allows businesses to innovate and market and redefine their own success. In politics, creativity allows future leaders to push beyond America's current famine of political and social imagination.

Across this bridge, we change leaders must march from imagination to innovation. *We* must do this because no one else will ever be sufficiently hungry and foolish enough to redefine what innovation means, what change means. *We* are the crazy ones just mad enough to change the world.

ACKNOWLEDGEMENTS

This book would not be possible without my colleagues, partners, clients, and teachers who are all part of this new approach to change leadership.

First, thanks to my great Mango Publishing team and editor, Gary Krebs, my talented DMG Global colleagues including the amazing Alan Axelrod and researchers Constance Warner, Ira Callier, and Alena McGonigle.

Second, a call out to the greatest partners any business leader could ever ask for, change leaders all of them: Scott Miller, Joel McCleary, Bobby Armao, Carl Ford, Sergio Zyman, the Fratelli Group, Michael Thaler, Tom Paolozzi, Darryl Carter, Jerry Wind, Tan Sri Lim Ewe Jin, Kabir Khan, Edgar House, Joe Michenfelder, Eugene Burger, Jeff McBride, Ross Johnson, Larry Hass, Bob Fitch, John McLaughlin, and the many others, you know who you are.

Finally, I could not have birthed this book without my teachers, many of whom are also my clients. From so many great business leaders, entrepreneurs, and CEOs, to my athletic coaches, Marty Stern, Jim Tuppeny, and Irv "Moon" Mondschein, hall of famers all, to my professors at Wharton, Princeton, and the London School of Economics, to my parents, brother, sister, nephews, and niece… and to my favorite teacher of all, my wife, Xie Zheng, this book is born from the strategies of change I continue to learn from each of you.

ABOUT THE AUTHOR

David Morey, Chairman and CEO of DMG Global and Vice Chairman of Core Strategy Group, is one of America's leading strategic consultants—and one of the nation's most sought-after speakers. Morey is the bestselling author of *The Underdog Advantage*, *The Leadership Campaign*, and *Creating Business Magic*. He has worked with and helped add billions of dollars in revenue and market value to some of the world's top companies. Morey has advised five Nobel Peace Prize winners, nineteen winning global presidential campaigns, and a who's who of Fortune 500 CEOs.

ENDNOTES

1 Wikipedia, "List of Edison patents,"https://en.wikipedia.org/wiki/List_of_Edison_patents. His patents worldwide totaled 2,332.

2 Nathan Myhrvold, "Move Over, Thomas Edison. Lowell Wood is Now America's Most Prolific Inventor," Intellectual Ventures (November 4, 2015), http://www.intellectualventures.com/insights/archives/move-over-thomas-edison.-lowell-wood-is-now-americas-most-prolific-inventor/. Wood was awarded 1,085 utility patents—patents for inventions. Edison's US total of 1,093 includes 1,084 utility patents and 9 design patents. Thus, Edison was beaten by a single invention patent.

3 Abraham Lincoln lost from 3 to 5 elections if you count both personal and technical losses. Some even argue Lincoln lost as many as eight elections before he won the US Presidency, including the following life challenges and set-backs:

- 1816 His family was forced out of their home.
- 1818 His mother died.
- 1831 Failed in business.
- 1832 Ran for state legislature—*lost*.
- 1832 Lost his job—wanted to go to law school; couldn't get in. (Unless you were wealthy in these times, you did not go to law school. As Professor George Conyne notes in assisting in this section: "The greatest of all American judges, Chief Justice John Marshall (1801-35), went to law school for a total of six weeks.)
- 1833 Bankrupt—spent the next seventeen years paying off this debt.
- 1834 Ran for state legislature again—won.
- 1835 Was engaged to be married, sweetheart died.
- 1836 Had a total nervous breakdown, in bed for six months.
- 1838 Sought to become state legislature speaker—*defeated*. (See note below as the Democrats controlled the state legislature, so this defeat was inevitable and was not a referendum on Lincoln himself.)
- 1840 Sought to become elector—*defeated*. (See note below: Lincoln lost because the Democrats won the state in the presidential election.
- 1843 Ran for Congress—*lost*.
- 1846 Ran for Congress again—this time he won.
- 1848 Ran for re-election to Congress—*lost*. (Note the Whig party in Illinois practiced the principle of "rotation in office" so they could accuse the Democrats of being "professional politicians." In Lincoln's case, he and two other Whigs contested the district in rotation, regardless of the outcome. Lincoln served his term, from 1847 to 1849, so, as a Whig, in 1848, he was mandated to give way to one of the other Whigs, who themselves had stood aside for him in 1846.
- 1849 Sought job of land officer in his home state—rejected.

- 1854 Ran for Senate of the United States—*lost*. (Note that until 1913, state legislatures chose US Senators—there was no popular vote. When a senator's seat was due expire, voters knew this and the legislature they voted for was an issue—but not the only issue. In 1854, as usual, the Democrats won in Illinois, but split into anti-slavery and compromise-with-the-South factions. At the outset, Lincoln got more votes than the two Democratic candidates, but failed to reach the needed majority. To resolve the deadlock, Lincoln threw his support to the anti-slavery Democrat, who was elected and, in the following year, became a Republican.
- 1856 Sought the Vice-Presidential nomination—*lost*. (Note that Lincoln lost because he was a westerner and the Republicans wanted to balance the ticket with an easterner, since the presidential candidate was John Fremont of California. William Dayton of New Jersey was put on the ticket.)
- 1858 Ran for US Senate again—*lost*. (Note again, as with 1854, the 1858 legislative elections resulted, as usual, in a Democrat-controlled body, so Stephen Douglas, then the most powerful politician in the country, was always expected to be elected over Lincoln, the designated Whig candidate.)
- 1860 Elected President of the United States.

An accurate historical reading, then, recognizes that throughout the period from 1830 to 1858, Lincoln's state of Illinois was, more than now, an overwhelmingly Democratic state—and Lincoln was a Whig up until 1854, and a Republican thereafter. Further, it is worth noting:

- Democrats controlled the Illinois governorship from 1830–1857.
- Democrats controlled the state legislature 1830–1859.
- Democrats controlled both US Senate seats from 1830–1855 and controlled one up until 1861.
- Democrats won Illinois in every presidential election from 1828–1856, including the two they lost in 1840 and 1848.
- Lincoln was the single Whig congressman, from 1847–1849, in a delegation of seven.

Thus, many of the electoral "losses" above are technical more than personal. But one point is certain: Abraham Lincoln knew a lot about losing in politics.

4 John Brooks, *Business Adventures: Twelve Classic Tales from the World of Wall Street* (Worthing: Littlehampton Book Services Ltd, 1969), 91.

5 Feloni, Richard, http://www.businessinsider.com/lessons-from-the-failure-of-the-ford-edsel-2015-9/?IR=T&r=MY.

6 Ron Adner, *The Wide Lens: A New Strategy for Innovation* (New York: Portfolio/Penguin, 2012), Chapter 1.

7 Business briefing at Anthony Robbins Business Mastery seminar, August 5, 2015, Las Vegas, Nevada.

8 Satoshi Nakamoto, paper titled *Bitcoin: A Peer-to-Peer Electronic Cash System* (October 2008).

9 Geoffrey G. Parker, Marshall W. Van Alstyne, and Sangeet Paul Choudary, *Platform Revolution: How Networked Markets Are Transforming the Economy and How to Make Them Work For You* (New York: W.W. Norton & Company, Ltd., 2016), 3-15.

10 Ibid, 5.

11 Scott Galloway, T*he Four: The Hidden DNA of Amazon, Apple, Facebook, and Google* (New York: Portfolio/Penguin, 2017), Chapter 1.

12 Ibid, 6.

13 Satya Nadella, *Hit Refresh: The Quest to Rediscover Microsoft's Soul and Imagine a Better Future for Everyone* (New York: Harper Collins, 2017), Chapter 6; Michio Kaku, Einstein's Cosmos: How Einstein's Vision Transformed Our Underst*anding of Space and Time* (New York: W.W. Norton & Company, Ltd., 2004).

14 Jeremy Rifkin, *The Zero Marginal Cost Society: The Internet of Things, The Collaborative Commons, and the Eclipse of Capitalism* (New York: St. Martin's Press, 2014), 2.

15 Ray Dalio, Principles (New York: Simon & Schuster, 2017).

16 Thomas Kuhn, *The Structure of Scientific Revolutions,* as quoted in https://en.wikipedia.org/wiki/The_Structure_of_Scientific_Revolutions#Copernican_Revolution.

17 Quoted in Tina Seelig, *Creativity Rules: Get Ideas Out of Your Head and Into the World* (New York: Harper Collins, 2015), 57.

18 See Aidan P. Moran, *The Psychology of Concentration in Sports Performances: A Cognitive Analysis* (London: A Psychology Press Book, 1996); Dr. James E. Loehr and Peter J. McLaughlin, *Mentally Tough: The Principles of Winning at Sports Applied to Winning in Business* (Lanham: Rowman & Littlefield, 1988); and Michael Bar-Eli, *Boost: How the Psychology of Sports Can Enhance Your Performance in Management and Work* (Oxford: Oxford University Press, 2018).

19 Quoted in Michael Bar-Eli, *Boost: How the Psychology of Sports Can Enhance Your Performance in Management and Work* (Oxford: Oxford University Press, 2018),9, and as reported by Rob Bagchi in The Guardian, "50 Stunning Olympic Moments No 21: Daley Thompson Wins 1984 Decathlon" (2012), www.theguardian.com/sport/blog/2012/apr/04/50-stunning-olympic-moments-daley-thompson.

20 Tony Robbins, "From Limitations to No Limits at All," https://www.tonyrobbins.com/stories/from-limitations-to-no-limits-at-all/.

21 Salim Ismail with Michael S. Malone and Yuri Van Geest, *Exponential Organizations: Why new organizations are ten times better, faster, and cheaper than yours (and what to do about it)* (New York: Diversion Books, 2014), 162.

22 Tony Robbins Business Mastery seminar and discussion, Las Vegas, NV, August 5, 2015.

23 Christian Sarkar, "Renovate Before You Innovate: An Interview with Sergio Zyman," Zyman Institute of Brand Science, http://www.zibs.com/zyman.shtml.

24 Napoleon Hill, *Think and Grow Rich Superset* (New York: Macmillan, 2008), 44.

25 Sergio Zyman, *Renovate Before You Innovate: Why Doing the New Thing Might Not Be the Right Thing* (New York: Portfolio, 2004).

26 Al Browning, *I Remember Paul "bear" Bryant: Personal Memories of College Football's Most Legendary Coach, as Told by the People Who Knew Him Best* (Nashville: Cumberland House, 2001). 247

27 Quoted in Salim Ismail with Michael S. Malone and Yuri Van Geest, *Exponential Organizations: Why new organizations are ten times better, faster, and cheaper than yours (and what to do about it)* (New York: Diversion Books 2014), 124.

28 Bill DeMain, *In Their Own Words: Songwriters Talk About the Creative Process* (Westport: Praeger, 2004), chapter 14.

29 Matt Cardin, "Billy Joel on Beethoven, the Beatles, Mozart, and Creativity," *The Teeming Brain*, http://www.teemingbrain.com/2013/05/27/billy-joel-on-beethoven-the-beatles-mozart-and-creativity/.

30 Ibid.

31 Alan Axelrod, *Edison on Innovation: 102 Lessons in Creativity for Business and Beyond* (San Francisco: Jossey-Bass,2008), 50.

32 In 1942, the great African American scientist George Washington Carver set up a laboratory in Dearborn, Michigan, and, financed by Henry Ford, perfected the process of creating rubber from goldenrod. Carver died the following year, and although World War II drove continued experimentation with goldenrod, the rubber it yielded was of a low molecular weight, resulting in rubber of insufficient tensile strength to be practical for tires and the like.

33 Billy Joel interview, "Billy Talks about His Songwriting Process (November 14, 2011), https://billyjoel.com/news/37747/.

34 Albert Einstein, "Induction and Deduction in Physics," *Berliner Tageblatt,* Dec. 25, 1919, CPAE 7: 28; quoted in Walter Isaacson, *Einstein: His Life and Universe* (New York: Simon & Schuster, 2007), 118.

35 Isaacson, 118.

36 Ray Dalio, *Principles* (New York: Simon & Schuster, 2017), 187.

37 See Pagan Kennedy, *Inventology: How We Dream Up Things That Change the World* (New York: First Mariner Books, 2016) for wonderful accounts of Robert Plath and Jack Dorsey innovation.

38 Eric Ries, *The Lean Startup: How Today's Entrepreneurs Use Continuous Innovation to Create Radically Successful Businesses* (New York: Crown Business, 2011).

39 "Richard Branson," Wikipedia, https://en.wikipedia.org/wiki/Richard_Branson.

40 See Richard Branson, *Screw It Let's Do It: Lessons In Life* (London: Virgin Books, 2006).

41 Harrison Jacobs, "Why Hot-Air Ballooning Is Richard Branson's Favorite Way to Travel," *Business Insider* (October 12, 2014), http://www.businessinsider.com/richard-branson-on-hot-air-ballooning-2014-10.

42 Ibid.

43 Kevin Ashton, *How to Fly a Horse: The Secret History of Creation, Invention, and Discovery* (New York: Anchor Books, 2015), 52.

44 Ibid.

45 Ibid, 55.

46 "OODA loop," Wikipedia, https://en.wikipedia.org/wiki/OODA_loop.

47 Verne Harnish & the Editors of *Fortune, The Greatest Business Decisions of All Time* (New York: Fortune Books, 2013), 152.

48 Ibid.

49 See David Morey and Scott Miller, *The Underdog Advantage: Using the Power of Insurgent Strategy to Put Your Business on Top* (New York: McGraw-Hill, 2004).

50 Richard McMurry, *Atlanta 1864: Last Chance for the Confederacy* (Lincoln: University of Nebraska Press, 2000), 111.

51 See David Morey and the Scott Miller, *The Underdog Advantage: Using the Power of Insurgent Strategy to Put Your Business on Top* (New York: McGraw-Hill, 2004), page 72. Scott Miller's football coach was Boyd Williams.

52 Jonathan R. Allen, "William Tecumseh Sherman Quotes," http://www.nellaware.com/blog/william-tecumseh-sherman-quotes.html.

53 W. F. Strong, "The Airline That Started with a Cocktail Napkin," *Texas Standard* (April 20, 2016), http://www.texasstandard.org/stories/the-airline-that-started-with-a-cocktail-napkin/.

54 Brook Barnes, "For Disney's Iger, a Bold Move That Will Define His Legacy," *New York Times* (December 15, 2017), https://www.nytimes.com/2017/12/15/business/media/bob-iger-disney-fox.html.

55 Marguerite Ward, "Warren Buffett's reading routine could make you smarter, science suggests," *CNBC Make It* (November 16, 2016), https://www.cnbc.com/2016/11/16/warren-buffetts-reading-routine-could-make-you-smarter-suggests-science.html.

56 Wired staff, "May 26, 1995: Gates, Microsoft Jump on 'Internet Tidal Wave,' " *Wired* (May 6, 2010), https://www.wired.com/2010/05/0526bill-gates-internet-memo/.

57 Robert A. Guth, "In Secret Hideaway, Bill Gates Ponders Microsoft's Future, The Wall Street Journal (March 28, 2005).

58 David A. Kaplan chapter, *The Greatest Business Decisions of All Time* (New York: Verne Harnish & The Editors of Fortune, 2013), 98.

59 Kevin Ashton, *How To Fly A Horse: The Secret History of Creation, Invention, and Discovery* (New York: Anchor Books, 2015), 195.

60 Ibid, 196.

61 Ibid, 196–197.

62 Georgia, "Steve Jobs: You have to start with the customer experience and work backwards to the technology," *iMore* (October 26, 2013), https://www.imore.com/steve-jobs-you-have-start-customer-experience-and-work-backwards-technology.

63 Sam Walton Quotes, BrainyQuote, https://www.brainyquote.com/quotes/sam_walton_146810.

64 Chris Lake, "10 Customer Experience Soundbites from Jeff Bezos," *Econsultancy* (August 6, 2013), https://econsultancy.com/blog/63184-10-customer-experience-soundbites-from-jeff-bezos.

65 Brad Stone, *The Everything Store: Jeff Bezos and the Age of Amazon* (New York: Little, Brown and Company, 2013).

66 John Cook, "Full memo: Jeff Bezos responds to brutal NYT story, says it doesn't represent the Amazon he leads," *GeekWire* (August 16, 2015), https://www.geekwire.com/2015/full-memo-jeff-bezos-responds-to-cutting-nyt-expose-says-tolerance-for-lack-of-empathy-needs-to-be-zero/.

67 Jacqueline Howard, "Americans devote more than 10 hours a day to screen time, and growing," CNN (July 29, 2016), https://www.cnn.com/2016/06/30/health/americans-screen-time-nielsen/index.html.

68 Sergio Zyman with Armin A. Brott, *Renovate Before You Innovate: Why Doing the New Thing Might Not Be the Right Thing* (New York: Portfolio, 2004).

69 See David Morey and Scott Miller, *The Underdog Advantage: Using the Power of Insurgent Strategy to Put Your Business on Top* (New York: McGraw-Hill, 2004), see chap 7.

70 Bob Beamon, *The Man Who Could Fly* (Columbus: Genesis Press, 1999), and Dick Schaap, *The Perfect Jump* (New York: New American Library, 1976).

71 Bob Beamon's World Record Long Jump—1968 Olympics, https://www.youtube.com/watch?v=DEt_Xgg8dzc.

72 Heather Brown, "5 Best Accidental Inventions," *Famous Scientists: The Art of Genius*, https://www.famousscientists.org/5-best-accidental-inventions/ and Darren Orf, "10 Awesome Accidental Discoveries," *Popular Mechanics* (June 27, 2013), https://www.popularmechanics.com/science/health/g1216/10-awesome-accidental-discoveries/.

73 Ohid Yaqub, "Serendipity: Towards a taxonomy and theory," *Research Policy* 47, no. 1 (February 2018), 169–179.

74 Editorial, "The serendipity test," Nature (January 31, 2018), https://www.nature.com/articles/d41586-018-01405-7.

75 Enzo Ferrari Biography, IMDB, http://www.imdb.com/name/nm0274060/bio.

76 NPR, "How I Built This with Guy Raz, *iTunes Preview,* https://itunes.apple.com/us/podcast/how-i-built-this-with-guy-raz/id1150510297?mt=2.

77 Jon Fine, "How Craigslist's Founder Realized He Sucked as a Manager, Inc., https://www.inc.com/magazine/201609/jon-fine/inc-interview-craigslist.html.

78 Ibid.

79 Susan M. Freese, *Craigslist: The Company and Its Founder* (Minneapolis: Essential Library, 2011), 37.

80 Ibid.

81 "Craigslist," Wikipedia, https://en.wikipedia.org/wiki/Craigslist.

82 David Morey, Eugene Burger and John McLaughlin, *Creating Business Magic: How the Power of Magic Can Inspire, Innovate, and Revolutionize Your Business* (Miami: Mango Press, 2018).

83 Ray Dalio, Principles (New York: Simon & Schuster, 2017), 34.

84 Ibid.

85 Roger Bannister, *The Four Minute Mile: 50th Anniversary Edition* (Guilford: The Lyons Press, 2004).

86 The New York *Times*, March 5, 2018, "Track Feat Achieved in 3:59.4 Changed the Measure of a Mile."

87 "The Roger Bannister Effect: The Myth of the Psychological Breakthrough," *The Science of Running,* http://www.scienceofrunning.com/2017/05/the-roger-bannister-effect-the-myth-of-the-psychological-breakthrough.html.

88 Walter Isaacson, *Einstein: His Life and Universe* (New York: Simon & Schuster, 2007), 6.

89 Ibid. 133

90 Ibid. 299

91 Richard Wike, Katie Simmons, Bruce Stokes, and Janell Fetterolf, "1. Many unhappy with current political system," Pew Research Center (October 16, 2017), http://www.pewglobal.org/2017/10/16/many-unhappy-with-current-political-system/.

92 Ron Adner, *The Wide Lens: A New Strategy for Innovation* (New York: Portfolio/Penguin), 177.

93 Weber Shandwick 2012; see thoughtLeadership@webershandwick.com.

94 "Gloria Steinem," Wikipedia, https://en.wikipedia.org/wiki/Gloria_Steinem.

95 http://www.gloriasteinem.com.

96 "George S. Patton," Wikipedia, https://en.wikipedia.org/wiki/George_S._Patton.

97 Alan Axelrod, *Patton on Leadership: Strategic Lessons for Corporate Warfare* (Prentice-Hall Press, 1999).

98 Robert J. Anderson and William A. Adams, *Mastering Leadership: An Integrated Framework for Breakthrough Performance and Extraordinary Business Results* (Hoboken, NJ: John Wiley & Sons, 2016).

99 Ray Dalio, Principles (New York: Simon & Schuster, 2017), 95-96.

100 Ibid.

101 Alan Axelrod, *Edison on Innovation: 102 Lessons in Creativity for Business and Beyond* (San Francisco: Jossey-Bass A Wiley Imprint, 2008), 110-112.

102 Dan Bigman, "Jim Collins on the Real Lesson of Steve Jobs," *Chief Executive* (November 7, 2017), https://chiefexecutive.net/jim-collins-real-lesson-steve-jobs/.

103 See Boris Groysperg, Jeremiah Lee, Jesse Price, and J. Yo-Jud Cheng, "The Leader's Guide to Corporate Culture," *(Harvard Business Review,* January–February 2018), https://hbr.org/product/the-leaders-guide-to-corporate-culture/R1801B-PDF-ENG.

104 Guy Kawasaki with Michele Moreno, *Rules for Revolutionaries: The Capitalist Manifesto for Creating and Marketing New Products and Services* (New York: Harper Business, 1999), 82.

105 Anthony Robbins, "7 Master Steps—for Coaching," *Facebook* (August 1, 2011), https://www.facebook.com/notes/rose-evans/7-master-steps-for-coaching-by-anthony-robbins/229044013803393/.

106 The Predictive Index, "Arnold S. Daniels" Late Founder of The Predictive Index," https://www.predictiveindex.com/arnold-daniels.

107 John Hopkins, *The Entrepreneur Coach* newsletter, http://inspiritgrowth.com or inspireme@inspiritgrowth.com.

108 Cheney/Peters, "Reward Excellent Failure, Punish Mediocre Success," Credit *Union National Association News* (May 16, 2012), http://news.cuna.org/articles/37752--reward-excellent-failure--punish-mediocre-success-.

109 Paul Stephen Hudson, "A Call for 'Bold Persistent Experimentation': FDR's Oglethorpe University Commencement Address, 1932," *Georgia Info,* http://georgiainfo.galileo.usg.edu/topics/history/article/progressive-era-world-war-ii-1901-1945/a-call-for-bold-persistent-experimentation-fdrs-oglethorpe-university-comme.

110 Franklin D. Roosevelt, "Address at Oglethorpe University in Atlanta, Georgia," May 22, 1932," *The American Presidency Project*, http://www.presidency.ucsb.edu/ws/?pid=88410.

111 Elizabeth Howell, "'One Small Step' Quote on Apollo 11 Briefly Confusted Legendary Broadcaster Conkrite," *Universe Today* (December 23, 2015), https://www.universetoday.com/113331/one-small-step-quote-on-apollo-11-briefly-confused-legendary-broadcaster/.

112 Rachel Maddow, "Space travel history made with SpaceX landing," MSNBC (April 8, 2016), http://www.msnbc.com/rachel-maddow/watch/space-travel-history-made-with-spacex-landing-662162499632?playlist=associated.

113 *Ashlee Vance, Elon Musk: Tesla, SpaceX, and the Quest for a Fantastic Future (New York: Ecco, 2015).*

114 "Elon Musk," Wikipedia, https://en.wikipedia.org/wiki/Elon_Musk.

115 "The World's Billionaires," Wikipedia, https://en.wikipedia.org/wiki/The_World%27s_Billionaires.

116 Roy Carroll, "Elon Musk's mission to Mars," *The Guardian* (July 17, 2013), https://www.theguardian.com/technology/2013/jul/17/elon-musk-mission-mars-spacex.

117 Ross Andersen, "Elon Musk puts his case for a multi-planet civilization," *Aeon* (September 30, 2014), https://aeon.co/essays/elon-musk-puts-his-case-for-a-multi-planet-civilisation.

118 See the work and book by Jerry Wind on the Architecture of Disruption, focusing on the all-powerful principles of adaptive experimentation, open innovation, and strategic disruption.

119 Kent Beck, James Grenning, Robert C. Martin, Mike Beedle, Jim Highsmith, Steve Mellor, Arie van Bennekum, Andrew Hunt, Ken Schwaber, Alistair Cockburn,

Ron Jeffries, Jeff Sutherland, Ward Cunningham, Jon Kern, Dave Thomas, Martin Fowler, and Brian Marick, *Manifesto for Agile Software Development*, Agile Alliance (2001), https://www.agilealliance.org/agile101/the-agile-manifesto/.

120 For original text, see ibid.

121 James Dyson, "How I Built This," interview with Guy Raz, https://www.acast.com/howibuiltthis/dyson-james-dyson.

122 "*Apollo 13* (1995) Square Peg in a Round Hole Scene," YouTube (August 3, 2017), https://www.youtube.com/watch?v=ry55--J4_VQ.

123 Marguerite Ward, "Billionaire Elon Musk credits his success to these 8 books," *CNBC* (February 21, 2017), https://www.cnbc.com/2017/02/21/billionaire-elon-musk-credits-his-success-to-these-8-books.html.

124 Scott Miller and David Morey, *The Leadership Campaign: 10 Political Strategies to Win At your Career and Propel Your Business to Victory* (Wayne: Career Press 2016).

125 *Fast Company*: "The World's 50 Most Innovative Companies," March/April 2018, 38.

126 Walter Isaacson, *Ben Franklin: An American Life* (New York: Simon & Schuster 2003), 2.

127 Jared Sparks, *The Life of Benjamin Franklin: Containing the Autobiography, with Notes and a Continuation (Boston: Whittemore, Niles and Hall, 1856) 408.*

128 C. J. G. Gersick, "Revolutionary Change Theories: A Multi-Level Exploration of the Punctuated Equilibrium Paradigm," *Academy of Management Review*, 16[1] (1991), 10–36.

129 E. Romanelli and M. Tushman, "Organizational Transformation as Punctuated Equilibrium: An Empirical Test, *Academy of Management Journal*, 37[5] (1994), 1141–1166.

130 "Punctuated Equilibrium," Wikipedia, https://en.wikipedia.org/wiki/Punctuated_equilibrium.

131 Charles Darwin, *On the Origin of Species by Means of Natural Selection, Or, the Preservation of Favoured Races in the Struggle for Life* (London: J. Murray, 1859).

132 "On the Origin of Species," Wikipedia, https://en.wikipedia.org/wiki/On_the_Origin_of_Species.

133 See David Morey, Eugene Burger, and John E. McLaughlin, *Creating Business Magic: How the Power of Magic Can Inspire, Innovate, and Revolutionize Your Business* (Coral Gables: Mango Publishing Group, 2018).

134 Walter Isaacson, *Leonardo Da Vinci* (New York: Simon & Schuster, 2017).

135 Steve Jobs, Commencement address to Stanford University graduates, June 12, 2005, *Stanford News* (June 14, 2005), https://news.stanford.edu/2005/06/14/jobs-061505/; "Steve Jobs Stanford Commencement Speech 2005," YouTube (March 6, 2006), https://www.youtube.com/watch?v=D1R-jKKp3NA.

136 Jobs, Stanford Commencement Speech, op. cit.

137 Thomas Jefferson to James Madison, January 30, 1787; accessed at *The Works of Thomas Jefferson*, vol. 5, http://oll.libertyfund.org/search/title/802?q=storms+in+the+physical.

138 Jeffrey Bezos, "To our shareowners," https://www.sec.gov/Archives/edgar/data/1018724/000119312516530910/d168744dex991.htm.

139 Quote Investigator, "There Must Be a Pony Somewhere," *Quote Investigator* (December 12, 2013), https://quoteinvestigator.com/2013/12/13/pony-somewhere/.

140 Presentation at Anthony Robbins "Business Mastery" seminar, Las Vegas, August 5, 2015.

141 "Steve Jobs—Apple Campus Memorial," YouTube (October 26, 2011), https://www.youtube.com/watch?v=Zj3x_3ZxA_8.

142 "Apple—Think Different-Full Version," YouTube (August 21, 2010),https://www.youtube.com/watch?v=cFEarBzelBs.

A

action 43, 64, 68, 80, 100-101, 113, 119-120, 145, 166, 177, 191, 198, 205, 220, 231, 240, 243, 283, 291, 296-297
agility 35, 65, 113, 265, 278-282
attitude 89, 92, 127, 145, 171, 176, 178
awareness 168-169

B

benefits 8, 16-17, 20, 91, 117, 139, 154-156, 158-159, 162, 167-170, 172, 174, 178-179, 254, 290
branding 168

C

capturing all ideas a
change 5-7, 9, 12, 16-17, 20, 24, 35, 42-45, 47-48, 54, 56, 59, 64-67, 89-93, 96-98, 100, 114, 117, 119-120, 123-125, 130, 139, 145-148, 150-151, 159-160, 164, 167-169, 172, 198, 202-204, 206-210, 212-220, 223-227, 231, 233, 235-238, 240-255, 260, 264-265, 267, 271, 278, 286-294, 296-301, 306, 311
choice 32, 61, 116-117, 119-120, 133, 144-145, 159-161, 163-164, 214, 223-224, 231, 243, 246, 264, 280
communication 177, 224, 236-237, 266
competition 58, 67, 71, 117-118, 122, 124, 165, 175, 178-179, 191, 225, 237, 242
Connection 63, 135, 159, 161, 164
context 12, 15, 24, 28, 37-39, 47, 55, 69, 85, 95-96, 99, 114, 163, 172, 198, 203, 215-217, 253, 289
control 6, 29, 36, 39-40, 45, 71-72, 94, 108-109, 117-118, 123-125, 127-128, 135, 159-160, 163-164, 167, 175, 182, 193, 201, 215, 217, 223-224, 235, 240-244, 247-250, 254, 261, 268, 272, 274, 294
Convenience 159, 161, 164, 176
creativity 13-15, 57, 68, 72, 76-78, 81-82, 84, 87, 99, 151, 157, 298, 300, 305-306, 309
Credibility 168, 170, 179
crisis 41, 55, 166, 202-203, 205-206, 244, 258, 276, 278
customization 159-160, 164, 223-224

D

decisions 38, 114, 159, 173, 221, 236, 307
delivery 34, 265-266
detail 39, 64, 175, 177, 191, 219, 224, 253
differentiation 33, 119, 139, 168-169, 174, 178-179, 255, 280
discovery 86, 90, 109, 134, 184, 186-187, 190-191, 300, 307

disruption 43, 65-66, 142, 147, 151, 287, 290, 310
diversity 249

E

emotion 173
empathy 220
empowerment 229, 234, 236-237, 239, 242, 244, 246, 251-252
equilibrium 9, 17, 20, 108, 282-283, 286-290, 298, 311
experience 42, 57-58, 62, 80, 98, 148, 156-157, 159-161, 163, 167, 169, 172, 177-180, 222, 224, 230, 238, 267, 278, 288, 298, 307-308
experimentation 17, 84, 90, 198, 259-260, 262, 264-265, 267, 269, 274, 306, 310
exploiting disaster 89

F

failure 17, 26-27, 30-31, 35, 37, 39-40, 72, 88, 111, 117, 253, 255, 276, 297, 300, 310
future 8, 17, 20, 34-35, 41-42, 47-48, 57, 65, 72, 95, 100, 116-117, 133, 147-149, 153-155, 158-159, 163, 167, 172-173, 175, 179, 192, 201-202, 209, 218, 220, 227, 231, 235, 238, 241, 243-244, 247, 249-250, 252, 254-255, 262, 272, 291, 294, 300, 305, 307, 310

H

happy accidents 190-191, 198, 200
Humility 153

I

imagery 168, 172, 179
imagination 27, 39, 58-60, 64, 68, 95, 137, 153-154, 211-213, 267, 298, 300
initiative 117-119, 203, 231, 255, 281
Innovation Not Invention 62
inside-out leadership 246

L

leadership 4-6, 12-13, 16-17, 25, 28, 31, 43-44, 56, 59, 61, 93, 117, 119-120, 146, 148, 160, 162, 200, 206, 214, 223, 225, 231, 233-236, 238, 240, 243-246, 248-250, 252, 254-255, 282, 293, 296, 298, 300-302, 309, 311
learning 47, 76, 86, 89, 92, 99, 117, 138, 198-199, 206, 212, 214, 232, 251
luck 72, 80-81, 105, 194, 197-202, 205-206, 226

M

management 14, 18, 26-28, 43, 62, 70, 204, 235, 239, 265, 271, 287, 305, 311
marketing 8, 13-16, 18, 20, 26-27, 30-31, 33, 36-40, 42, 45, 61, 63, 67, 73, 122, 141-142, 150, 160, 162-163, 165-168, 171-175, 177-178, 180, 201, 203-206, 218, 223, 225, 264, 271, 278-282, 289-293, 298, 310
mobility 28, 65, 121, 148, 218
momentum 27, 33, 36, 70, 101, 117-118, 152, 169, 220-221, 223, 243-244, 254, 277-279, 282, 289, 293, 297

P

pain 46, 65, 67-68, 88, 95, 100, 157, 162-163, 167-169, 172-174, 179, 188, 194, 238, 295, 298
perception 34, 71, 157, 159, 170, 172, 223
peripheral vision 8, 129-130, 132, 189
playing offense 61, 98, 117, 120, 126, 198, 217, 225, 236, 255
preparation 104, 189, 198, 296
problems as gifts 88-89, 97
prototyping 116, 294

R

relevance 169, 174, 179, 239
Renovation, 166
revolution 44-45, 47, 54-56, 63-64, 80, 83, 119, 132, 139-140, 161, 193, 223, 230, 246, 260, 264, 271, 285, 287, 289, 300, 305

S

serendipity 189-191, 308
strategy 14, 18, 21, 35, 39, 62, 68, 97, 114, 117, 119, 121, 138, 142, 150, 166, 171-172, 175-178, 180, 197, 215, 217-219, 225, 236, 239-241, 243-244, 248-249, 251-252, 254, 281, 302, 304, 307-309
success 15, 17, 27-28, 33, 35-36, 56, 59-64, 69-72, 92-93, 98-99, 101, 111, 118, 141-142, 147-149, 153, 162, 165, 171, 175-176, 178, 192, 198, 202, 217, 219-220, 225, 235-237, 242-243, 255, 272, 275, 278, 282, 290, 293, 296-297, 300, 310-311

T

thinking 18-19, 21, 24, 34-35, 40, 42-43, 46, 48-49, 54-56, 61-62, 64-68, 81-82, 89-93, 98-99, 105, 122, 125-126, 130-131, 133, 148, 152, 162, 166-167, 187, 201, 211, 235, 290, 299
thinking anew 40
tools 5-6, 16, 30, 59, 97, 101, 193, 196, 251-252, 296

transformation 36, 44, 52, 56, 67, 83, 166, 215, 249, 311
trying 30, 62, 83-84, 89, 107, 117, 120, 122, 150, 156, 174, 199, 220, 222, 248, 269, 295, 297

urgency 8, 101, 103-104, 110, 113-117, 119, 126-127, 219, 239, 253, 264, 277, 282, 285

workshops 8, 75, 78, 87, 93, 100, 252